Organisational Learning

T0341141

Organisational Learning: An integrated HR and knowledge management perspective draws on a broad and multi-disciplinary base to look at the origins and practice of organisational learning. It critically considers: the nature of organisational knowledge as a social construct; pedagogical issues around learning as individuals, groups, teams and whole organisations; and technological issues around the development of knowledge-based information systems. Supporting case studies are provided throughout the book, and readers will also benefit from a companion website which expands on the key themes of the text.

Organisational Learning will enable readers to develop and implement strategies for ensuring long-term access to the embedded knowledge and experience of an organisation. This textbook will be invaluable reading for undergraduate and postgraduate students on organisational learning, human resource management and knowledge management courses.

Roderick Smith is a Senior Lecturer in Information and Knowledge Management at the Robert Gordon University, UK.

'A timely, clarifying navigation of the complex array of research that has emerged since organisational learning took hold as a key feature of the leadership and management portfolio. This will become a central textbook for our students.'

Dr Michael Bell, *Coordinator of Educational Leadership and Management, Flinders University of South Australia*

'An excellent piece of work for both academics and practitioners involved in organisational learning. The author creates a compelling interdisciplinary read and I can recommend this book to all of my colleagues.'

Hetty van Emmerik, *Full Professor of Organizational Theory and Organizational Behavior, Maastricht University, the Netherlands*

Organisational Learning

An integrated HR and knowledge
management perspective

Roderick Smith

Routledge
Taylor & Francis Group

LONDON AND NEW YORK

First published 2016
by Routledge
2 Park Square, Milton Park, Abingdon, Oxon OX14 4RN

And by Routledge
711 Third Avenue, New York, NY 10017

Routledge is an imprint of the Taylor & Francis Group, an informa business

© 2016 Roderick Smith

British Library Cataloguing in Publication Data
A catalogue record for this book is available from the British Library

Library of Congress Cataloging in Publication Data
Names: Smith, Roderick, 1961- author.
Title: Organizational learning: an integrated HR and knowledge management perspective/Roderick Smith.
Description: Abingdon, Oxon; New York, NY: Routledge, 2016. | Includes bibliographical references and index.
Identifiers: LCCN 2015044171 | ISBN 9781138860803 (hardback) | ISBN 9781138860810 (pbk.) | ISBN 9781315716251 (ebook)
Subjects: LCSH: Organizational learning. | Knowledge management. | Personnel management.
Classification: LCC HD58.82.S6125 2016 | DDC 658.3/124—dc23
LC record available at http://lccn.loc.gov/2015044171

ISBN: 978-1-138-86080-3 (hbk)
ISBN: 978-1-138-86081-0 (pbk)
ISBN: 978-1-315-71625-1 (ebk)

Typeset in Bembo
by Sunrise Setting Ltd, Brixham, UK

I would like to dedicate this text to my wife Fiona and children Martha and Sandy

Contents

x *Contents*

Illustrations

Figures

Tables

Acknowledgements

I would like to thank Fiona Smith and Sylvie Davies, colleagues at RGU, and David Millar from Wood Group, Aberdeen for their support and help in completing this text.

Introduction

The purpose of this textbook is to present a coherent and practical view of how organisations might embed organisational learning (OL) as a discipline within their operational, tactical and strategic practices. Throughout the text this will be referred to as the organisational learning programme (OLP). The coherence of the text will be based on the consistency of its theoretical basis, which will be outlined and discussed. Here there is choice for the reader. If we are to reject this theoretical perspective, then we must also reject the validity of the questions that are being addressed and that form the core of this text. So, there is an initial and important 'buy-in' being expected here. Essentially, this is the *socially constructed nature of knowledge production and the implications of this for the development of an OLP.*

The SPADES model will draw on the content of the first two parts of the book in order to present a practical plan of action for embedding organisational learning. This will be consistent with the theoretical position outlined and will be referred to and elaborated upon throughout the text. Central to this is the recognition of knowledge as a valuable organisational resource and that the purpose of the OLP is to devise practices that will recognise the nature of this resource and how best to 'manage' it. The theoretical perspective is crucial here and drives the formation of the questions that are being posed by the emerging environment within different organisational contexts. Given this, it is necessary to clarify the key distinctions being made here and to consider briefly what distinguishes a positivist perspective from a more socially constructed one.

Positivist knowledge emerged from the Enlightenment and from the steady development of the scientific methodology. The embedding of a rational approach to human understanding and progress ultimately presented the comprehensive and relatively stable knowledge context associated with modernity. Modernity, therefore, rested initially upon a utopian view of social fulfilment and purpose and has been characterised by:

> A deep confidence in the ability of human thought to comprehend the essential structure and meaning of human existence and reality itself.
>
> (Gill 2000: 2)

Scientific knowledge represented modernity's belief in the directional sense of the Enlightenment agenda of human progress through scientific discovery and the rational methodology that this presents. This is the grand narrative associated with the emergence of modernity and its goal of attaining a state of human fulfilment through the application of the scientific method. The epistemological position of scientific knowledge rests upon this method of deductive rationality and it is a position that has proven to be both enduring and robust. Its application to the production process drove the practices associated with the early Ford Motor Company and it drove the 'time and motion' initiative associated with many British industries in the post-war period, which in turn is based on the scientific management principles associated with Frederick Winslow Taylor (1856–1915).

Positivism would, therefore, determine a quite distinct OLP. It would be empirically based in its methodological approach and it would seek to determine value primarily through statistically measurable elements. To construct an OLP that stands opposed to this view might be considered illogical, irrational and perhaps unjustifiable. However, in considering the nature of organisational knowledge, the socially constructed view of knowledge will be presented as the key defining basis for the development of any OLP. To do this we must explore this perspective and justify its position as the guiding theoretical perspective. As this, it will also present a particular and equally distinct OLP.

From a socially constructed perspective all knowledge is recognised as being the product of the social context from which it emerges. For example, decision making in organisations is determined more by the structure of that organisation than any rational identification of what is 'true'. All decisions are subject to the variables that constitute any group and the ideological underpinning of that group. Here an organisation that is dominated by individuals with a particular world view will produce decisions that align themselves with this view. These might be entirely different from another organisation that does not share this world view. This is similar to recognising that any problem that is given to any two groups will not necessarily come up with the same solution. The solution will be determined by the dynamic within the group, by dominant 'voices' or by prevailing attitudes. Alter and shift these values and attitudes and the solution itself will shift.

Within this socially determined context, therefore, the context is everything. Who, for example, has a legitimate voice? Legitimacy here is particularly significant, in that each individual within a group will tend to seek out the opportunities to acquire this legitimacy in order to acquire dominance within the wider discourse. So, within a traditional context the hierarchical structure of an organisation attributes legitimacy via seniority within the hierarchy. Those higher up have more legitimacy and their opinion will inevitably carry more weight. Similarly, in an academic setting a tutor is afforded legitimacy by the symbols that they represent. Being a member of a university, having a higher qualification and publications afford legitimacy and allows an individual to be able to have a voice in relation to the discipline that they are associated with – much as this text will/may add to my legitimacy.

So, legitimacy is a key concept. It is represented by various symbols that characterise individual organisations. This might be in relation to specific aspects of behaviour including dress codes or other privileges. It is the old 'key to the executive washroom'. The primary benefit here is not the access to the, presumably, more luxurious washroom facilities but the legitimacy that is acknowledged by others who know that a specific individual has access. This knowledge lends weight – legitimacy – to the voice of the recipient.

Within the context of organisational learning this more traditional form of legitimacy is problematic. If knowledge is acknowledged as being embedded in the practices of all, if it is seen as an inclusive rather than exclusive resource, then there is an inherent challenge to this notion of legitimacy. Voices need to be more equal and this then requires a reconsideration of the context which is responsible for producing the knowledge asset. Rather than this being based on who has the loudest voice, it requires all voices to be accepted as more equal and therefore, more legitimate.

The first questions for organisational learning, therefore, are often structural questions as it is these that will determine the social configuration within the organisation and it is also these that will make OL practice appear to be both idealistic and unrealistic. *It is not easy to tackle or challenge embedded models of behaviour within organisations and yet this is the first and most crucial question for OL practitioners.*

This question is about the very structure of the organisation and how this then manifests itself in the power dynamic which in turn will determine how any individual voice will acquire legitimacy and, therefore, influence in the decision-making process. This decision-making process is the outcome of whatever learning has been embedded within it. This may be part of a collaborative effort, but it might equally be an expression of an individual's power, 'I make the decisions around here'. How decisions are contested is indicative of the way in which this process is embedded. Contestation itself, along with legitimacy is a key concept. It raises questions around the nature of discussion and collaboration. Is it one-way, are we told what to do, or is it two-way, do we have a say in what happens? Most organisations will fall between these two positions, but the organisation that is capable of learning will lean towards the latter.

How we might acquire a voice – legitimacy – and how we might use this voice – contestation – are the cornerstones of any OLP. The questions that need to be formed and asked, will be around these two concepts. Because of this OL is often presented as utopian and idealistic, but if we are in the midst of an information revolution, then we must expect questions that are challenging and formidable.

It is vital, therefore, that the overall focus is clear and that the approach is applied consistently. In order to be able to achieve this clarity and consistency it is necessary to have a clear understanding of what organisational learning is 'asking' of an organisation and this can be done by a consideration of the key theories and models. These highlight the nature of the questions that need to be asked, for example, Senge in the *Fifth Discipline* (1993), is asking questions around our embedded mental models as one of his key disciplines. This is a question about our individual position in relation to the organisation. The purpose of asking this is to better understand the relationship between the individual and the organisation. The relationship will determine the extent to which individual learning will transform itself into organisational learning. What might be different here is the interpretation of the question. It might be regarded as a quantitative question, such as how many hours were spent on individual training or professional development, or how much has been spent on developing the Learning Management System? Alternatively it might be regarded as more qualitative in nature, how do individuals feel about the current working environment or how supportive is their direct supervisor or manager?

The same discipline can be interpreted in many different ways. The intention here is to try to ask these questions more consistently and from a specific position, namely from a more socially constructed perspective and one that views the organisation as being embedded in a context characterised by fluidity, dynamism, complexity and rapid change. This might be viewed as a postmodern perspective.

In the first instance this will inform the consideration of the **nature of the organisation** (see Chapter 5) and the **ethical** basis for organisational action (see Chapter 6). Similarly, the focus on the individual and their collective action, as the basis for organisational learning has impacted upon the role of **human resources** and the organisational functions associated with this element of the organisational system (see Chapter 7). The organisation itself, the ethical position upon which it is based and the role of HR form the wider context for the questions that relate to the development of OL.

Within this wider context the questions for the OL practitioner are further enhanced or refined by key technical and cultural elements. Specifically, the emergence of the concept of **knowledge management (KM)** has allowed the information and knowledge asset to take centre stage (see Chapter 8). In considering the impact of KM there is an inevitable debate between those viewing knowledge as a discrete entity that can be managed in much the same way as any other asset, be it raw materials or financial assets and those who see it as a more socially embedded resource. However, the notion of tacit knowledge makes this asset a personal asset that is acquired through the transformation of individual learning to an explicit form that is available to all. **Learning and development** is clearly significant here (see Chapter 9), as is the use of **information and communication technologies** (see Chapter 10) to support and facilitate this learning. Each of these elements sit within the wider context and need to be developed and understood in accordance with a clear and consistent position or perspective. Otherwise, they lose focus, become too complex and ultimately lose meaning and clarity.

The **SPADES** model (see Part 4 and Chapter 11) is an iterative process that presents a series of elements designed to support the development of an OLP. Each tool or technique within the individual elements is an example of the type of activity associated with each stage of the model. It is not meant to be comprehensive and it cannot be more than an introduction to each tool or technique. For example, critical discourse analysis and web page design are very different, but both are crucial and the practitioner needs to engage with them if they are hoping to develop and sustain the OLP. Only a brief view of both of these can be provided here.

The first element of the SPADES model focuses on the organisational environment, and seeks to identify the nature of the questions that any organisation might face. For example, this might relate to the technical ability to provide an environment with the appropriate functionality to sustain the rich dialogues associated with an OLP. However, it might also relate to the extent to which the dominant discourse is understood by OL practitioners, giving them an informed view of how best to nurture the appropriate organisational culture. This blend of technical and cultural elements characterises many of the challenges that the OL practitioner will face in developing an OLP. This is what it means to **plant** an OLP (see Chapter 12).

To **nurture** an OLP requires the organisation to explicitly focus on the development of the relationship between the individual and the organisation (see Chapter 13). This will draw on a process of socialisation that goes beyond a 'traditional' induction programme and commits itself to an ongoing engagement that allows the establishment of a dialogue between the individuals within the organisation and the identification of aims and objectives that will remain pertinent to the individual as they look to support the aims of the organisation. This is the basis of postmodern ethics within an organisation, where it is recognised that appropriate ethical behaviour is not a series of discrete and explicit actions but itself an ongoing process, based on dialogue.

As this engagement with the ethical dimension of the postmodern organisation progresses then the establishment of appropriate relationships allows for the OLP to **grow** (see Chapter 14). Being based on dialogue, as it is, the OLP will look to become adept at the communication associated with dialogue. It will develop the ability to tell rich stories and will establish the necessary trust for these dialogues to have meaning, based on integrity. The skills developed here are communication skills, but they are developed in tandem with the development of an environment that is collaborative, sharing and ultimately trusting.

Dialogue is, therefore, the basis of both the operational process of an OLP and the stimulus to the creation of the environment within which it will thrive. Ultimately, these capabilities will allow for the growth of the OLP and its **propagation,** or spread, into all aspects of the organisation (see Chapter 15). The organisation will be a community based on trust and the individual members will be able to effectively articulate and share the knowledge they acquire through their ongoing experience.

To a large extent the lack of clarity associated with the emerging environment has undermined the development of OL as a discipline. It has allowed a range of different perspectives to create a miasma that clouds the view of what organisational learning is. Is it technologically driven, as many early KM initiatives were, relying on the emerging functionality of technology to define and apparently encapsulate complex knowledge bases? Is it an enhancement of already embedded training and development functions? The simple answer is that it can, potentially, be all of these and it is this that has caused the lack of clarity in relation to OL. It can be interpreted in many different ways, it can be viewed from multiple perspectives, but attempting to do so will begin to blur the view, lose clarity and ultimately present an unknowable and incompressible set of practices. Clarity can be achieved if we attempt to take a consistent view, and focus on the questions that this view helps us to form and ultimately seek to apply tools and techniques from the point of view of this perspective. This text seeks to present OL from a specific perspective and to justify doing so.

Part 1

Organisational learning

Key theories and models

Part I

1 The relationship between the individual and the organisation

---

Learning outcomes:

1 Identify the humanistic characteristics of organisational learning.
2 Understand the collaborative nature of organisational learning.
3 Identify the characteristics associated with experiential and work-based learning.
4 Understand elements of organisational behaviour relating to *theories-in-use*.
5 Identify the elements in key models of the learning organisation (LO).
6 Understand the implications associated with the application of the LO models.

Organisational learning (OL) can be regarded as emerging from the more humanistic approaches to management. These have challenged more scientific approaches, associated with Frederick Winslow Taylor (1856–1915) and the production processes of Henry Ford (1863–1947). Organisation development (OD) associated with Richard Beckhard (1928–99) has focused on the 'connect' between the extent to which an individual is disengaged from the aims and objectives of the organisation and the non-achievement of these aims and objectives. To become an organisation that is capable of meeting the challenge of change, this relationship needs to be brought to centre stage. Humanistic management styles have attempted to address this and are based on three key elements:

- The concept of human dignity.
- An ethical basis for decision making.
- Decision making based on dialogue.

Human dignity addresses the relationship that the individual might have with the organisation. It forms the basis of both the structure and the process that define the organisation. It seeks to embed autonomy as a principle of practice, itself based on the assumption that there exists a positive correlation between employee satisfaction and efficiency and, ultimately, productivity. In looking to achieve and embed this there is a need to address the ethical dimension to organisational practices and processes. Difficult as this is to consistently interpret, in relation to practice, there is nevertheless a key relationship between the concepts associated with postmodernity and humanistic management. This is based on the acceptance of the fluidity and dynamism associated with the postmodern and the need to base decision making on rich and constantly evolving dialogue. Embedded within this dialogue is the necessary opportunity to constantly seek the ethical 'route' and to a large extent it is this commitment to engage in dialogue at this level and to this extent, that forms the basis of the postmodern approach to ethics.

Organisational learning and the perceived need to develop a learning organisation (LO) requires a fundamental review of the relationship between the individual and the organisation, and as such is concerned with aspects relating to organisational behaviour. Here theorists, such as Elton Mayo (1880–1949), have driven the development of humanistic approaches to understanding behaviour in organisations and the importance of the relationship between the individual and the organisation. As an element of organisational practice this places OL within the context of human resource management (HRM).

Theories of organisational behaviour draw on a range of disciplines including:

* Psychology
* Social psychology
* Sociology
* Anthropology.

Key theories consider specific characteristics of organisational behaviour and seek to illustrate that collective learning is at least a possibility, if all of the factors necessary are identified and supported.

However, this identification and support only takes us so far. The issue of why we might want to learn collectively and how an organisation might encourage us to do so is a very personal and individual matter. Nobody can force you to think what you don't want to think! Could we even begin to justify, ethically, attempts to manipulate individuals in this type of way? These are important questions for OL, particularly when viewing the management of knowledge within a less structured context.

Marsick and Watkins (1999a) identified the development of learning as an organisational practice (see Table 1.1). The shift here is from directed to undirected, from one-way to two-way, and from learning being the identification of specific skills to a more holistic need to develop understanding. This shifts responsibility from the manager to the individual and in doing so it impacts upon the structure of the organisation itself. It will ultimately challenge the more structured models of organisational design and replace these with open, more egalitarian models.

> Action-based learning models frequently lead to changes in the system as a whole because learners question collective values, belief systems and ways of organising work in their search for solutions. The action project causes dissonance, which enables unfreezing of old ways.
>
> (Marsick and Watkins 1999b: 206)

Table 1.1 Learning and organisational practice

Metaphor	Nature of work	Organisation's Structure	Learning
Machine instruction	Highly structured	Hierarchical	One-way
Open system	Interactive	Networked	Negotiated
Brains	Self-regulated	Autonomous	Informal/continuous
Chaos/complexity	Self-initiated	Decentralised	Action-based

This creation of dissonance is a characteristic of the environment and of the ongoing experience of the organisation. An experience has value where it might add to existing experience. Unless an experience is different it will lack any real value and therefore, the context of surprise, the experience of puzzlement and even confusion are valuable as learning experiences. Likewise, the explicit experiences of others to challenge and counter embedded views adds to this rich mix of experiential learning. It is founded on uncertainty and doubt and because of this requires the wider learning environment to be one that is supportive and where each learner has at least learnt to trust the others. Uncertainty is a positive ingredient where it is a common universal experience and can in itself help to build the required trust through the sense of shared uncertainty.

2 The centrality of experience

In exploring OL it is important to remain focused on the wider theoretical and ethical context within which it sits. It is necessary to look at manifestations of collective learning and collective learning contexts. Specifically, we need to examine learning itself, followed by learning in work-based contexts and the notion of experiential learning. In doing this we ultimately emphasise the need for reflective professional practitioners. Practitioners who can understand the extent of their knowledge, drawn from their experience, and are willing to share this with others for the benefit of the organisation, will be effective OL practitioners.

As an emerging discipline, OL has drawn on the recognition of knowledge as an organisational asset and that if this asset is to be of value to the organisation there needs to be an explicit mechanism for its management. Given the nature of the knowledge asset and its roots in the day-to-day experience of individuals, there is a need to consider the nature of experiential learning (EL).

> Experiential learning (EL) recognizes and celebrates knowledge generated outside institutions. If learning can be defined as change or transformation, in the sense of expanding our range of possibilities and action, experiential learning is expansion that challenges the hegemonic logic of expert knowledge, refuses disciplinary knowledge claims of universal validity, and resists knowledge authority based solely on scientific evidence.
>
> (Fenwick 2003)

Tara Fenwick's comment above at once illustrates the inherent separation that we feel between work and learning. Learning has become associated with formal education, but this perception has been developed from a point where this separation was not recognised. In other words, there was a time where we learnt directly from others and knowledge was transferred from one to another without necessarily the interjection of the 'educator'. Lave and Wenger (1991) are often associated with the coining of the related concept of 'legitimate peripheral participation' which closely considers this idea of the individual being drawn away and separated from learning – or the imposition of the educator.

> 'Legitimate peripheral participation' provides a way to speak about the relations between newcomers and old-timers, and about activities, identities, artefacts, and communities of knowledge and practice. It concerns the process by which newcomers become part of a community of practice. A person's intentions to learn are engaged and the meaning of learning is configured through the process of becoming

a full participant in a socio-cultural practice. This social process includes, indeed sub-sumes, the learning of knowledgeable skills.

(Lave and Wenger 1991: 29)

What we can identify here is a changing relationship between work and learning. The learning organisation is an expression of this still fluid and dynamic relationship. It has flowed from Lave and Wenger's position above, to learning being seen as an intrinsic good in its own right and back to the need to marry learning with work-based practice. However, when we come to examine and consider learning as it occurs in the workplace we face a number of issues. Not least:

*   What is the role of the educator?

If you place yourself within a familiar organisational environment and ask yourself, where you learnt, the likelihood is that you will say that you learnt from the social group around you, and largely informally. You might also have experienced the formally arranged train-ing sessions that form the basis of induction and ongoing programmes of professional development. These programmes are reflecting the need to formally embed learning as an organisational practice and OL differs from these programmes only in its more full engage-ment with the knowledge asset itself. Primarily, this focuses on the need to impose a formal, managed structure upon something that often and intrinsically recoils from this formality and indeed thrives on its inherent informality. On the one hand there is a need to manage explicit knowledge and there is an equal need to have this knowledge circu-lated effectively through the mechanisms and networks that form the basis of the organi-sation's information system.

Experiential learning forms the basis of knowledge creation and OL concerns itself with the transformation of this knowledge into an organisational asset. Experiential learn-ing and OL are key components of an organisational learning programme (OLP), and they feed the knowledge-based information system that completes the engagement necessary to realise the transformation of personal experience (referred to as our *tacit* knowledge) to a form that can be used and applied by the group or the whole organisation (referred to as our *explicit* knowledge). The OLP concerns itself with the making of tacit knowledge explicit.

Experiential learning is, therefore, a crucial element of the socially embedded nature of the knowledge asset. It asks questions of the organisation and in turn places certain pres-sures on the organisation. David Boud (2003) has identified these new pressures that are being placed on practice as a result, to some extent, of this need to learn, to identify the learning processes and ultimately to understand how it is we learn at work.

> We are asking ourselves now, how is it that people actually learn in real settings? And, how can learning be promoted everywhere? The answer is not the one we expect. It is not just more RPL [Recognition of Prior Learning], more courses and more web-based programs. But I suspect it will be a more reflexive development in which the major learning interventions involve noticing what we are doing, what gets in the way of doing it better and how we do it in congenial ways with those we interact with.
>
> This has been called informal learning, but that term undervalues the most important learning of all. The new challenge to practice is to find ways of acknowledging how

we and others learn in our many locations and build on that without the act of for-malising learning destroying what we are trying to foster.

(Boud 2003)

Lave and Wenger (1991) identify the crucial link between education and management. Clearly the two come together with OL. Even if it is the individual that learns, rather than the organisation this does not mean that the external context within which learning takes place is of no significance. Clearly this context does have a bearing and it is this that has moved the consideration of learning, to some extent, away from it being a process of internalisation and towards one that places merit in the external environment. In a prac-tical sense it considers the learning that a learner can achieve through collaboration, as opposed to working alone. Most of this work is based on Vytgotsky's concept of *proximal development*, of which there are many interpretations. Essentially, it asks us to consider social forms of learning. This has led to the development of *communities of practice* (CoP), identified and promoted by the work of Lave and Wenger (1991). This places learning fully within a social context where learning takes place within practice:

> Learning, thinking, and knowing are relations among people in activity in, with, and arising from the socially and culturally structured world. This world is socially con-stituted; objective forms and systems of activity, on the one hand, and agents' subjec-tive and inter-subjective understandings of them, on the other, mutually constitute both the world and its experienced forms.
>
> (Lave and Wenger 1991: 51)

One of the most important distinctions that we begin to see emerge here is the redefini-tion of the purpose of learning. Rather than individuals learning abstract facts and gener-alisations while sitting at the feet of an expert, it is more about learning how to effectively learn within a supportive and collaborative context or environment. Within an organisa-tion this might be learning how to be able to apply knowledge to any particular issue that may arise. Brown and Duguid (2000) have touched on this in their consideration of social learning. It is about being *knowledgeable* over having knowledge. Within the more fluid organisational context where truths are more difficult to pin down, it is the ability to react and to act knowledgeably that is clearly the more appropriate. Does this not express more effectively the experience of an individual, rather than some representation of the amount they know – their technical expertise?

As the author of this text I am presented as the expert who has knowledge to share about OL. However, no text can say it all and even what it does say will be open to both doubt and contestation. For very good reasons you may disagree with the interpretation of the content being presented to you here. Learning takes place when you are able to internalise the content that is being presented to you (in doing so this may fundamentally alter this content) and re-present it in your own terms. Despite all of the material pre-sented to you here in this text there needs to be questions raised about how any individual might engage with this material. Where is the internalisation of this material, where and how will you be asked to illustrate (externalise) your understanding of this material? Much effort in recent years has gone in to considering not the technical transfer of facts and figures, but the means by which the learner is able to construct their own meaning. In recent years, for example, *constructivism* (Jean Piaget, 1896–1980 and Lev Vytgotsky 1896–1934) or *constructionism* (Seymour Papert, b. 1928) has been recognised as a process or theoretical position that supports this. It was Vytgotsky who presented the *zone of proximal development* which argues that we learn when our experiences resonate with what we already know. Piaget, similarly, identified that learning was a spontaneous activity that we all engage with and that instructional techniques that were the basis for traditional teacher-led learning were less effective. Around this there is a structure, it is not an entirely free process and individuals can be supported in their learning. However, it is a social process, one where a supportive and collaborative environment will facilitate a more effective form of learning.

Learning activities in constructivist settings are characterised by:

- active engagement
- inquiry
- problem solving
- collaboration with others.

Rather than a dispenser of knowledge, the teacher is:

- a guide
- a facilitator
- a co-explorer.

They encourage learners to:

- question
- challenge
- formulate their own ideas, opinions and conclusions.

Constructivism focuses on the socially constructed nature of learning. In doing so it requires the re-examination of the cultural assumptions that underpin the context within which learning takes place. Specifically, within our context this would require us to consider the power relationship that might exist within an organisational context. John Coopey (1995), in his critique of the learning organisation raises the issue of how the literature of the learning organisation has largely ignored the need to perceive how its goals might impact upon the ideological structure within the organisation. He rightly identifies a democratic element to the learning organisation, an underlying egalitarianism, but also identifies in the nature of organisations an equally fundamental position that is contrary to this democratic element.

> Actors within an organisational setting are involved in a 'dialectic of control', attempting to maintain some semblance of control over their work lives. To safeguard their interests through relationships of mutual dependency, they take advantage of imbalances in personal access to resources – raw materials, finance, equipment and information; of opportunities to command the use of these factors; and of 'authorisation', which enables one person to exercise command over another. Over time, the dialectic serves as an adaptive process through which structures and their associated systems are confirmed or transformed and, with them, the bias in the distribution of resources.
>
> (Coopey 1995: 197)

In relation to constructivism the comment above highlights the fundamental notion of there being no objective truth or reality. A criticism of this view might be that it allows or justifies any view of reality, a position that might be referred to as *relativism*. However, if we attempt to maintain a focus on how constructivism might inform our understanding of OL we can at least suggest that it draws us towards a presentation of learning as a social process and, importantly, what we mean by that. We are, therefore, able to associate constructivism with developments such as Action Learning (Reg Revans, 1907–2003). Similarly, Stephen Brookfield (1996), whose work primarily has been in the area of adult education, has presented the *good practice audit* (GPA). This audit is split into three phases:

- formulating the problem
- analysing the experience
- compiling the suggestions.

As he goes on to say:

> It involves a mix of individual reflection and collaborative critical analysis and is focused on helping people deal with difficulties they have themselves identified ... once the GPA gets going, the reflection, sharing and analysis become much more spontaneous and unstructured than the method seems to suggest. The conversations that ensue are open and unpredictable, yet they happen under the guise of a well-structured series of tasks.
>
> (Brookfield 1996: 27–8)

We can still turn to fundamental questions of why we should share our knowledge and to a large extent none of the above satisfactorily answers this question. However, in identifying the nature of learning within social contexts we do move some way to also identifying managerial priorities in relation to this most fundamental of questions.

The principles upon which both OD and OL are based inherently value the individual and look to support those activities that can enhance the individual. This requires us, amongst other things, to address some of the issues that were raised by Coopey (1995). We can also equate these principles with learning activities and provide an opportunity for individuals to be productive, to be innovative and to meet the challenges inherent within a fluid and constantly changing context. In doing this we must value those opportunities that enhance sharing. In identifying learning in this way we have now moved a long way from simply regarding this as the implementation of an intranet, a learning management system or other technologically based tool. Similarly, we have moved away from the concept of knowledge being recognised as solely an explicit asset. We may have knowledge that can be made explicit, but not knowledge that will remain uncontested. Explicit knowledge and the process by which it is contested, forms the basis of any OLP.

In understanding and appreciating OL we bring to centre stage the theoretical definitions of knowledge that are less structured. The social context is more appropriately attached to the crucial development or creation of tacit knowledge, which underpins OL. Indeed we have a view of knowledge as a process, essentially a learning process. This process forms the basis of an OLP and in turn this is founded upon the key models of the learning organisation.

3   The learning organisation

All organisations will be defined by the dominant discourse embedded within their strategy, structure, culture and systems. This discourse will have been derived from the interaction of the individuals who have formed and developed the organisation. It will also reflect the power dynamics that make up the organisation. This discourse will determine what can be said by individuals within the organisation. It will form the patterns of their behaviour and ultimately it will determine the extent and nature of its learning capabilities. To affect change in an organisation and to be able to apply the knowledge embedded in organisational practices we must start with an understanding of the dominant discourse. Critical discourse analysis is a technique that can be used to identify the characteristics of the dominant discourse.

 Key points

Critical discourse analysis will be considered further in Part 4 and will inform the *Planting* element of the SPADES model.

To meet the challenge of change, that characterises the contemporary organisational environment, knowledge production is central. What we knew cannot be relied on to form the basis of what we will need to know. Rather we need to have the capability to constantly produce knowledge – we need to be able to learn. This means that organisations need to be flexible, adaptable, responsive and agile in order to avoid the vulnerability associated with obsolete knowledge. These *new capabilities* are those associated with the LO.

The organisation is dependent upon individual learning being transformed or translated into learning for the organisation. An individual may learn but this will not necessarily mean that the organisation learns, in other words, individual learning remains tacit. Something at the level of individual learning needs to form the trigger for the transformation of individual knowledge into an organisational asset and it is the elements of the LO which claim to do this. For OL to be successful there is a need to change or adapt crucial aspects of organisational behaviour, with the aim of creating a positive interaction between the individual and the organisation.

Collective learning is necessary. Just as a football team made up of the best individual international players can be beaten by an amateur outfit, we can identify with the strength to be gained from being part of a good team – the individuals, if good, will contribute, but they must be good collectively. This ability is not the same as being good individually!

Pause for thought – collective learning

As we have just said:

Just as a football team made up of the best individual international players can be beaten by an amateur outfit, we can identify with the strength to be gained from being part of a good team – the individuals, if good, will contribute, but they must be good collectively. This ability is not the same as being good individually.

Brian Clough is recognised as one of the most successful English team managers in history. He was often considered eccentric and this manifested itself in a number of ways. He famously claimed **not to talk tactics** with his team and rather than give a team talk at the end of a cup game and ahead of extra time he remained seated in his dug out and let the players get on with it.

It was all about personal responsibility within the structure, a team shape defined by its balance.

(Wilson 2011: 425)

Consider the importance or significance of taking personal responsibility for something within a collective context.

OL is a learning process that addresses the 'organisational dilemma' (Chris Argyris, 1923–2013). This refers to our approach and attitude to the organisation in relation to our own personal aims and objectives. Where these objectives are diverging from those of the organisation then we can say that the dilemma is strong or prominent. Where this dilemma is strong, little or no OL will occur. Individuals will be learning through their ongoing engagement and experience but this will not be successfully translated into OL. One of the aims of learning within the organisation is to address this dilemma and it will do this through a consideration of:

- organisational routines
- levels of participation
- communication
- accountability.

Where and how we begin to form the relationship between individuals and the organisation is of particular relevance to the OLP. We are all aware of the way in which we become integrated into an organisation. It is linked to onboarding, and other induction programmes as well as ongoing development and training which in turn underpin the socialisation process that is central to the establishment of a positive relationship between the individual and the organisation. Beyond this it becomes part of the continuing professional development (CPD) programme that is in place in many organisations, recognising that the individual constantly needs to maintain and push forward their professional knowledge.

Key points

Onboarding and socialisation will be considered further in Part 4 and will inform the *Nurturing* element of the SPADES model.

However, much of this knowledge is based upon an implicit understanding of this relationship between the individual and the organisation. Making this relationship explicit does not mean writing it down but externalising the relationship through a more open discussion and ongoing consideration of issues that relate to this relationship. This, for example, begins to address one of the main tenets of an LO and that is of a 'no blame' culture. Correction, and therefore learning, becomes possible when there is a more explicit and open approach.

As individuals we will form a view or an opinion of the organisation. This will form our attitude to the organisation, which in turn will determine our behaviour or actions in relation to the organisation. In studying organisational behaviour we are looking to form a more coherent view of individual action. Chris Argyris (1923–2013) and Donald Schön (1930–1997) considered this relationship throughout their work and offered an influential insight into individual actions.

Argyris and Schön (1978) identified two theories related to action:

- The actions that represent one's *beliefs*.
- The actions that one actually *uses*.

This latter was called *theories-in-use*.

Individuals can employ theories-in-use that differ strongly from their espoused beliefs and surprisingly construct mechanisms to justify this. These theories are represented within the models of single-and double-loop learning.

Single-loop learning: the tendency to detect errors without questioning to any great extent the underlying policy that is ultimately responsible for these errors. Change that takes place in this context is responsive to a perceived need and will in fact show positive results, at least initially. For example, a marketing manager may identify a downturn in a product's sales and devise a strategy to boost this – with positive results. However, this does not necessarily address the underlying values and norms, which will be supporting this situation in the first place and these, if left unchanged or unchallenged, will continue to impact negatively on the organisation.

Double-loop learning: the underlying policy reasons for errors is actively examined and does take a more recognizably systemic or holistic view of organisations. It will change the value of the theory-in-use, as well as the strategies that underpin it

Errors that occur do not necessarily mean that underlying values or norms need to be addressed and in these cases single-loop learning is appropriate. However, the organisation must be in a position to identify where there is a need to challenge these norms and apply double-loop learning.

Theories-in-use are an example of how organisational behaviour can be understood and represented. In this instance they represent ways in which people operate in actuality.

Argyris, in his research, has claimed to have identified a core number of limited theories that are employed by individuals. This does not necessarily undermine their individuality, as individuals will employ these theories as individuals.

An example of this would be *face saving*. This behaviour varies widely but the root of face saving as a form of behaviour, is common. It is often presented as a response to embarrassments or threat. When faced with either embarrassment or a threat there is a tendency to attempt to bypass it and to cover up this bypass. Therefore, the theory-in-use related to face-saving produces actionable knowledge – it defines the action strategy (to bypass). This action is essentially defensive and is associated with what Argyris calls:

- Model I Theory-in-Use

Model I essentially identifies an organisation that acts defensively, and where there is a limited learning environment *Model O-I* learning environments exist. So, in this organisation we can avoid feeling threatened, but at the same time avoid any understanding of why we felt this threat or the reasons behind there being a threat in the first place. As Argyris himself says, Model I over protects the individual within the organisation. The learning that is in place in the Model I organisation will perpetuate and reinforce this behaviour and is the *Model O-I learning system*.

The individual will internalise their theories-in-use, governed by the values and actions below:

- Achieve your intended purpose.
- Maximise winning and minimise losing.
- Suppress negative feelings.
- Behave according to what you consider rational.
- Advocate your position.
- Evaluate the thoughts and actions of others.
- Attribute causes for whatever you are trying to understand.

These values and actions are self-perpetuating and the challenge is to try to break the cycle and move on to what Argyris called a *Model II Learning Organisation*. Model I is largely characterised by negative and defensive theories-in-use, Model II has the ability to identify negative behaviour and to counter it. Model II will look to re-engage with what we actually believe, but tries to place this within a set of organisational values for the individual, where the individual to some extent believes that they are actually acting in accordance with these values.

So, we behave in particular ways as individuals within organisations. This behaviour can be defensive and in this in turn can be justified by the individual. Where this behaviour becomes embedded in organisations then they not only lose the ability to affect change, they will also build this as an organisational mentality that can be very difficult to shift. For the OL practitioner this is often the first question or task. Identifying the nature of theories-in-use requires an ability to uncover not only existing practices but also the reasons for these practices. With Model O-I learning systems this will take considerable time and effort to, in the first instance, identify, and then begin to combat this embedded behaviour.

4 Models of the learning organisation

The LO is an organisation that has at least accepted the challenge of trying to embed the characteristics of social forms of learning. This will almost certainly be based on the recognition of the value of this learning to the organisation, even if some of the implications of implementing these programmes are not fully appreciated.

The LO can be defined through how embedded learning is within the strategy, structures, culture and systems of the organisation:

Strategy: mission directed; short and medium term; rational and intuitive; active and proactive; various foci.
Structure: loosely combined units and teams; decentralised; mixing thinkers and doers; coordination through discussion.
Culture: flexible; problem oriented; creative.
Systems: information for reflection and action; dealing with complexity.

The purpose of an LO is to identify and solve problems. It should anticipate problems and it is the ability to continually learn that will allow it to solve problems. A key capability is the shifting of learning from an individual to a social action. To approach this there is a need to initially recognise that the ability to shift a concern from oneself to the 'other' is fundamentally an ethical question, where a position where there is a strong sense of the collective is created and sustained. More specifically, there is a need to draw individual and collective values together. Anything that counters this, will counter the development of the OLP. This careful construction of the collective means that any differences need to be addressed openly and through suitable compromises. The task is to create a collaborative learning environment. Coopey (1995) emphasises this importance of difference and that dialogue needs to be used to resolve conflict and create trust within a collaborative rather than competitive context.

Argyris also emphasises trust and Coopey supports this. However, on the other hand, Argyris envisages the momentum for the development of the learning organisation as coming from the leader – a *philosopher king*, as outlined by Plato. However, Coopey argues that power and the exercise of power is not conducive to this development and there is therefore a need to consider checks and balances from within the organisation to ensure that the leader acts appropriately.

These checks and balances are designed to better define the relationship between the individual and the organisation. They are the basis for the discursive nature of the OLP. As Gheradi (2011) has pointed out, discursive practice requires an engagement with a 'trajectory of learning' that has three elements:

Feeling: an awareness of our sensory impressions.
Describing: an ability to articulate, openly, the nature of our sensory impressions.
Using: an understanding of the application/implication of these sensory impressions.

These elements are attempting to identify the 'practice' associated with the dialogue that is at the centre of the OLP. What is it we need to talk about? Peter Senge (1993) similarly attempts to identify the areas (or disciplines) that form this discursive practice.

Senge's five disciplines

Senge, in presenting his model of the learning organisation is attempting to present a practical model that will ultimately embed learning practices within the organisation. For Senge, there is a need to consider five key issues or disciplines:

1   systemic thinking
2   personal mastery
3   mental models
4   shared vision
5   team working.

Systemic thinking

This can perhaps most famously be illustrated by the butterfly flapping its wings in the Amazon. This subsequently causes a series of events culminating in a hurricane on the other side of the world. What this is essentially suggesting is that everything in the world is inter-related and even the smallest parts will have an impact on the whole.

Systemic thinking has developed over a long period of time and has been largely ignored up until quite recently. It can be said to have begun with Ludwig von Bertallanfy's (1950) *Open Systems Theory* that largely opposed reductionist thinking which sought to understand things, largely in physics, through taking them to bits and considering their component parts. It was Senge, and others, who began applying this to organisations and thus began to oppose mechanistic or scientific forms of management that had appeared to be successful in increasing operational efficiency and effectiveness through a detailed study of routine activities.

This style of management was concerned with control and power being placed largely at the top. However, the down side of this was seen to be demotivation of the workforce, for example, with tasks being performed mechanistically and thus causing drudgery and lack of any interest for the worker in the functions being carried out. There was a realisation that it was more beneficial to consider the functioning of the organisation as a whole including the environment within which it operates.

Peter Checkland (1981) is associated with the *soft system methodology* that itself is normally identified with the mnemonic:

C – Customer
A – Actor
T – Transformation process
W – Worldview
O – Owners
E – Environmental

This seeks to ensure that systems designers are asking themselves questions relevant to the user of those systems at the design stage.

Checkland is also associated with *action research* that seeks to ensure that there is a collaborative process of critical investigation into the organisation and that this is placed within a social context, in other words it is seen in terms of how people interact and that there is an opportunity to be reflective throughout the process.

C. West Churchman (1913–2004) is associated with the need to constantly be considering the *others'* view and seeing the situation through the other person's eyes. In doing so he is stressing the fact that scientists must take responsibility for the social consequences of their actions. This introduced an ethical dimension to the development of systems within organisations.

 Key points

Ethics will be considered further in Part 2 and will inform all of the elements of the SPADES model.

Systems themselves and the inter-relationships that they represent are all around us. They appear in our basic observation of the world. This might be the weather system or the movement of tectonic plates. One event causes a subsequent event in a series of relationships that will impact on the whole. The operation of systems is fundamental to existence and we do have an intuitive understanding of this and the relationships that it represents.

Systemic thinking in a practical, organisational sense has led to a series of different tools and techniques. These try to provide some understanding of the way in which basic organisational procedures operate.

At this point we will consider two basic tools described by Senge:

- links and loops
- archetypes.

Links and loops

If you carry out any piece of research you are looking, essentially, to identify relationships that exist between different variables. Links and loops identify these relationships and represent them diagrammatically in order for us to better understand them.

The initial link is often an increase or a decrease in the level of service provided which links to a rise or drop in sales or use of the service. The loop in this suggests that a drop in sales might negatively impact upon staff morale which in itself then leads to a further drop in levels of service and so on. It becomes a vicious cycle.

Where this situation is allowed to continue the exponential growth rate of this type of problem will soon swamp the organisation. Where this is happening it is often referred to as the *reinforcing loop*.

Equally significant here are what are called *balancing loops* which, although not bad in themselves, tend to inhibit growth and controlled development. They are characterised as being a rollercoaster ride on which we are hurled about a bit! Where you attempt to adjust an element within a system and where you throw it off balance there will be a tendency for the system to right itself and fight to return to the natural balance that exists. We can relate this to the workload of school teachers increasing and there subsequently being a drop in extramural activities such as the school football team and so on.

Archetypes (first of its kind)

Archetypes are an attempt to represent complex relationships between variables with a view to illustrating aspects of organisational behaviour. Again, in relation to research, archetypes essentially ask you or encourage you to consider a hypothesis – or an *archetype*. An example might be:

Fixes that backfire

An example of this archetype would be the *squeaky wheel* analogy where an inexperienced individual solves the problem of the squeaking wheel by putting water on it. This works initially but the problem soon returns and is worse. Again water is applied to solve the problem and it is solved for a short time, but ultimately the wheel will rust up entirely. This can be related to customer complaints and the solution that we choose to meet this problem. How do we know that it is the right solution and not just a solution that will initially placate, but will then return worse than before?

This illustrates that the long- and short-term consequences of decisions can oppose each other. It is the problem of the *quick fix*! We are probably all familiar with this and indeed this is why it is recognized as an identifiable characteristic of behaviour within organisations.

Strategies to counter something similar to archetypes relates to the way in which individuals can confront the real issue, related to their action.

- Consider the frequency of applying a 'fix' and attempt to cut down on it.
- Consider what alternative fixes there might be.
- Identify the root problem and address this rather than the symptom.

 Pause for thought – systemic thinking and the 5 whys

Senge (1993) offers a range of exercises and activities to support the five key disciplines. This activity is called the 5 whys and seeks to illustrate systemic thinking and the inter-related nature of the organisation.

With this activity you are asked to think of a question that is relevant to a specific organisation, beginning with why.

- Why have our levels of sickness been increasing over the last few months?
- Why is there a leak in the bund?
- Why has the price of sandwiches gone up in the canteen?
- Why are profits down?

The aim of the activity is to illustrate that from whichever point one starts in relation to an organisational problem we can or should be able to watch it meander through the organisation as we attempt to search for the root cause of this problem. In carrying out this activity try to avoid blaming individuals or groups and focus on the problem.

The classic story is, the pool of oil on the factory floor:

> A manager is walking through the factory with a systems thinking friend. They both observe a pool of oil on the floor and the manager turns to a worker nearby and asks if they would clean up the oil. The manager is happy with the prompt and efficient way the problem has been solved. However, the systems thinker asks why there was a pool of oil on the floor and the worker says because the pipe above their heads is leaking. The manager then asks for the pipe to be fixed, but the systems thinker again asks why the pipe is leaking. Again, the reply is that the seal used at this joint in the pipe is corroded. Getting the idea the manager asks why the seal has corroded and the worker says that they have been using an inferior type. Feeling a little sheepish the manager asks why and is told that there was a recent directive from the finance department to cut their budgets forcing them to use this cheaper seal. Finally, the worker replies that why there was this current cost cutting exercise was because senior management had upgraded their corporate hospitality suites to try to improve relations with important customers and clients.

Systemic thinking is the key discipline, for Senge. It is the ability to recognise the organisation as a collective, as a series of inter-related an interdependent elements. Each requires the other, and the actions of one element will have direct consequences for all of the other elements that make up the system. Again, this emphasises the ethical nature or basis of the LO. For an individual to operate they need to be aware of the existence of the 'other' and this is at the root of effectively ethical behaviour.

Personal mastery

This ethical basis reflects itself, also, in the discipline of personal mastery. In building the relationship between the individual and the organisation there is a need for individual and organisational aims to support and reflect each other. Where this does not occur there is likely to be little willingness of individuals to cooperate, share or learn for the organisation.

Personal mastery is about, in the first instance, defining the objectives of the individual and quite simply asks the individual to define what these might be. An activity associated with this is *personal vision* where Senge asks a group of individuals a simple question:

Personal vision

In this activity I am going to ask you a dangerous question and that is to imagine that you have achieved your most fondly held dream in life, ignoring how possible or impossible it might seem. Describe what it is. Having done this, reflect on what you have thought of and ask why this might have been difficult to do, perhaps you find it difficult to say you want something, perhaps it reflects somebody else's expectation of you, your mother or a friend.

Having identified your goal, now attempt to imagine what it might be like to achieve it. What is it going to do for you? For example, it might impact upon your own self-image, or your own tangible belongings, perhaps a home. It might be related to a relationship – again, in achieving this, what is it doing for you? Ask yourself also, if you could have it now, would you take it?

In asking these questions Senge is attempting to identify the aims and objectives of the individual. In the classic scenario an individual says that they want to *own a castle beside their sister's home*. In pursuing this, the individual is asked to say why they want it. As an explanation they say that they like the feeling of *security* and of *belonging* that comes from being close to a family member. At this point there are two identified elements that engage with the organisation.

Security and a *sense of belonging* are issues for organisations and all organisations can ask themselves how well, or otherwise, they provide these for their employees. For example, short-term rolling contracts provide little security and little or no involvement in any aspect of decision making and can make individuals feel detached from the governance of the organisation.

Where an organisation is capable of enhancing both a sense of security and of belonging, being part of the whole, then the individual's stated aims will be drawn closer to those of the organisation – where the organisation is looking to embed the social and collaborative principles associated with the LO. In externalising their aims, the individual is being asked to make themselves more visible and, therefore, more vulnerable.

For this to be a meaningful activity and for this discipline to have any value then there will need to be a certain degree of trust existing between the organisation and the individual. This trust cannot be taken for granted, nor should it be regarded as an operational requirement. Rather, it needs to be embedded with the overall mission of the organisation.

Mental models

Mental models as a concept stems from, amongst other things, educational psychology and cognitive processes that are concerned with how we construct and adapt our understanding. This was expressed by Jean Piaget (1896–1980) in what came to be regarded as the biological model of intellectual development – *schema* – and refers to our own personal constructs of the world around us. For example, we all have our own political opinions and these are formed from a series of influences throughout our lives. Perhaps this might be parental and other social concerns, or personal experiences. Once we form schema, they tend only to be adapted and are rarely completely replaced. So, learning is a process of assimilation and interpretation in relation to these formed opinions. Intelligence or our intellectual capabilities relate to how effectively we are able to carry out this process.

Within an organisational context we bring these schema to our relationships and importantly we form or construct schema or mental models about the experience we have of the organisational environment, again perhaps formed from any number of different experiences. It will impact on our attitude to individuals and groups within the organisation.

Do we regard people as being trustworthy or are they to be considered potentially devious? An LO seeks to make people aware of these models and work with them, or reflect upon them in order to attempt to ensure that they do not form a barrier to effective individual participation. It will ask you to identify and reflect upon your mental model and seek to reconcile issues that might affect the organisation.

Left-hand column

One of the techniques that is used here is called the *left-hand column*. It starts with a problem, perhaps there is a feeling that somebody is not pulling their weight or that you are being treated unfairly. You are asked to describe the situation and imagine a context in which you are having a conversation about this issue, perhaps with the person concerned or with your line manager. The suggestion is that in these conversations there are really two dialogues going on at the same time. If you took a piece of paper and drew a line down the middle you could write the actual conversation in the right-hand column but then also write what was not said in the left-hand column. In this column is what was being thought or felt during the conversation.

In exploring these mental models we are again learning about the relationship between the individual and the organisation and this learning perspective is an important component of the LO, as much as the ability of the organisation to share its knowledge through formal and informal networks.

Again, this is requiring the individual to externalise what has 'not' been said and a question needs to be asked and considered about the willingness of individuals to do this. There was, presumably, a reason behind why it was not said in the first place. For individuals to be willing to externalise the content of their mental models they need to trust the organisation and to trust the organisation it must be explicitly ethical in its own actions.

Shared vision

Shared vision again is dealing directly with the relationship between the individual and the organisation. It is essentially assuming that where there is shared vision, then the organisation has a balance between individual and organisational aims.

In terms of building or creating the vision for the organisation (perhaps, the mission statement) there are different ways in which it might be approached:

Telling: this is a rather authoritarian approach but nevertheless telling is a form of vision and is argued by many to have a powerful impact on action. It is leadership from the front and has drive and commitment inherent within it. It will require direct communication techniques and clearly set limits for participation from 'others'. It lacks any real sense of commitment from those who are told and often people only remember 25 per cent of what they are told.

Selling: this approach attempts to persuade people to come on board with the vision. The recipients have some right to say 'no'. Requires open channels of communication and moves to a more personal style of leadership. It is still 'boss-centric'.

Testing: this includes an important element where the vision is tested and comments sought. It further involves people and should have mechanisms by which their opinions can be acted upon and the vision altered. It must provide adequate information and the mechanism for response should not intimidate, it should also preserve privacy in terms of response to the plan.

Consulting: this accepts that the boss does not have all of the answers. However, it begins a process that can be potentially lengthy and ultimately may lead to a compromise that suits nobody. This requires a staged approach to information gathering and the analysis of information. This is still based on a plan coming from the top rather than being built from the bottom.

Co-creating: this is where everybody has a creative input into the development of the organisational vision. This will start with establishing personal visions, with the treatment of people as equals and to seek alignment rather than simple agreement, which might hide negative feelings, possibly held within mental models.

Where we *co-create* rather than *tell* we are illustrating a better ability to embed meaningful learning within the organisation. Shared vision as a discipline is a more explicit expression of the maturity of the organisation as an LO. The two-way dialogue necessary for the co-creation of the organisational vision will employ information technologies in a particular way, they will facilitate open dialogue and this clearly plays to their strengths. The ownership of the vision will be more broadly based and this helps to build further trust.

Team working

This is based on sound communication, where individuals are willing to participate in dialogue. It is based on the fundamental OL belief that individuals have more to gain than lose through collaborative learning. In the LO the structure and environment will facilitate team working. It will cross boundaries, it will be open and in doing so it will encourage two-way dialogues. The capabilities required by individuals include sound communication skills and an appreciation of how to share the knowledge that is being accumulated through experience. This cannot be taken for granted and if necessary key capabilities need to form part of individual development plans.

Each of the disciplines described above blend themselves into a series of actions that support organisational learning. The relationship between the individual and the organisation is central and within each discipline discursive practices drive their agenda and actions. They seek to externalise the relationship between the organisation and the individual. Through this we can positively work to create an effective OLP, as an environment suitable for social learning.

Its bedrock is dialogue:

> If you take a *systemic view* of the organisation and appreciate the complex inter-relationships that impact upon, and are the consequences of, individual and collective actions; if you seek to understand the *aims of the individual* and provide some support to the achievement of these aims; if you address the *negativity of individual attitudes* and foster a *common sense or feeling* for the organisation; if you can develop and implement *effective team working* — then you will be creating an organisation that is capable of learning, that is positively addressing issues that impact negatively upon the organisation's ability or willingness to learn.

Senge's model has remained both popular and controversial since its inception and development. It is inherently idealistic, as many models are, and whether or not any organisation can achieve success in relation to all of the disciplines identified is questionable.

Nevertheless, the basis or foundation of each discipline is discursive. Individually, how do we talk about our mental models of the organisation? Organisationally, how do we communicate our vision or how do the groups or teams talk to each other? Our ability to talk or to communicate is facilitated by technologies embedded in our information systems or our learning management systems, but the LO models help to guide the content of this context.

The learning company

Pedlar, Burgoyne and Boydell (1997) presented four key characteristics of the LO, or what they referred to as the learning company:

1 Has a climate in which individual members are encouraged to develop their full potential.
2 Extends this learning culture to include customers, suppliers and other significant stakeholders.
3 Makes human resource development strategy central to business policy.
4 Is a continuous process of organisational transformation.

In this model of the learning company there are 11 characteristics:

1 a learning approach to strategy
2 participative policy making
3 informating
4 formative accounting and control
5 internal exchange
6 reward flexibility
7 enabling structures
8 boundary workers as environmental scanners
9 inter-company learning
10 a learning climate
11 self-development opportunities for all.

A learning approach to strategy

In the development and presentation of strategic policy statements the organisation will ensure that a learning process informs this crucial organisational activity. In order to do this there is a need for a degree of flexibility and dynamism in terms of how plans are initiated and allowed to evolve. This suggests a style of leadership and direction setting that is open to dialogue and is a visible process that can be seen largely as experimentation rather than the creation of definitive statements.

Central to this is the willingness of managers to openly reflect on their practices and the case example here is Shell's 'management challenge' where managers observe each other's working practices on a three yearly rota basis. The idea here is to test norms and assumptions. It seeks to challenge any practices that have become embedded.

Identifying where you want to go as an organisation and basing it on this reflective process is similar to Senge's disciplines of shared vision and mental models, where the former seeks to embed collective/social practices in management decision-making processes and the latter to challenge embedded ideas or patterns of behaviour.

Participative policy making

As this characteristic suggests, the aim here is to ensure that there is as much participation across the organisation in policy formation as it is possible to achieve. The benefit to be gained here is in, for example, the ability to reduce the time it takes to embed ideas and innovations into the production process.

The case of Toyota being able to embed these ideas quicker than General Motors, despite spending more time on planning, is presented as the main benefit to be gained from managing dialogues. We can look to key information technologies that allow even large multi-national organisations to create these dialogues despite their obvious problems of geography and so on.

Informating

Here we have the role of ICT in facilitating the OL strategy of the organisation. In managing explicit knowledge, knowledge-based information systems can store, retrieve, manipulate and move data and information in increasingly, if not bewilderingly, diverse and complex ways. We have data warehouses where we once had databases, we apply data-mining techniques to make sense of data sources that we as individuals are simply not capable of doing. Last but not least we have network technologies that connect us to whoever we might wish to connect to, at whatever time and in whatever place we might wish to be connected.

The functionality of these technologies has driven many KM and OL initiatives and appears to be central, as Pedlar, Burgoyne and Boydell (1997: 92) say:

> British Airways told us in one of our data gathering sessions that they would rather sell their aeroplanes than their computer system, because while you can always lease a plane, the computer system is at the heart of the business. With its tentacles, like the roots of a tree, reaching out to all travel agents, it sucks in business; on the operations side (the branches and twigs) it reaches out and coordinates the flights' planes, aircrews, catering and so on.

At an operational level there is no doubt that these systems play a very large part, but as any gardener will tell you trees also cause damage, they deprive other plants of moisture and nutrients, their roots can block and crack drains and their shade can prevent sunlight getting to other parts of the garden. In other words, without extending this analogy to breaking point, systems themselves need to be controlled and managed for the purpose or purposes they were intended. Information systems can get out of hand, they can focus too much on operational level activities and they do tend to focus on the management of explicit knowledge rather than the creation of tacit knowledge or the way in which this tacit knowledge might become explicit.

 Key points

Knowledge-based information systems will be considered further in Part 3 and will inform the *Planting* element of the SPADES model.

These systems need to be user-friendly and should aim to facilitate learning processes. Technologies for learning within organisations should first and foremost reflect the cultural dynamics embedded within the organisation's preparedness for learning. This important point highlights the issue simply, where the functionality of the technology is not aligned we find technologies that do not fulfil their assigned roles, individuals do not share in the expected way and these systems can become expensive white elephants.

Formative accounting and control

How we account for our actions is an important part of the learning process. In the first instance, this can focus on the financial side of things and with this characteristic, this is the primary focus. Individuals can benefit from a greater awareness of financial implications and these can be made available more effectively through the information system.

However, being accountable goes beyond finance and budgets and extends to responsibilities and codes of practice and ethics. Embedding within any learning programme an opportunity to reflect upon the extent to which individuals and groups meet or are unable to meet these types of responsibilities can highlight important aspects of learning readiness. Can we admit mistakes, openly without any fear of the consequences? Can we respond to any failure in a measured and constructive way?

Internal exchange

At the heart of knowledge sharing, according to this and other models, is the relationship between the individual and the organisation. Senge and Argyris have both emphasised this point and with internal exchange, Pedlar, Burgoyne and Boydell are also presenting the need to develop some understanding of how this relationship can in the first instance be perceived, with a view to then developing and enhancing it.

> The quality of relationships has a very marked effect on how much learning is likely to happen in the company. Without good relationships the dialogues required between the different parts of the organisation, in order to deliver the best product or service, will not take place. Behind good quality dialogue is a sense of the whole company.
>
> (Pedlar, Burgoyne and Boydell 1997: 111–12)

Establishing mechanisms to assess the level and nature of the internal exchange within any organisation is a complex undertaking. It will require a focus on specific techniques, perhaps already in place, for example, peer review or mentoring programmes. In analysing these techniques a further dialogue will need to be created, one that allows the OL practitioners to gain an understanding of this exchange. Here qualitative research techniques such as critical discourse analysis can play an important part.

Reward flexibility

The essence of the knowledge-economy is fluidity. This results in a need to sustain a level of organisational flexibility that has not previously been required. This flexible approach is one of the 'new capabilities' associated with the LO.

If we accept this, then as managers we need to review how we express this flexibility and how we respond to practices that can be seen to demonstrate flexibility. This should be done with a view to reviewing, amongst other things, rewards and pay structures. We should, essentially, be paying those who work flexibly more than those who do not.

The implications of this are not inconsiderable as there is a need to address well established, if not embedded, organisational practices. Not least, there is a questioning of the organisational structure where your remuneration is dependent upon your position and not your ongoing contribution or way of working. In this way LOs are often seen to be less hierarchical in the traditional sense, with more opportunities to progress and to regress on an ongoing basis.

Pay is only one type of reward and in this characteristic, rewards such as support, encouragement, development opportunities and so on can all be added to the mix. Where organisations have complex reward systems they will also tend to be organisations that have a strong need to ensure high levels of innovation and creativity.

> The basic principle in encouraging people to feel part of the whole enterprise is to treat them that way.
>
> (Pedlar, Burgoyne and Boydell 1997: 120)

This relates closely to Senge's view of both personal mastery and shared vision. In the former there is an element of empowerment, whereby individuals are encouraged to show initiatives and where there is a realistic expectation that this will be rewarded either in terms of money or other forms of recognition.

Enabling structures

Flexibility underpins this characteristic and recognises the need to be able to respond when circumstance change, even when a previously successful model requires to be abandoned and replaced. Having the 'bottle' to challenge the organisation in this way and to this extent is not inconsiderable. This is the 'adapt or die' scenario which can be associated with organisations that have been initially successful but fail to recognise that this previously winning formula is no longer valid.

Enabling structures highlight the need to assess the organisation's ability to offer a sufficiently flexible learning environment. Is there space and time for individuals to make the necessary changes, to identify the shortcomings as they emerge, to decide on a suitable means of responding? This has led to some interesting organisational developments and the one that often raises some eyebrows is the notion of sleeping pods. Here individuals are encouraged to recharge their batteries by taking a 'power nap'. Organisations have begun to install these facilities and to a large extent they are a recognition of the need to ensure that enabling structures are in place to facilitate and enhance learning capabilities. It remains an intriguing question – how ready is your organisation to sleep?!

The main point being made here is an 'old' pedagogical one – make sure that you have the proper environment for teaching and learning. Make sure that the room is not too hot or too cold and so on. Pedagogy is increasingly informing our understanding of the LO but at this point we are emphasising the type of issues associated with 'moving the deck chairs round on the Titanic'. In other words, avoiding making small and unnecessary changes and ensuring that there is a structure in place that allows these small changes to be made in an informed way.

Boundary workers as environmental scanners

Senge's principal discipline is *systems thinking* and we have identified a shift from closed to open systems where the environment is recognised as having a direct impact upon the organisation. This environment informs action at all levels from operational to strategic.

The work carried out to understand these contextual matters is an important part of the organisation's ability to learn. Specific work needs to be done to collect and use this type of information and to a large extent this characteristic falls into the classic remit of information management. An information need has been identified and we need to ensure that there are mechanisms in place to gather this information and to store it effectively. This in turn should ensure that those who need to use this information can access it in the most efficient way possible. They should receive this information when they need it and in a form that is useful to them.

By doing this, existing products or services can be kept as relevant and current as possible and indicate where the future might lie.

Inter-company learning

This characteristic is very much a subset of the above characteristic where organisations within an environment are brought into a close relationship that will benefit both parties.

> Getting through this process with some business partners might take several meetings, especially with tricky relationships such as competitors or those with a poor history. Yet a company's ability to make alliances and operate in networks is emerging as one of the key areas of organisational capability for the future.
>
> (Pedlar, Burgoyne and Boydell 1997: 147)

A learning climate

Two crucial, culturally based dynamics are being highlighted with this characteristic. First, there is the need to ensure that the facilitation of learning is seen as a primary task of organisational managers and second is that the blame culture is comprehensively undermined. With the former there is an active realignment of responsibilities and an expectation that formal job descriptions begin to reflect this. By recognising the latter there is a clear statement being made that failures to learn are not the fault of the individual but carried collectively by all. Blame, to a large extent, is being recognised here as a failure in the learning programme as a whole and the organisation's failure to the individual rather that the individual's to the organisation.

Where a learning climate is being maintained there is an ability to sustain improvement through a constructive dialogue that is able to question and challenge practices. Learning becomes a normal activity. Pedlar, Burgoyne and Boydell (1997: 153–4) suggest a quick questionnaire to assess learning capabilities, based on the following ten items:

1   Sexist and racist remarks are commonplace and tolerated by management.
2   Praise is much rarer than criticism.
3   You get little information about your own performance.
4   There is competitive pressure from fellow employees to work long hours.
5   There is little concern shown for members' health and welfare.

6 Making admissions of mistakes or failure is career limiting.
7 All management decisions are justified in terms of the bottom line, that is, solely on financial grounds.
8 There are a lot of hierarchical distinctions made in terms of conditions, perks and so on.
9 There is little diversity in management – most are male, white etc.
10 It is very hard to get people to listen to you and your ideas.

Questionnaires of this type are tools to understand the nature of the learning environment. This ranges over a number of different areas. We can assess both the suitability of the existing environment and the perception of individuals as to the value placed on their engagement with learning. So we have a blend of practical pedagogical issues and more sociological/psychological issues. These latter are not exclusive to social or collective learning contexts but they do appear to be enhanced.

Self-development opportunities for all

Egalitarianism appears to be central to the LO and this obviously extends to the development of the OLP. Staff development programmes that allow individuals to be trained, to attend conferences, to join professional bodies, to get involved with external initiatives and so on, all form part of the mechanisms by which individuals continue to learn – they continue to professionally develop. This is embedded to some extent in all organisations but the LO draws this to the centre and again emphasises that this type of activity is not in itself new but is a reconfiguration of existing activities.

The LO emphasises the importance of these activities, it does not allow the organisation to see this as a peripheral activity. Rather, it should be a structured activity that is available to all and there should be mechanisms in place to ensure that the whole organisation benefits from these activities. For example, when individuals attend conferences it is often the case that there is no mechanism to share what has been learnt. Often no formal reports are necessary. The opportunity to maximise the benefit of this activity is lost.

So, detailed development planning is one way to encourage a more systematic approach to this type of learning opportunity, but it is recognised that this can act as a demotivator if managed poorly. Here there is seen to be an opportunity to offer control to individuals, with only periodic/light reviews to ensure that expectations are being met.

> The aim is to give control and responsibility for managing themselves to each person and then create opportunities to review learning and development on occasions such as annual appraisals.
>
> (Pedlar, Burgoyne and Boydell 1997: 165)

Personal development planning (PDP) forms an important part of most contemporary organisations and is, or should be, linked directly to the OLP. Again, these are not new activities but enhancements to existing activities. They are a *re-emphasis* or a *repositioning* of what might have been seen as marginal or peripheral in terms of their overall significance to the organisation.

Both of the above models have highlighted characteristics (disciplines in Senge's case) and these help to form the relevant questions. They, at best, help us to identify the relevant questions but they certainly do not address these questions. Both models are very much aligned to the externalisation of personal knowledge and this has always been embedded in organisational practice. So, OL is as much about identifying current practice as it is about introducing any new or unique practices.

OL is equally a response to the perceived nature of the organisational environment. Specifically, change is presented as the key feature. If organisations are to survive and to thrive they need to be good at dealing with change. Change itself reflects the uncertainty that often drives learning. Where we feel uncertain, where we feel confusion and doubt, there is a heightened sense of the need to learn in order not to be a 'victim' of change. Similarly, where we face competition from within the organisation there is also a heightened sense of a need to learn in order to 'keep up'. Where there is less of a sense of external or internal competition there is often said to be less of an impetus or incentive to learn. Public sector organisations offer fewer example of OL for this reason, but this does not mean that OL is of less significance. Rather the challenges of developing the OLP will be different for different organisations. Uncertainty in the external or internal environment will create an impetus for OL that may not necessarily exist to the same extent in public sector organisations.

Exactly how an organisation might look to develop its OLP will be dependent upon the type of organisation and just how able it is to form the right questions, at the right time. A range of different tools and techniques have become associated with both knowledge management (KM) and OL, from simple email to complex learning environments and communities of practice. The SPADES model is looking to identify a staged approach to the development of the OLP, starting with technical and cultural environment. It suggests that the success of any tool will be dependent upon the individual context and that it can be the wrong time to consider the introduction, in particular, of the CoP model. This model is for organisations that can be said to be *mature* as far as OL is concerned.

In terms of context, there is no more critical a context than the armed forces, where the need to ensure that they have the capabilities to respond in key situations can literally be a matter of life and death. Because of this it is no surprise that the armed forces have identified the need to be able to create and embed OL practices. The Center for Army Lessons Learned (CALL) is part of the United States Army and has developed the use of After Action Reviews to drive OL, their current mission statement is:

> The Center for Army Lessons Learned facilitates the Army's lessons learned program by identifying, collecting, analyzing, disseminating and archiving issues and best practice; and by maintaining situational awareness in order to share knowledge throughout the Army as well as our unified action partners utilizing tools like networks, workshops and interviews.
>
> (Center for Army Lessons Learned 2015)

Major global organisations similarly have pioneered the deployment of OL tools, including Royal Dutch Shell which from the early 1970s developed and became associated with scenario planning.

> Scenarios give us lenses that help us see future prospects more clearly, make richer judgements and be more sensitive to uncertainties.
>
> (Royal Dutch Shell 2015)

Scenario planning and lessons learned are just two examples of how organisations are responding to the need to embed OL.

 Key points

Scenario planning will be considered further in Part 4 and will inform the *Growing* element of the SPADES model.

The SPADES model is looking to illustrate how OL can be aligned with an organic process that provides the right environment for growth before looking to establish and stabilise this environment ahead of actual growth and ultimately the ability to sustain an iterative process of propagation. Different tools and techniques are considered at each stage of the model, starting with the context and ending with communities of practice which are primarily a learning context. Many of these tools and techniques are not new and will currently form part of the HRD strategy of the organisation. OL, therefore, emphasises key practices some of which will be embedded, others not.

Concluding remarks

For all of these tools and techniques associated with OL and for all of the elements, disciplines or characteristics of the LO model it is the collaborative and social context of learning that drives the OLP. Trust and respect are central to the ethos of the OLP and in relation to all organisational practices these need to be identified and embedded. This is the ethical structure that can be associated with the fluid and dynamic contemporary organisational context. These are the humanistic principles from which OL has emerged.

Part 2

Organisational learning

Key principles and contexts

This part is an overview of the key principles and contexts that have contributed to the development of OL. Understanding the organisation and the significance of group working focuses on the need to communicate and in particular to create meaningful organisational dialogues. Organisation development (OD) has contributed to the embedding of collaborative models of working and in turn has allowed the organisation to meet many of the challenges associated with constant change.

The emphasis on collaboration has identified the need for an underlying ethical position that supports both the fluidity inherent within the environment and the trust and respect that is necessary for those engaged with OL. This needs to embed an ethical position that respects the individual. Here, the HR function will be drawn to the centre, focusing specifically on the need to define organisational culture and the role of leadership. Similarly, mechanisms of learning are associated with the key KM models that look to make our personal experience available to all in the organisation.

OL as an inclusive discipline is challenging our understanding of the organisation, it is founded upon an ethical position that respects the 'other' and this builds the trust that allows for the embedding of more egalitarian organisational structures and drives learning as a social and collaborative action.

5 The nature of the contemporary organisation

Learning outcomes:

1. Understand the organisation and the shifting perception of its purpose.
2. Identify the dynamics of collaborative group working.
3. Appreciate the significance and importance of communication.
4. Identify the key role of OD as an agent for change.

Introduction

Organisations are clearly central to any consideration of organisational learning. How we have understood organisations will inform how they might be mechanisms that support learning as a key dynamic in the management of change. There is often a choice presented to us here, to either take a *positivist*, a more *interpretive*, a *critical* or a *postmodern* view. Many arguments have been presented about the efficacy of each of these views and they have a direct impact upon how we might view the development of learning within the organisation. Positivism is often associated directly with behaviourism of the Pavlovian kind, which focuses on direct behaviour and largely ignores the context as a determinant of action. However, this is not entirely justified as a positivist study of action will focus on the individual's justification for their action and that this in turn is derived from the social context within which they sit. Just as the individual subject will interpret meaning so will the researcher. Interpretive studies, however, place a more substantial emphasis upon the human social characteristic of action. Rather than employing more empirically based data collection tools, interpretive studies rely on more qualitative tools, such as ethno-methodology, content analysis and semiotics. To an extent it is a difference in data-collection method that defines the approach, rather than an argument based on one being more or less scientific than the other. Critical and postmodern views challenge the way in which the organisation can be understood. Specifically, the production of knowledge from a critical perspective is based upon communication and that dialogue forms the basis of our action, rather than any force based on crucial power dynamics. Postmodern theories will reject this position and the divorcing of power and knowledge production. What we might know in a postmodern sense is based on the power structures that will determine what we might claim as right or wrong. Although this is not the place for a detailed consideration of the claims and counter-claims, it is important to be clear that this text draws more on critical and postmodern approaches to our understanding of organisations.

The centrality of power dynamics and of dialogue is crucial. Power will determine knowledge production, which in turn will determine what it is possible for us to learn. However, the nihilism associated with postmodern thought can be countered by a recognition that these power structures are themselves fluid and any move towards more egalitarian models will enrich the wider knowledge discourse embedded within the organisation.

Organisation theory

A great deal of the early work on organisations was based on the belief that they were structures that ought to be geared towards maximising efficiency as a prerequisite for maximising profitability. Scientific management principles associated with the classical theory of organisations attributed to F. W. Taylor (1911) presented a rational view, producing a bureaucratic model and the hierarchical structures that we are still very familiar with today.

Organisations have long been considered as bureaucratic entities with well-defined structures and clear hierarchies of authority governed by explicit rules. Shifting this has required significant advances in relation to technical and key cultural concepts, including education. Printing encapsulates this, to an extent by representing both a technical development but also one that drove literacy.

The key question for the organisation has also had some clarity, namely it is looking to be more efficient. To do this it must be managed and this concept of management initially focused on the administrative functions that defined the operational actions of the organisation. On the other hand there has also been a more sociological perspective on organisations, which brought both psychology and sociology into the consideration of the organisation as a collective entity. The theory of organisations, has, therefore, always drawn on a cross-disciplinary base, following trends in sociological thought as well as in management science. It continues to blend these disciplines in pursuit of what is meant by efficiency and within the current context it is looking to consider the implications associated with the emergence of the knowledge-economy and the information society.

This has drawn education to the fore and the need to acknowledge the contribution of a broader base of individuals within the organisation as the key source of its much sought after efficiency. Rather than this being the guidance of those at the top to those at the bottom of the formal hierarchy, it is the collaborative contribution of all that will 'unlock' the value of the intellectual capital that is accumulated through experience. This highlights the relationships that exist within the organisation and the sociological underpinning of our understanding of the approach to 'managing' an organisation that is capable of learning.

Rensis Likert (1903–1981) is associated with the presentation of organisations as falling into four broad categories:

1   Exploitative – where the relationship between the individual and the organisation is one-way and very much from top to bottom. These would normally be highly structured organisations with clear and transparent lines of authority.
2   Benevolent – where the relationship between the individual and the organisation is very much like that of a parent to a child. There is little opportunity for two-way communication and leaders as decision makers expect compliance, which will be rewarded. Equally, non-compliance can expect some form of punishment.
3   Consultative – where the relationship between the individual and the organisation is based on a certain but limited degree of two-way communication. This can enhance

the sense of individual responsibility within the decision-making process. This in turn can have a beneficial impact upon both motivation and performance.

4   Participative – where the relationship between the individual and the organisation is based on two-way communication and the identification of the strategic and operational goals of the organisation is collaboratively formed. This further enhances individual levels of satisfaction.

This approach to understanding organisations can very much be described as *normative*, in that it is proposing a single favoured model of the organisation. In this case model 4, the participative organisation is presented as the favoured model. To an extent, Senge's model of the LO is normative in that it is presenting key disciplines that need to be embedded within practice in order for the organisation to learn.

Similarly, contingency theories, such as *structural contingency theory* (associated with the work of Jay Lorsch (b. 1932), draws on this positivist perspective to focus on the structural context to determine and drive the direction of decision making within any organisational context. Essentially, it is not the individual that will determine the course of action to be taken but the structural context within which the individual sits. This context may vary from one organisation to another and therefore the decisions to be taken may vary but the determinants remain constant.

There is also a differing perspective in terms of what the value or purpose of the organisation might be, with the former more focused on 'managerialism' and the latter on employees and their engagement with or relationship to the management of the organisation. In radical and postmodern schools of thought that can be associated with more humanistic principles, it is the underlying power dynamics within organisations that have formed the principal focus for understanding the organisation. The challenge here is in seeing the organisation as not representing any form of 'reality'.

> ... postmodern theorists work on the assumption that there are different realities for different people.
>
> (Crowther and Green 2004: 4)

The significance of these differing perspectives can clearly be identified in the questions that they raise for organisations and the priorities that they ultimately identify. In studying OL we need to be aware of these differing approaches as the development of this area has centred on the role of the OL practitioner and the interventions that they represent.

 Pause for thought – positivism

Positivism is a theoretical perspective first outlined by Auguste Comte (1798–1857) and is based upon the substantial claims of the scientific methodology. In order to identify a 'truth' a test needs to be established which in its replication and consistent result will determine what can be regarded as a fact. All knowledge is based upon this approach and it is one that has been embedded in our view of the world for many centuries. In aligning ourselves with this view we are to an extent identifying the ability of all areas of knowledge to be broken down into their component parts and ultimately to produce a definitive truth. This process of investigation would ultimately result in an absolute understanding that would fulfil the social purpose of humanity.

Where this has a direct bearing on organisational learning is in relation to how we might form or develop a learning programme for organisations. From a positivist perspective we would emphasise a more technocratic view with an emphasis on empirical evidence and statistical analysis. It will align itself with Durkheim's view of *sui generis* where social action is identified by general facts. All social actions can be understood, can be predicted and will follow a discernible pattern. Positivism searches for these patterns, these facts and positively looks to place the endeavours and approaches of the scientists who have uncovered patterns and 'laws' of the natural world – the natural sciences – within the social world and the social sciences.

In this sense organisations are changing, in terms of their structure, in response to the perceived need to manage individuals as assets. In considering how and why people work, it is inevitable that we must consider the structure, form, nature and operating processes of the organisations in which they work. Organisations perhaps can be seen as quasi-organisms that have lives of their own. They are born, grow, flourish and sometimes die. They form relationships and foster offspring and have lifestyles and attitudes.

Organisations are human creations and consist of people rather than buildings, machinery and so on. The term 'organisation' itself is not limited to industry or commerce and people within organisations are (to some extent) working towards common goals where informal groups can be as important as formal organisational structures. Essentially, organisations are social structures and we need to understand them in these terms.

The structure of the organisation is said to be influenced by three basic factors:

1   How activities are structured
         ... how employee behaviour is controlled by job design and procedures.
2   Where the power is concentrated in an organisation
         ... where is the centre of decision making?
3   How much line personnel control there is over the work-flow

In smaller organisations the third factor is often prominent, while with larger organisations this would be the first element. In large bureaucratic organisations, such as local government, it is often the second element.

It is more difficult to identify any concrete link between organisational structure and performance but the systemic view is one that helps to illustrate how organisations are embedded within their own context. Through an awareness of how the parts or the elements constitute the whole and how this whole sits, itself within its environment, emphasises the social basis of organisational activity. No organisation exists external to its own environment or even in terms of its own composition which is itself a fluid and dynamic social construct as open to change as any market or any individual's 'mood'.

This 'new perspective' on organisations is reflected in the fluidity and dynamism that OD and OL seek to address. OL and KM recognise that within this type of organisational context the knowledge asset or the intellectual capital of the organisation is the principal resource. The more rational approaches to understanding organisations are being questioned:

> Perhaps the most important failing of the narrow view of rationality is not that it is wrong per se, but that it has led to a dramatic imbalance in the way we think about managing.
>
> (Peters and Waterman 2004: 52)

According to Peters and Waterman (2004) organisations can reflect this new understanding through the development of eight key attributes:

1   bias for action
2   close to the customer
3   autonomy and entrepreneurship
4   productivity through people
5   hands on – value driven
6   stick to the knitting
7   simple form, lean staff
8   simultaneous loose–tight properties.

This person-centred approach has, again, highlighted how we might define the knowledge-based organisation and how the human element at least of intellectual capital might be managed, if not exploited. Organisations will miss opportunities where they are unable to give staff the flexibility to pursue new ideas and develop new products. Innovation needs to move away from new products and new ventures being the exclusive domain of the strategic planners and R&D departments into the *line*. Cultures should be created which aid and encourage innovation and old barriers eradicated. Again, this conforms to the model of the knowledge-based organisation, as Charles Handy (1985) has pointed out when he talks about 'smart' people coming to the fore and recognising that there are no success blueprints but a series of models that can or may lead to success.

Handy identifies three generic styles of organisation that he argues will dominate in the future:

The shamrock organisation

•   Like the shamrock, the organisation has three 'leaves':

1   core workers
2   flexible/part-time workers
3   contract workers.

The federal organisation

•   Allied together under a common flag.
•   Modern organisations need not only benefit from the flexibility that comes from smallness but also command the resources of large corporations.
•   Can be characterised by having a federal centre with a number of autonomous or semi-autonomous divisions.

The triple I organisation

- Based on the premise that in the future an organisation's employees will be at its core and will need three basic capabilities:

  1   The ability to use Intelligence to analyse ...
  2   The available Information to ...
  3   Generate Ideas for new products and services.

The triple I organisation does not so much define a structure – much more a system of operating standards. Their form can be shamrock or federal or any other particular model but staff are recruited on the basis of their skills or 'smartness'. Staff are unsupervised in the traditional sense and seek to keep their skills, knowledge and abilities up to date in an organisation that is capable of learning. These capabilities emerge from the relationship that individuals will create within the organisation and it is important to identify how this relationship between the employer and the employee is created and sustained.

The clear 'drift' in relation to our understanding of organisations and the elements that help us to understand, if not determine their operation and function, is towards a more humanistic or even postmodern perspective. In Likert's normative model it is the characteristics associated with participation and collaboration that are emphasised and this can also be equated with Senge's disciplines. For Handy, in the triple I organisation the level of individual responsibility and engagement is clearly enhanced. The focus is on the relationship between the individual and the organisation and the embedding of collaborative practices. This then raises questions around how this relationship needs to be formed and developed. What elements will determine behaviour at both a transactional and a transformative level?

Transactional – is the level of everyday action and how individuals relate to each other and conduct themselves in relation to one another.
Transformative – is the 'higher' level of change to the embedded culture and to the understanding of how relations are to be conducted.

The Burke–Litwin model (1993) attempts to identify the elements or variables that need to be considered in relation to performance and change. In terms of transformational change the key elements are:

Mission and strategy: identifying the aim and objectives of the organisation and how these are to be achieved.
Leadership: the perception of the role of managers in 'delivering' the aim or strategic goal of the organisation.
Culture: the rules, values and principles that determine action.

These elements sit within the organisational environment and will determine individual performance. They form the top part of the Burke–Litwin (1993) model. The bottom part covers the transactional dynamics (see Figure 5.1)

The Burke–Litwin model can be used to identify the questions that need to be asked in order to assess the capabilities of the organisation in relation to change. These tie in with Senge's disciplines, for example, there may be an investigation into the extent to which the vision of the organisation is based on telling, selling, testing, consulting or co-creating. Where telling is embedded as, at least, the perception of individuals within the

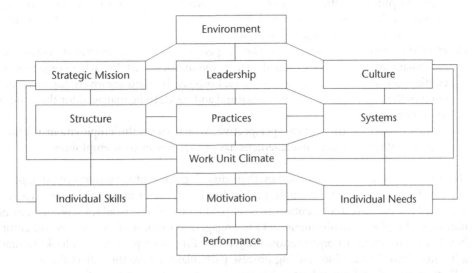

Figure 5.1 Burke–Litwin model of organisational performance and change

Source: Burke and Litwin, 1993.

organisation of how the strategic goal is determined then the type or nature of intervention is clarified both for the OD and OL practitioners. In this case there is a need to better understand why this is the way things are done.

- Is this an embedded expectation, widespread throughout the organisation?
- Does it have its roots in the alignment of efficiency with authority and control?
- Do employees at operational levels actively look to avoid the responsibility associated with co-creation?

The formation of questions such as these is at the heart of the development of the OLP. The OL practitioner is one that has the capabilities associated with this question formation. Therefore, OL practice looks to 'unpack' the relationship between the individual and the organisation and this goes beyond pay and benefits to include the conduct of the power relationship between employer and employee.

There is no doubt that across the world, there has been a move away from collectivist employee relations, which stressed union–employer bargaining arrangements, towards individual-based negotiations, which are underpinned by personal contracts and performance-related pay systems. However, collective bargaining continues in many countries and in many employment sectors – for example, in the UK, collective bargaining is still common in the public sector.

Throughout the European Union, legislation is bringing a common approach to some aspects of employee relations: for example, the requirement of all large multi-national companies operating in more than one EU country, is that they have European-wide works councils. This ensures an enhanced role for collective representation.

Different perspectives can be presented in relation to this important relationship:

The unitarist perspective: from a *unitarist* perspective, an organisation is viewed as a unified whole. It takes the view that everybody who works in the organisation has a sense of common purpose within an overarching paternalistic style of management. In such an organisation conflict is seen as unhelpful, and caused by *troublemakers*. The *unitarist* view is implicit in American models of HR.

The pluralist perspective: by contrast, the *pluralist* perspective sees organisations as coalitions of separate interest groups presided over by top management. In such an organisation, conflicts are seen as inevitable. They can, however, be used creatively for the wider good of the organisation. Conflict is natural and needs to be managed for the good of the organisation.

The radicalist perspective: the *radicalist* perspective, which views the employment relationship as conflictual, where management has greater power than employees.

These perspectives are characterised by their differing sense of *involvement* or *participation* by both the employee and the employer. Neither involvement nor participation is a new concept. However, greater attention is now paid to the ways in which conflict can be minimised. Employee involvement seeks to engage and support all employees and ensure their full commitment to organisational objectives. Employee participation looks to draw individuals into the decision-making process, particularly where they affect them.

Participation, therefore, indicates that the subordinate has greater influence over matters, but within the superior's responsibilities. Participation is seen as a process of delegation where workers can influence the work mix which is delegated to them, and the freedom that subordinates have to choose their own preferred methods of achieving agreed objectives.

 Pause for thought – the technologies of participation

As we have seen, there is always a choice about how to go about something like employee involvement. In Senge's discipline of shared vision he talks about a spectrum where at one extreme there is *telling* where individuals are told what the vision is to be and at the other *co-creating* where all those involved (everybody) have some meaningful input into the creation of the final vision – the mission statement perhaps.

The organisation will have a choice of how to approach involvement through participation. However, as well as there being a will to shift from telling to co-creating there also needs to be the capability. Social media such as Facebook have facilitated a broadly based opportunity for individuals to engage in a range of activities. BBC Trending (bbc.co.uk/trending) often picks up and comments on these, including a recent debate around individuals first presenting themselves as 'ugly' and then as more 'attractive'. The intention was to try to make the point not to 'judge a book by the cover' but this was criticised because it was suggesting that people with glasses and other characteristics were ugly. This as an opportunity to debate, across a potentially global audience and for these to potentially go 'viral', to an extent illustrates the opportunity this type of media offers organisations. It can certainly facilitate discussion, which is at the heart of collaboration.

Take some time to think about how different social media tools might help to facilitate the introduction of co-creation.

Social media can facilitate co-creation, they can provide a platform from which a dialogue can be sustained and developed. The individual needs to be inclined to participate with this dialogue and they will be if they have a strong and positive relationship with the organisation. In the first instance this will be determined by the relationship that forms between the groups that make up the organisation. Here again the OL practitioners need to recognise their role in understanding and building the appropriate relationships.

Collaborative group working

All organisations are collections of individuals and inherently social. However, they will organise themselves in many different ways to achieve what it is they want to achieve. They all, however, require group working and therefore our understanding of how groups form and achieve, or not, the goals set for them by the organisation is crucial:

> Groups in organisations are sources of powerful forces that need to be managed because they can be both constructive and destructive.
>
> (Xenikou and Furnham 2013: 3)

Fundamentally, it is the relationship between the individual and the organisation that will drive the effectiveness of group working and since the ground-breaking Hawthorne studies in the early part of the twentieth century it has been recognised that the study of the social environment within any organisation is necessary and will ultimately drive its efficiency. OD emphasises the importance of these human social systems in relation to organisational efficiency. Here, the study of the performance of the group is prioritised over the performance of the individual. The presence of others is itself regarded as a stimulant to a more positive engagement with the goals of the organisation and this has manifested itself in open-planned offices and glass walls where there might have been opaque solid walls. However, there is also evidence that suggests that the presence of others inhibits the potential productivity of individuals, that it might encourage 'loafing' and more passive engagement with tasks. Individuals can be pressured by other members in a variety of different ways, there can be a lessened sense of responsibility in group focused tasks, an individual's contribution is less explicit in a group context and there is potentially a lessened sense of value felt by the individual.

The purpose of group working and of collaborative learning is to enhance decision making in organisations. The crucial question here is around the extent to which it can be said that group decisions are better than those made by individuals. On the one hand the group has more resources available to it and therefore should be better placed to make better decisions. However, groups often fail to realise the potential of the resource available to them. They often polarise themselves around a dominant voice or idea and fail to adequately identify and externalise the knowledge that is held overall by the group.

Xenikou and Furnham (2013) identify three characteristics of collective decision making and their tendency to become polarised:

Persuasive argument: where individuals reinforce their current position when they hear new arguments in support of it.

Social comparison: where others hold similar views to that on an individual group member, that individual will have their view reinforced and will be more inclined to defend this view, even in its more extreme form.

Self-categorisation: a group may look to distinguish itself as a group, from other groups and
    will adopt a position that fulfils this role. This may also be in a more extreme form.

The role of the OL practitioner is to ensure that these tendencies are made explicit to those
that are involved with collaborative learning. Heightening awareness here might not avoid
these issues but will raise awareness of them. All group decision making needs to be a part
of the wider organisational process and should avoid becoming self-contained, where the
significance of the decision is not seen as having any impact upon the rest of the organisation. Others should have an opportunity to comment upon group decisions and rather than
this being seen as an example of how cumbersome collaborative learning might become, it
should be seen as a safeguard against poor decision making and an opportunity to further
build organisational trust. In this way the question manifests itself around how effectively
we might manage the collaborative process. How might we facilitate this level of dialogue?
    Group working is, therefore, complex but crucial. At times individuals will manifest a
range of different characteristics, they will compensate for colleagues unable to perform
to a given level, they will attempt to motivate themselves to match a perceived expectation
of other group members and feel guilt where they perceive their own underperformance
or resentment when their own perceived value is not adequately recognised. One key
element, therefore, is the extent to which the individual members of a group perceive the
value of what they are attempting to achieve. This helps to form a crucial question around
how this might be achieved.

 Pause for thought – identifying goals

Is it necessary to stress the importance of identifying the goal at an early stage and
    maintain this by a mantra-like repetition of it *or* should the members of a group
    themselves be allowed to identify the goal?
Does the latter empower the group but at the expense of clear leadership?
Does the process of identifying the goal through the group unnecessarily prolong
    the time taken to achieve the goal?

Group working raises questions regarding the overall structure of the organisation, what
its key cultural characteristics might be and how these might inhibit or support the sense
that individuals will have of the value of the work that they are being asked to do.
    Group working is about communication and the management of how any conflict
might be resolved in order to ensure effective and positive engagement. This is achieved
through appropriate *negotiation*, but exactly what this might be depends upon the type of
conflict that is being identified:

Relationship conflict – this might be personal antipathy towards another group member.
Difference of opinion – a conflict regarding how best to proceed.

In the latter case the conflict might be positive, opening up issues and providing a range
of different perspectives. This in turn should drive *innovation* which itself springs from the

creativity of the individuals who form the group. To manage this there needs to be built a context based on *trust* where individuals will be encouraged to externalise their expertise and risk potential criticism or even ridicule when new ideas may impact upon existing processes and practices. Creativity and innovation, ultimately, are at the heart of group working and through it, it is hoped that this creativity and innovation will be enhanced and maximised. This leads back to the *organisational dilemma*, or the extent to which individuals align themselves with the aims and objectives of the organisation as a whole:

> Person-organisation fit has been shown to affect task performance and organisational citizenship behaviours.
>
> (Xenikou and Furnham 2013: 176)

To make the necessary changes to ensure organisational prosperity or survival it is clearly necessary to understand and work with the culture of the organisation. Much of this is based upon a need to positively engage with individuals who make up the groups that in turn make up the organisation. Ultimately, the process that is being described here is a collective learning process where all members of the organisation feel enabled or empowered and inclined to externalise their own knowledge creation and make it an asset not just for themselves but for the group as a whole.

Just how the emerging digital environment is having an impact upon the issues that have been described above is an interesting and engaging question.

* How does this emerging context enhance or inhibit group working?
* How does this environment address the central issue of building organisational trust in order to facilitate effective organisational learning?

All of the major facets of our contemporary life are looking to engage and have a presence within the emerging digital environment. Political action can be organised through the web (the flash or smart mob) and our social relationships are conducted and to an extent determined through our engagement with social networking sites, such as Facebook, LinkedIn, Twitter and so on. Our working lives are rapidly being blended into this digital environment.

> The mind-seizing characteristics of interactive media, multimedia and hypermedia and the immersion of human minds in online environments and virtual realities must have a tremendous impact on our mental life. The question is, what impact?
>
> (Van Dijk 2006: 210)

There are many facets to this emerging environment and indeed it is not an uncontested concept. We can legitimately ask whether or not we are actually justified in presenting the emerging environment as a revolutionary 'new' context that is worthy of our consideration. However, the amount of academic and other study and concern both through the mass media and elsewhere is indicative of a major shift. Ultimately, from a practical, professional point of view we can see significant changes that represent equally significant challenges for professional practice. Woolgar (2003) presents us with five 'rules' of being virtual as follows:

1 *The uptake and use of the new technologies depends crucially on the local social context.*
  Here, context is everything. Questions are formed around who has formed, and is forming, the web and how this equates to the way in which it is being used.

2   *The fears and risks associated with new technologies are unevenly socially distributed.*
      Here, engagement is everything. Who expects what of the technological 'advances'
      and how is this distributed across the community?

3   *Virtual technologies supplement rather than substitute for real activities.*
      Rather than replacing practices and ushering in revolutionary change, the impact of
      technology is actually less pronounced. Here there is perhaps more of a socially con-
      structed view of technological change rather than a more deterministic view.

4   *The more virtual the more real.*
      Rather than streamlining and simplifying many 'real' practices, new virtual practices
      actually stimulate more real practices by making existing operational processes more
      efficient.

5   *The more global the more local.*
      Many tools designed for global outreach are often applied in local context.

Each of the 'rules' above is contestable and what we often assume to be happening is often
contradicted in practice. Below are two comments on key contexts: the social and the
psychological.

Social context, the digital divide

How can we judge the social nature of this digital environment? Does it make us less
social or does it open up new opportunities for communication and contact. Both of these
views are present in the 'popular' view of the digital environment.

Two key theories give us some insights into the nature of this when they consider the
idea of *social presence* and *media richness*. With the former, communication and its effectiveness is judged by the degree to which it supports or facilitates social presence and with the
latter the media of communication is judged by its ability or otherwise to communicate
ambiguous information. In relation to both of these, computer mediate communication
(CMC) is not highly regarded. To a large extent this is based upon *communication bandwidth*
which itself rests upon the idea that communication is essentially the transferral of information. Alongside this is the theory of *de-individuation* where there is a sense of anonymity
experienced by individuals when they are part of a group. There is often evidence presented to support the view that more 'extreme' views are held or decisions made within
computer-based group contexts, but there is also evidence to counter and challenge this.

> ... whereas CMC may indeed filter out many interpersonal cues that identify and
> individuate the communicators, group and category level cues are frequently defined
> by the interaction context.
>
> (Watt, Lea and Spears 2002: 69)

The *social identity model of de-individuation effect* (SIDE) is a more critical model of the way
in which groups operate and in particular the way in which anonymity impacts upon an
individual's behaviour within groups.

> Whereas the de-individuation approach views CMC behaviour in relation to the
> rejection of general norms prevalent in society, accentuated by the lack of interper-
> sonal cues in the medium, the SIDE approach has shown CMC behaviour to be more
> consistently explained as instances of conformity to local group norms, accentuated
> by the lack of interpersonal cues.
>
> (Watt, Lea and Spears 2002: 72)

Rather than the – relatively – anonymous environment of the web leading to less normative behaviour on the part of individuals in group situations there is clearly evidence now that suggests the opposite. Neither position can be presented as definitive, I don't think! Rather they illustrate the need to understand this environment and to investigate the impact of CMC on group behaviour. We need to do this in order to effectively operate within the environment.

This level of ambiguity and complexity also relates to the wider notion of the digital divide. Here the digital divide highlights the uneven nature of the engagement with technologies. Specifically, access to the Internet is not the same everywhere and there are areas with more 'advantages' than others. Also, within this largely geographical divide there are further divides, for example, in relation to age and to gender. The Internet was initially regarded as a male domain, and largely a young male domain. Generation X and the Baby Boomers were largely excluded while Generation Y is so immersed in these technologies they are unable to conceive of a context that does not include these technologies. The divide here also relates as much to income with the 'better off' tending to be the group most often having access to the Internet.

Just how accurate these generalisations might be is debatable but there is, nevertheless, a concern for us in relation to this divide, as Castells (2001) has pointed out:

> The differentiation between Internet-haves [sic] and have-nots adds a fundamental cleavage to existing sources of inequality and social exclusion in a complex interaction that appears to increase the gap between the promise of the Information Age and its bleak reality for many people around the world.
>
> (Castells 2001: 247)

The nature of the Internet is the significant factor here because it is an environment very much shaped by its users. If we are moving towards a more equitable distribution of access and use, we nevertheless need to recognise that the origins will have determined at least an initial direction. Or, they might have been, and may still be, determining the main purpose and agenda for this medium!

> ... first users may have shaped the Internet for the latecomers, both in terms of content and of technology, in the same way that the pioneers of the Internet shaped the technology for the masses of users in the 1990s.
>
> (Castells 2001: 255)

In very simple terms, Iceland has led the way with 97.8 per cent penetration of the Internet. The Scandinavia countries are also well ahead and it should be no real surprise that the USA is not leading, despite having over 245 million Internet users, as it has proportionately been overhauled since the early days of its total domination.

The digital divide itself is more complex than simply being the *haves* and the *have-nots*. There are those who choose not to use the Internet for reasons associated with what the Internet has been and is becoming. The dynamic growth of the Internet is not random, rather there will be a dominant discourse shaping it and this will marginalise as much as it includes.

Psychological context, group dynamics

The shift that we are largely observing here is one that has moved from physical experience of our environment or context to a virtual one. This is often referred to as a 'mediated' environment. In this mediated environment we live in a world of images and representations. We often see this world as more superficial, where attention span is under threat and we are less able to process complex information. We live in an era of sound bites, throwaway phrases and change for change's sake. But there is little evidence to suggest that the engagement with multimedia is potentially less challenging.

> In spite of all the myths about the stultifying impact of modern visual culture, almost all psychological research shows that reading in general has a more compelling but not necessarily greater appeal to our mental efforts than perceiving audio-visual message.
>
> (Van Dijk 2006: 215)

Engaging with the rich multimedia of the digital age is a challenge to us and requires us to be adept, versatile and capable if we are to fully appreciate the potentially subtle and complex messages that can now be presented to us.

> ... an optimum use of the new media requires full grown and versatile mental development and a multifunctional use of these new capabilities.
>
> (Van Dijk 2006: 215)

This impacts upon all communication and here we are going to focus on the impact on group communication where there are significant issues around the coordination of communication and where the visible cues associated with face-to-face communication are missing. In the first instance let's look at what makes good group communication!

The key component elements of successful group working are factors relating to belonging. A sense of loyalty, commitment, pride and value all play their part in creating a strong sense of being part of something that is worthwhile and that it is 'good' to be part of. Many groups and organisations have used tried and tested methods to embed this sense of belonging, from initiation ceremonies to key 'symbols' – *the key to the executive washroom* and other feelings of exclusivity!

In a virtual context can such elements exist? In cyberspace the level of fluidity is enhanced, groups form and re-form, they disappear at an alarming rate and form themselves around a range of different issues and topics. Is it possible in this context for the same sense of loyalty and commitment to emerge?

As Wallace (2001) considered, conformity is crucial in the development and maintenance of groups and to an extent operating in cyberspace impacts upon this:

> For better or worse, it appears that a computer-mediated environment strips away some of the features that contribute to our tendency to conform in a group setting.
>
> (Wallace 2001: 61)

Nevertheless, as she goes on to say:

> ... customs and conventions have emerged, and tightly knit and successful groups flourish on the Internet. It seems that new strategies were needed to bring about the compliance and conformity so essential to a viable community.
>
> (Wallace 2001: 61)

Email has emerged as a less formal means of communication but it has nevertheless created conventions, as has messaging and texting. It is almost necessary for an email or a text to align itself with the appropriate level of informality and for users to understand, to use and to conform to this informality.

We might not go so far as to say that there is a standard 'netiquette' in place on the web, simply because the level of detachment is such that we do not acquire or pick up the conventions of behaviour as quickly as we might with face-to-face communication. This has required there to be more explicit instruction to be presented on the web, more bold statements of what is and is not acceptable. This is often said to be driven by the users' need to believe that the medium will survive and that it will be endangered if there is not created an explicit understanding of what it is and how it will operate.

On the Internet, groups will attempt, therefore, to create a norm but when it comes to forming opinion there has long been a belief that the web is an environment that will bring individuals together who share similar views and that even extreme views will be affirmed and made even more extreme by the proximity of other similar views. This is true of groups outside the web and this is due to the absence of any moderating voice.

> The loss of that moderate voice is partly due to the exaggerated group polarization effects that can occur on the Internet.
>
> (Wallace 2001: 76)

Where groups identify a sense of being part of a group then this polarisation is enhanced, but, interestingly where there is less of a sense of being part of a group the individuality associated with the isolation and anonymity of the web has the opposite effect.

Central to the success of any group is the sense of trust that might or might not exist between the members. The advantage to be gained from virtual groups is the extension of the knowledge pool made available once it has been released from its geographical constraints, but the ability to establish trust might be more of a problem.

Virtual groups do form and are successful but the key elements that make them successful are based on the ability to create a group dynamic at an early stage. This in turn is based upon early and frequent exchanges based on a shared leadership and generally a more egalitarian approach. Where this more 'rapid' team engagement is present the team tends to create the necessary momentum to make considerable positive progress. However, where this is missing the team or group can find it immensely difficult to reverse it and very quickly 'bad practices' become established. Here, the virtual nature of the group is itself a barrier to the addressing of this type of issue and can make these groups more difficult to manage effectively.

Group dynamics, therefore, exist in a virtual environment in much the same way as they do in face-to-face environments. The belief that virtual environments bring a more open and democratic engagement where race, gender and so on are less of a barrier only exists to an extent, but the level of 'invisibility' in a virtual environment is not absolute. Position and status remain and individual members continue to vie for a more 'favourable' position within the group. Internet groups often create levels and difference in order to identify newcomers and to illustrate their own established status. This can be quite explicit with newcomers being required to 'pass' some process of initiation and even complete a test. Wallace highlights this as 'expert-ism' which relates to this practice of devising mechanisms or creating opportunities to replicate social structures or dynamics within the virtual environment:

> ... the insider knowledge of the group's history and norms can be the dividing line between the ingroup and the outgroup, with little reference to race, age, gender or ethnicity.
>
> (Wallace 2001: 101)

Trolling is a particular expression of this where individuals will attempt to mislead in order to illustrate to those 'in the know' the position of the individual who responds to the message. Here it is not about being right or wrong but about illustrating your own position in relation to the group – in these cases as either expert or novice! The message YHBT (you have been trolled) makes the troll's status explicit in relation to a specific group.

The emerging digital environment appears to be replicating more than replacing existing cultural dynamics. This challenges the work of individuals such as Marshall McLuhan and his popular concept of the *global village* where prejudice is being broken down by the removal of geographical barriers. Perhaps our psychological characteristics are more prevalent than geographical proximity and although geography might well be history this does not mean necessarily that we will engage with one another any differently!

The individual, the group and the organisation

Groups operate within an organisational context and their purpose is to enhance the achievement of organisational aims. This in turn is achieved by the positive engagement of the individual with the organisation's aims. Within the emerging organisational context there appears to be more similarity between face-to-face, traditional, forms of contact and that experienced within the virtual environment. Key dynamics appear to operate in both environments, both good and bad.

Given this we can expect to be able to develop and sustain group working within the digital context. Global organisations might be able to expect a level of engagement between geographically dispersed colleagues that is at least equal to that of more traditional models of the organisation. Digital media, it might be fair to say, moulds itself to the requirements of the social group rather than fundamentally altering the dynamic of the group. This is a less technologically determined view of our engagement with the digital age and more aligned with social constructionism.

Organisations are, therefore, a series of relationships that form themselves around dynamic group formations. These in turn construct the dialogue that will represent the learning of the organisation. So, participation is a core activity and active, positive involvement is being sought. There are a number of methods of involvement and participation available to employers and employees.

These include:

- collective bargaining
- joint consultation
- team briefing
- problem-solving groups
- empowerment
- european Works Councils
- quality circles.

Team briefing, problem-solving groups and empowerment all involve direct individual participation, whereas collective bargaining and joint consultation involve indirect representative participation. Under problem-solving groups and empowerment, people are forced to be free, and in collective bargaining and problem-solving groups, workers have a voice in management.

The relationship that is beginning to emerge is one where the individual is emphasised and their needs are considered as relevant if not central to the well-being of the organisation and ultimately the achievement of its overall aims and objectives. The LO is an organisation that embraces the involvement of the individual, where conflict is addressed through dialogue as an active and positive opportunity to reflect on current practice.

This reflection will, in turn, ensure that the organisation is able to respond to its environment and make the necessary changes. However, explicit change programmes within organisations often fail:

> Change is both continuous and often ugly in organisations because of resistance. Clever business plans (about change) rarely survive the first attempts to put them into practice.
>
> (Xenikou and Furnham 2013: 183)

All organisations face change and have, indeed, always faced change. This can be at an environmental, organisational, group or individual level and it can impact upon any aspect of the organisation's practices from strategic direction to operational actions. The size and age of the organisation can determine the agility of the organisation with larger and older organisations likely to have centralised procedures and to be organised hierarchically. These two latter characteristics tend to create a formality within the organisation that places a greater degree of formality, with explicit rules and procedures. These embedded structural elements will impact upon the ability of the organisation to change and to an extent it is a conflict between the perception of stability, consistency and certainty, against the chaos of change, fluidity and uncertainty. To successfully change an organisation needs to be comfortable with this chaos.

Individuals who have a perception of something to lose (usually those who have acquired something) are less likely to want change. This would seem to indicate that younger individuals are more inclined to accept the potential consequences of change. It takes some explicit effort to make changes, to challenge the status quo, to disrupt the patterns of habit and, to an extent, to potentially undermine the patterns and actions that have been in the past successful and adequate. Change needs to be seen as positive and ongoing, the patterns need to embed themselves in dynamism and to an extent it is this that defines OL. Learning is both continuous and progressive, it accepts that there is something to be learnt and that this is a good thing!

For organisations there is a need to embed change strategies, to make change an integral part of the organisation. This might focus on the power structures of the organisation. Who has the power, who shapes and drives the culture of the organisation? Alternatively, the change strategy can be presented openly and in detail. Presented in this way the assumption is that if all individuals have enough information they will be convinced of the need. Different organisations will require different change strategies, focusing on the power dynamics is inherently challenging as it is looking to inevitably undermine this structure, but cannot make this explicit. Similarly, an inclusive and open strategy is also challenging. Not everybody will perceive the attempt in the same way, some will feel marginalised and that the process is favouring others.

Avoiding and resisting change can be a reflection of key cultural characteristics. This may point to mental models that favour individual strategies of blame avoidance which can be subtle and difficult to detect, or a lack of genuine team working, where crucial power dynamics creates a lack of balance in terms of the voices being heard. All of this needs to be identified if meaningful dialogue is to become established. How we are saying what we are saying becomes more significant than what we say. Something that it genuinely critical has greater value than something that pays lip-service to any prevailing position.

Opposition to change is, therefore, the testing ground of the organisation's capacity to sustain dialogue. Here it is important to be clear that meaningful dialogue is positive, it is not a mechanism that facilitates avoidance by creating endless discussion that goes nowhere. Rather it is a mechanism that views any active resistance to change as indicative of an underlying issue or issues. No change strategy is going to satisfy all, but it is important that members of an organisation are willing to accept that their view is only one of potentially many and that their view may not prevail at all times. Trust, at the heart of group working is crucial here and individuals need to trust the motivation of others as being genuine and not aimed at undermining them or their position in the organisation. This needs to be built in and embedded as part of the OLP.

OL is, therefore, a mechanism for managing change in the organisation, through collaborative dialogue. At the heart of dialogue is communication.

Communication

Communication becomes a key element within this participatory or collaborative process and is at the heart of what and how we might learn through the OL models. The communication within groups is significant for OL, and Lewin (1997) presented these groups as discrete entities. When they were functioning properly they created a meaning that transcended the individuals that made them up. This remains a valid and popular view and has informed our understanding of the nature of leadership, motivation, innovation and creativity.

Whether we are looking at embedding a process of co-creating or addressing a question around authority, control or empowerment, we are effectively looking to embed a richer dialogue within the organisation, where individuals have the opportunity to speak. With this comes the responsibility associated with the model of collaborative learning. This might align itself with the self-directing characteristics of mature adult learners but OL practitioners need to concern themselves with ensuring that the necessary capabilities are identified and embedded within organisational practices.

It cannot be taken for granted that everyone in an organisation will automatically want to accept the responsibility that inevitably comes with more collaborative forms of learning and be empowered, nor that they are capable of effectively exercising the responsibility of being empowered. This responsibility will include the willingness to acquire the capabilities that will be appropriate and effective within the emerging environment. In order to operate effectively and to engage positively with the rich dialogues that are becoming central to the organisation there is a need to be able to effectively communicate and to understand the principles associated with communication, particularly in organisations.

Communication is a key component of all social activities. It is used to not only send and receive information but also to more broadly frame our understanding of the world around us and to represent that understanding for us. Communication, therefore, is not neutral, and according to the theories of semiotics the communication of the same information will be open to alternative interpretation by different groups receiving that information. This has a significance for all of the ways in which we communicate, be it:

- intrapersonal
- interpersonal
- group
- organisational
- intercultural.

Communication is affective in that it can be expected to have an impact upon the individual and this in turn will impact upon the personal nature of the information embedded within any communication. We all embed information that we receive according to the context or construct of our own understanding. This is based on our experiences, background, cultural and social heritage and so on. As Price (1997) says, communication is:

> An activity in which symbolic content is not merely transmitted from one source to another, but exchanged between human agents, who interact within a shared situational and discursive context.
>
> (Price 1997: 51)

Price goes on to identify five uses and purposes of communication.

1. Communication is an *instrument* to gain control over the physical and social environment. It has a conscious aim to inform, to gain information and to entertain, making it a strategic activity.
2. Communication is *persuasive* aiming to change the attitudes and behaviours of others, to gain compliance for mutual benefit or for the exclusive benefit of one.
3. Communication is about *socialisation* in that it mediates culture through language and communication practices, it channels information which helps shape human behaviour, creates an awareness of the expectations of others and encourages conformity to norms.
4. These norms represent the *social functionality* of communication and seek to create a unity that is reflected in behaviour and manifested in social cohesion. This can be seen in our shared symbols, such as our key rites of passage – weddings and funerals, or from our phatic communications, our small talk that takes up so much time and effort!
5. This in turn represents the *expressive* function of communication that represents feelings, our intuitive senses and our aesthetic feelings. This is communication as emotion and although it might not always be creative, it often is.

Communication is, therefore, central to our ability to engage with and create the dialogues that will form the basis of any OLP. Collaborative learning will use language to transfer and share the experiences acquired by individuals for the benefit of the group and ultimately the organisation. As the engagement with the processes associated with externalisation become more significant, it is language and communication that is being emphasised. There is a need to embed more fully a capability associated with understanding how both language and communication 'work' and part of this is an understanding of semiotics.

Semiotics focuses on both the generation of meaning through the text and the *reader* (not receiver) who is seen as *active* rather than passive (Fiske, 2011: 38). Structuralism is an approach within semiotics linked to the analysis of texts. A text can be anything that communicates, or that can be made to communicate, a message – a statue, a photograph, an advertisement, a corporate brochure or a newspaper's sports page. A structuralist approach tries to identify the language or *code* that makes the text meaningful to a reader. This code is not necessarily open to the gaze of the reader in an obvious way. There is a system of signs in which the *signifier* becomes associated with what is *signified*.

In advertising, objects like cars (signifiers) are associated with ideas like freedom, adventure, sexual prowess or artistic taste (signified). Objects do not have such meanings in any *natural* sense. They are acquired through social consensus, or class or corporate conspiracy. Roland Barthes (2009, but originally published in 1957) said that systems of signifiers/significations constituted *mythologies* which helped to represent the social world as *natural* and hence unchangeable. *Hello!* magazine's celebration of status and wealth, through its signifiers of fashion and celebrity, might be said to be a form of class ideology. Certainly, it seems to communicate a sense of class superiority and confidence through the signifiers of wealth. In order to be able to effectively communicate the addresser and addressee must use the same code of communication. If they do not then the message will be obscured.

The key elements in semiotics are:

- Sign … any mark, symbol, bodily movement, token and so on used to indicate and convey thoughts, information, commands.
- Code … a system of signs governed by rules agreed explicitly or implicitly between members of the using culture.

One might say that a news item, say about a strike or a war, has its accompanying signifiers, a whole range of stereotypes of heroes and villains, dramatic music and so on. In Barthes' semiotics, *denotation* concerns the 'what' of communication – that to which we make signs refer.

- Literal description of a cat = *four-legged furry creature that drinks milk*.
- Connotations associated with the cat = *female, sly, cunning, resourceful, graceful*.

Connotation is determined by the form of the signifier. Objects can acquire connotations that go beyond their functional uses to the symbolic. Clearly the same word spoken differently or the same object photographed differently can have different connotations.

Metonymy is a figure of speech that works by using a part or element of something to stand for the whole. News is metonymic, where a reported event is interpreted as standing for the whole of the reality of which it is a part. Two or three strikers on a picket line are metonyms for a strike; tanks and soldiers are metonyms of the American army in Baghdad; a line of police behind riot shields is a metonym of the forces of law and order opposing civil anarchy.

With metonymy we construct the rest of the 'story' from the part we have been given. However, metonyms can present things in dramatically different and simplified ways. The statement 'Nixon bombed Hanoi' simplifies the inordinately complex process of decision making. A picture of one, violent part of an otherwise peaceful demonstration involving thousands can misrepresent the whole.

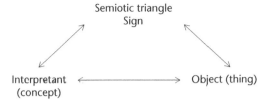

Figure 5.2 Peircean model

Source: Fiske, 1990: 42.

Sign refers to *objects* in reality and when understood by somebody and has an effect in someone's mind becomes the *interpretant*, where the interpretant is not the user of the sign but the mental concept produced by both the sign and user's experience of the object (see Figure 5.2).

As a linguist interested in language Saussure's dyadic model focused on how signs related to other signs rather than the object.

sign = signifier + signified

There are clear similarities between Peirce's sign and Saussure's signifier and Peirce's interpretant and Saussure's signified. Although Saussure is less concerned with how the sign corresponds to the object, where this does occur he calls it *signification*.

Signs have mental concepts attached to them, broadly interpreted by each of us in the same way and this might vary sometimes with cultural readings. The shared concept, says Fiske, relates to these objects in reality. Signifiers in the form of words change from language to language and the signified is also culturally determined. Signs in systems – signifieds are:

> . . . mental concepts we use to divide up reality and categorise it . . . signifieds are made by people, determined by the culture or subculture to which they belong. They are part of the semiotic or linguistic system that members of that culture use to communicate with each other.
>
> (Fiske 1990: 45)

The example of the traffic light is one that we are all familiar with, we understand what is being communicated to us, but it also reflects embedded norms and behaviours (see Figure 5.3). For example, we know the function of the traffic light is to ensure road safety and that we obey it in order to ensure our safety and that of others. We expect others to also obey. This relates to our wider appreciation of rules and regulation, our inherent understanding of what it is to be 'law-abiding' and, wider still, the place of the individual within a social context. This positions us as citizens, as part of the polity, as part of society. For many this goes beyond the key issue of road safety and ensures that at 2.00 am on a quiet road when we can clearly see that moving through a red light will endanger nobody, we remain stationary until the light changes. What is being signified by the traffic light is our deeper understanding of our social responsibility.

All codes convey meaning: their units are signs that refer by various means to things other than themselves. A code conveys meaning which derives from agreement among

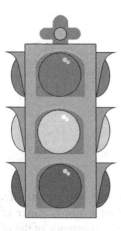

Figure 5.3 Common cultural symbol

its users, and from their shared cultural experience. Codes are transmittable via appropriate media/channels of communication (Fiske, 2011). We can talk about two types of meaning here:

paradigmatic meaning – is a code consisting of a network of signs from which individual units may be chosen:

♂ or ♀ ↑ or ↓ ← or →

syntagmatic meaning – is where the chosen units may be combined by rules or conventions into a message or text:

I♥NY

Language is a cooperative activity where references are socially and culturally determined and meaning is not absolute or permanently fixed. We use units of language (sounds/letters, words, phrases, sentences, paragraphs, text) to determine meaning through word form, word choice, grammar, sentence structure, paragraph construction or punctuation. Here the sameness of meaning is not related to the sameness of the sign. Different signs have the same meaning, for example, rich/wealthy or monarch/sovereign or the same sign can have different meanings, such as pitch which might be a type of tar or a football playing field or a throw. It is the context that allows us to assign meaning to these words, phrases and sentences. Language is, therefore, a cooperative activity, not an individualistic construct, and reference is *socially* and *culturally* determined. Meaning is not absolute or fixed permanently.

> The meaning of a word is its use in the language.
>
> (Ludwig Wittgenstein 1976)

Semantics is the branch of linguistics and logic concerned with meaning. A text is a series of cues which might point the way to its ideal 'preferred' reading, but which can never impose or determine this reading. In the completion of the text's meaning the consumer has much interpretative work to do. Meaning does not involve just individual words. In any consideration of meaning we also have to take account of what is conveyed by pragmatics, sentence meaning and discourse meaning. *Pragmatics* refers to how context influences the interpretation of meaning. It includes personal, spatial and temporal factors.

Mortensen (1972) identifies five postulates of communication:

Dynamic: subject to change, not fixed or static but fluid and evolving.
Irreversible: once it is in process it cannot be undone.
Proactive: it is proactive in that it facilitates some sort of advancement of meaning or meaning generation regardless of whether you want it to or not.
Interactive: information is exchanged and meaning is created by two or more people coming together and exchanging messages.
Contextual: it occurs in particular settings.

On top of this, communication is a continuous process that is unavoidable, we must communicate, it is multi-dimensional, occurs between equals and un-equals and to some extent is predictable.

> Communication never takes place in a vacuum; it is not a pure process, devoid of background or situational overtones.
>
> (Mortensen 1972: 21)

To understand communication we need to understand the situational context. Where has communication taken place, who is involved, what is the purpose of this communication or the intention of the communicators and what is the relationship between the participants? All of this collectively helps to convey meaning. For Price (1997: 57) contextual intention is:

> ... the idea that individuals produce meaning appropriate to the context in which they find themselves, and that their intentions to communicate cannot be separated from that context.

Context can also mean the wider social context in which an event takes place, which could be described as the universal form of all public discourses – the freedoms and constraints conferred by society as a whole.

Contexts of communication:

Interpersonal communication

Interpersonal communication is often in a face-to-face setting but can also include one-to-one communication mediated in some way e.g. telephone, Skype/FaceTime and so on. It will be between one individual and another, dyadic (interactive), spontaneous, will employ non-verbal behaviour, involve informal, reciprocal roles and there will be an absence of *clearly defined* goals. It involves some sort of *relationship* between two people where trust and openness may be key. It will be two-way communication and therefore, differs from traditional models showing linear flows in communication processes and will concern itself with the creation and exchange of meaning as opposed to a simple exchange.

Group communication

Group communication is face-to-face and involves interpersonal interaction within the context of the group. There would normally be three or more participants where roles are normally defined and differentiated, common norms of behaviour are established and there is an equally clear understanding of group identity. As well as norms in relation to behaviour there will also be common goals and aims. The communication exchange will be via recognisable codes and channels and smaller group communication will be distinct from bigger social groups that may be larger in structure, do not always require members to be in contact and there may also be issues around the formality and informality of the group.

Organisational communication

Here there will be a larger number of interactors who will not always be face-to-face. It will be within a defined structure where there will be a specialisation and formalisation of roles. Feedback will be less spontaneous and direct, and the purpose of the communication will be goal-oriented. The challenge in communicating effectively to large numbers of people involves using strategies to filter messages from management to departments, between members in departments, from staff to management etc. There will be different organisational sites, different geographical locations and time zones. The choice of media can vary with bulletins via email, blogs, newsletters, talks or Q&A sessions, video conferencing and so on.

Intercultural communication

Communication between individuals/groups from different cultures often involves assuming different ways of behaving, thinking and/or speaking to adapt to cultural differences. There is a need to minimise miscommunication and causes of offence. With globalisation this has led to the assumption that there are fewer cultural diversities but this also assumes that people are 'standardised' in much the same way as products might be. There remains here an issue of ethnocentrism, the view that one nation is central or 'right' or more important than any other. Some theorists see this in terms of media imperialism, where global news prioritises the First World (economically stable) as more important and uses stereotypes to convey meaning about other areas of the world.

Communication is at the heart of group dynamics; it is not neutral but will be enmeshed within our deeper understanding of the social context within which we are placed. Organisations will communicate, they will use their own signs and individuals will understand these signs in their own way. This understanding will be based on the organisation's shared values and will be as dynamic and changing as the organisational environment itself.

Our understanding of organisations and the key dynamics associated with both group dynamics and communication underpin our ability to intervene in the organisation. OL is very much an interventionist strategy that looks to not only understand current practices but to also embed specific ways of operating within the organisation. It seeks to understand the readiness of the organisation to collaborate and central to this is trust. OD, as a humanistic approach to understanding the organisation, seeks to embed the principles that will facilitate the introduction of an OLP. It concerns itself with the way that we view the organisation and the way individuals work together and communicate within the organisation.

Organisation development

Many individuals can be associated with the development of OD and although Frederick Winslow Taylor (1856–1915) and his association with scientific management principles might be far removed from the key elements of OD, nevertheless he was concerned with how we might go about understanding the nature of the organisation. Similarly, Max Weber (1864–1920) is associated with the concept of 'bureaucracy' as a mechanism for managing organisations, stressing hierarchy, division of labour and the adherence to strict procedures. However, it was the *Hawthorne Studies*, originally conducted by Elton Mayo (1880–1949) at the Western Electric Company's Hawthorne plant in the late 1920s and early 1930s, that brought social factors to the fore.

In the late 1940s and early 1950s, a more significant focus was placed on the social implications of employment and how individuals and groups related to the organisation. In the UK this is embedded within the wider political and social movement that drove the development of the welfare state and a wide ranging programme of nationalisation, in the post-war Labour government led by Clement Atlee. The UK sought to re-emerge from the Second World War, to tackle the crippling effects of war and to question the role of the UK in the post-imperial age. The social reforming governments that established the National Health Service (NHS) were supported and influenced by such groups as the Tavistock Institute which was founded in 1947 and which still works in the field of OD, as they state themselves on their current web pages:

> We were formally founded as a registered charity in September 1947. In our early work we brought together staff from different disciplines to find ways to apply psychoanalytic and open systems concepts to group and organisational life.
>
> (Tavistock Institute 2015)

As Burke says;

> The approach pioneered by the Tavistock consultants is based on the premise that an organisation is simultaneously a social and a technical system.
>
> (Burke 2000: 34)

This concern and interest in the inherent balance between technical and social systems continues to characterise much of the debate and discussion of how contemporary digital technologies are being applied in a range of organisational contexts. To an extent the concern over fragmentation is as current now as it was at the beginning of the 1950s.

In the US, similar developments focused on the need to drive organisational efficiency through the management of key change dynamics, specifically, the National Training Laboratory (NTL) and the concept of the T Group. Kurt Lewin (1890–1947) is central to the development of this field and helped to frame and define many of the key areas of concern. In particular, he was the first to write about group dynamics and to apply the theories of behavioural science to organisational practices. Similarly, Edgar Schein (b. 1928) has helped to focus on the concept of 'organisational culture' as central to the study of organisational efficiency, Warren Bennis (1925–2014) consistently supported and promoted the principles associated with democratic management and leadership, Richard Beckhard (1928–1999) pioneered the first non-degree training programme in OD at NTL and Chris Argyris (1923–2013) was the key in developing the direct connection between the wider consideration of OD and OL. From this foundation the OL literature can be said to have emerged.

From the beginning, therefore, the OD movement has been aligned with a distinct ideological perspective, one that has been associated with the concepts of democracy, egalitarianism, respect for the individual and the value of information to inform action and inspire creativity and innovation.

> OD is a consideration in general of how work is done, what the people who carry out the work believe and feel about their efficiency and effectiveness, rather than a specific, concrete, step-by-step linear procedure for accomplishing something.
>
> (Burke 2000: 1)

It is, therefore, possible to identify core values and ethics that inform OD practitioner's actions. These have been variously described as a combination of humanistic, optimistic and democratic values. Within these values there is an inherent respect for the dignity of the individual, that the individual is basically good and that all individuals should be treated equally and not subject to the misuse of power or authority.

The role of OD is to embed these principles in our understanding of the organisation and to help to drive the policies and processes that will reflect this understanding. However, there are many different and competing perspectives on organisation theory that either draw on more rational or *positivistic* views of practice or on more *humanistic* principles.

> Positivist social theories explain human behaviour by causes that lie in the situation and constrain the individual to act in certain ways, thereby conforming to the pressure of the environment. In organisation theory, positivism explains aspects of the organisation or its members by the environing situation.
>
> (Donaldson 2003: 42)

OD concerns itself with the ability of the organisation to adapt to its environment. Key to this is the extent to which the internal mechanisms (everything from its operational processes to the organisation-wide culture) allow the organisation to meet the challenges inherent in the change that defines this environment.

The OD practitioner looks to be able to identify an appropriate path or strategy that assists the organisation in meeting the challenges associated with change and in doing so they apply key OD principles:

- Collaborative relations between clients and consultants – from jointly deciding the consultant brief and outcomes to deciding how to collect valid data, how to jointly analyse the data and how to choose the best route of intervention, what to evaluate at the end.
- We are the helper, not the guru and expert to direct the change work. Those who direct the change work are the leaders and managers of the organisation.
- Consultants honour and dedicate time and effort to build high quality, authentic and trusting relations with clients in order to build the platform to help.
- We focus on supporting and educating clients to do sustainable change work so that without us they can continue to support the successful implementation of the change programme.

- While we can advise on content, our primary role is to pay attention to the processes that are needed to get the clients to their destination.
- While our practice intervention work mainly focuses on working with the basic unit of change within the systems, e.g. groups, and people within the group, our primary approach is a total system one.
- We hold tight to our belief in lifelong learning – hence the practitioner's need to do their own work while delivering work within the client system.

(Cheung-Judge and Holbeche 2001, loc. 844 of 7543)

OD is about engaging with practice and about ensuring appropriate change, both from the point of view of the individual or group and the organisation as a whole. It is as much a code of conduct as it is an explicit body of knowledge. It seeks to balance the need to allow the client to direct the dynamics within any change initiative and the ability to direct this based on the embodied knowledge of the OD practitioner. Various interventionist models are used to support this, all of which follow a basic five stage model:

1   *Motivating change*: here the OD practitioner is engaged with a process of socialisation that focuses on ensuring that individuals understand and appreciate the need for change and have a sense of their own ownership of the process by which change will be affected.
2   *Creating a vision*: here the OD practitioner is engaged with the process of setting the goals or objectives for the organisation. These must be based upon the current perceptions of the purpose and value of the organisation and be both realistic and achievable.
3   *Developing political support*: here the OD practitioner seeks to identify the key individuals who have the power to progress and achieve the desired change. These individuals need to be fully onboard and willing to promote and drive the intervention.
4   *Managing the transition*: here the OD practitioner is looking to ensure that the necessary momentum is maintained to achieve the changes that have been identified as necessary. Planning the actions or activities and ensuring that these are fully supported by the relevant individuals, as the intervention progresses are the two key components of this stage.
5   *Sustaining momentum*: here the OD practitioner ensures that the necessary resources are made available as required and that the value of the intervention is sustained by regular updates and messages that can be delivered through a range of mechanisms. Keeping the message of the intervention fresh!

Clearly, OD concerns itself with the relationship between the individual, the groups that these individuals form and how this then manifests itself as the organisation. The culture of the organisation will drive this crucial relationship, it will present to the individuals the norms and standards that are, to some extent, expected of them as part of the organisation and help form the group dynamics that will be able to sustain and progress the organisation through its own life cycle.

Kurt Lewin is often associated with the development of our current understanding of group dynamics. As a social psychologist in 1930s Germany he was forced to leave Germany and ultimately emigrated to the USA. He is associated with two key theories: field analysis and action research.

Field analysis seeks to identify the forces that either impact negatively or positively on the formation of any action within social situations. The 'field' is the environment or context within which an individual will construct their understanding of any situation – it is their values, goals, anxieties and so on. These values, goals and anxieties will change as an individual interacts with their environment and internalises the stimuli from this environment. This draws Lewin's position close to that associated with experiential learning where the ongoing stimuli present in the environment causes change to occur in what Lewin called the 'life-space'.

Action research uses a cyclical model to investigate social actions. The model focuses on workplace practices and encourages a reflective approach that aims to improve strategy and generate knowledge for the organisation. This draws the model close to Wenger's concept of communities of practice (CoP) where the investigation is an ongoing and iterative process and where the process itself forms an important part of the perceived 'outcome'. As individuals engage in this reflective process they become more adept at it and can more readily apply the knowledge that is generated.

One example of how this model has developed is *participatory action research* (PAR). Those who are participating in the research are the objects of that research and will be directly connected to the outcomes of that research. In this model our understanding is being determined by the actors within it, rather than being seen as emerging from the environment. This model, therefore, challenges a positivist view. Like field analysis, PAR draws some inspiration from theories of adult education, not least the concepts of self-direction and autonomy where the traditional model of teacher/learner is broken down into a more collaborative model where the learner has content to offer as well as to receive.

Lewin's basic model of change can be seen in Figure 5.4.

Unfreezing is the challenging of existing behaviours and requires a recognition that specific issues or problems will exist. In acknowledging this, there is some momentum created to tackle it, but only if this is done constructively for those involved. In other words, there needs to be trust between the participants engaging with this type of model or process.

Changing is the alteration to practice where individuals have already perceived the need to change and are actively engaged with a process that will identify alternative actions. Here there is a need to view multiple perspectives, to critically and objectively review alternative courses of action and be capable of doing this in an effective way. Here finding information and its critical consideration is significant. We might ask, how able are we to find information? What are the levels of information literacy within this organisation? This illustrates the existence of this model within itself, it is layered. Where poor information literacy skills are identified then these need to be developed before the change process can be progressed.

Refreezing will integrate the changes into practice. This will happen at individual, group and organisational levels. In doing this, the impact of change will be further considered and indeed identified as an ongoing process.

Figure 5.4 Lewin's basic model of change

Lewin can, therefore, be placed at the very origins of OD, which in turn can be regarded as a key element within the discipline of OL. Not least, it is the focus on a specific learning context, a collaborative learning context that is clearly emerging from these origins. Theoretical models such as *action research* are attempting to identify change management as a discrete process within the organisation and highlight this need to embrace change as a positive and creative part of organisational practice. Descriptions of the 'interventions' associated with action research tend to highlight the discrete nature of this change. To identify what needs to be changed is a collaborative effort (often amongst senior staff) and the 'thing' requiring change is directly addressed and changed. However, the acceptance of change as an ever-present phenomenon that impacts upon all within the organisation is crucial:

> The underlying value of this model for change is that it created within the client system the expertise to solve its own problems in the future, at least those problems that fall within the same universe as the original change problem.
>
> (Burke 2000: 62)

Here there is a sense of empowerment and of shared responsibility but a more tentative recognition of the localised nature of change as a discrete problem. Change, adaptation, flexibility, agility, all underpin the actions that are associated with OD and key to this are the learning mechanisms that have emerged in relation to the concept of the LO and the technical and cultural dynamics that are associated with the disciplines of information and knowledge management. OD can therefore be used as an umbrella term covering a range of discrete disciplines that have emerged as the concept has been explored in theory and this theory has been applied in practice.

OD concerns itself with the whole organisation over the long term aimed at enhancing effectiveness and efficiency, importantly via a *humanistic* approach to the key relationships within the organisation. Where the organisation can be said to exist within a context of change, organisation theory, collaborative group working and communication are placed within a broadly democratic framework:

> ... democracy in industry is not an idealistic conception but a hard necessity in those areas in which change is ever-present and in which creative scientific enterprise must be nourished. For democracy is the only system of organisation that is compatible with perpetual change.
>
> (Bennis 2009: 108)

Although change has been a constant, its current scale and impact is being felt and experienced to a degree of intensity that is largely unique. Unique in the sense that it is the obsolescence of knowledge that has driven a recognition of the need to be able to embed learning as an ongoing organisational process. It is this alone that can sustain organisational practices.

Concluding remarks

OD seeks to actively engage with the organisation both within its changing environment and with its own fluid boundary. The dynamic of change is met by the need to embed learning as a process and the OL practitioner requires the capability to understand and work with the language of the organisation, how the individuals talk to each other, and to recognise where and how this may or may not inhibit the process of OL. To do so there is a need to recognise the shifting variables, in particular the way in which the emerging digital environment brings both opportunities and challenges. The opportunity is to build a richer collaborative environment, the challenge to appreciate just how to understand and manage this environment. Collaboration itself forms the basis of the relationship between the individual and the organisation, but this in turn requires a more egalitarian outlook that is capable of giving a voice to all those who can contribute. In the LO this is everyone. If everyone is to be given a voice then those who are disinclined to use it, or unaware that they have it or unable to use it need to be supported and helped to ensure that they are able, willing and made aware of the their responsibility to use it well. This is where OD and OL blend together in creating an organisation that is capable of nurturing and growing the capabilities that are required to learn from experience and to do this in a sustainable way.

6 Ethics

Learning outcomes:

1   Understand how ethics relate to both the organisation and to the discipline of organisational learning.
2   Be able to identify the characteristics of postmodern ethics as outlined by Zygmunt Bauman.

Introduction

Having considered the nature of the organisation and identified the humanistic basis for OD, which in turn has informed the development of OL, it is necessary to consider further the position of ethics as a crucial organisational dynamic. Clearly, there is an ideological basis for OL, drawing on principles associated with more democratic models of the organisation. Here, inclusiveness fits with the need to establish meaningful collaboration amongst those who make up the organisation. However, here too we are faced with the issue of a context characterised and defined by constant change. Postmodern ethics wrestles with this ill-defined and multi-faceted context and offers a foundation for building ethical behaviour within what is a context that has moved beyond modernity and the certainty associated with it.

Ethical behaviour is the mutual understanding of the responsibilities that individuals have for one another. Organisational ethics identifies this responsibility in relation to the individuals within an organisation. It forms the basis of the relationship between the individual and the organisation and as such it determines the extent to which a trusting environment or context is created. Trust underpins collaborative learning as without it there will be no willingness to externalise individual experience, it will remain tacit and as such prone to the vagaries of power dynamics that will determine the efficacy of its application from the individual rather than the organisational perspective.

Business ethics

The UK based Institute of Business Ethics (2015) defines business ethics:

> Business ethics is the application of ethical values to business behaviour.

There is no single agreed definition of what these ethical values might be, but they relate to standards and to performance. The individual as part of an organisation has a role to fulfil. However, they must not be put in a position where they are either being asked to operate outside their own areas of competence or feel that their need to highlight any shortcomings in relation to the duty of care they have to individuals or groups is compromised.

The challenge for an organisation is not necessarily the production of a clear statement of what is and what is not the standard expected of individuals, but is the ability to ensure that these standards are appropriately embedded in practice. Here the issue is more to do with the method by which these standards are produced and how they are able to be reflected upon, on an ongoing basis. Rather than being written in stone, there is a need to recognise that ethics form a part of a fluid organisational environment where ethical issues are required to be examined, changed, amended or altered constantly. The need here is to have a mechanism to allow this to happen and it is at this point that ethics will form part of the rich dialogue within organisations that characterise organisational learning programmes. Where ethics becomes a part of what 'we talk about' then there is created a resolve to ensure that their ownership is aligned with those expected to perform and practice in relation to these ethical standards.

Universality and pluralism

Ethics are the agreed standards and constraints that determine what is and what is not acceptable action or behaviour. The key term here is 'agreed'. In here we have the contestation associated with the social context within which organisations, and society more generally, operate. The key issue here is who will determine what mechanisms will be used and how are these mechanisms created, applied, controlled or manipulated?

These questions have become more significant in a postmodern era where the search for the universality of ethical behaviour that had been perceived to be present in modernity can no longer be acknowledged. A universal code of ethics underpinning moral action was presented through the concept of the grand narrative with first the church and then the enlightened state claiming their own legitimacy in the statement of the universal ethical structure. The latter was based, not on the teaching of scripture but on an enlightened view of rational individuals who placed themselves in a position that justified their right to determine proper enlightened behaviour and to articulate the ethics and morality upon which this behaviour was based.

In the postmodern context this justified position is challenged and ultimately rejected. The enlightened can no more justify their right to determine ethics than scriptures. The concept of there being a grand narrative and with it a universally applied set of ethics has been challenged. Not least, Francois Lyotard (1984) has illustrated the breakdown of these grand narratives and in doing so drawn the consideration of ethics into the postmodern.

If there are no grand narratives, then where do or might our ethical structures come from? Who has the right or is in the position to suggest or determine what is ethical? Again, as Lyotard has said, it is now within the realm of local narratives that this will be determined. However, local determination is itself subject to the mechanisms that will allow some to have more influence over others.

The choice or the change here relates to the source of our ethical structure. With the concept of grand narratives we have an attempt at universality and the production of a comprehensive ethical structure. The source of this has been through both religion and through the concept of enlightened rationality. The former rests upon scriptures and the latter upon the scientific method or upon 'philosophers'.

> The ethics of the philosophers were to replace the Revelation of the Church.
>
> (Bauman 1988: 25)

The alternative to universality is pluralism where within the context of local narrative the focus shifts to the production of ethical structure and moral statement onto, not only an élite, but everyone.

> With the pluralism of rules (and our times are the times of pluralism) the moral choices (and the moral conscience left in their wake) appear to us intrinsically and irreparably ambivalent. Ours are the times of strongly felt moral ambiguity.
>
> (Bauman 1988: 21)

Such ambiguity can breed a sense of insecurity and it is often the case that individuals are seeking certainty – they want to know what the rules are and what the regulations are that they need to abide by. The difficulty is that there is no definitive authority to provide these rules or these regulations.

> ... the authorities we may trust are all contested, and none seem to be powerful enough to give us the degree of reassurance we seek. In the end, we trust no authority, at least, we trust none fully, and none for long: we cannot help being suspicious about any claim to infallibility. This is the most acute and prominent practical aspect of what is justly described as the 'postmodern moral crisis'.
>
> (Bauman 1988: 21)

 Pause for thought – hierarchism and efficiency

We need to consider how this has a direct bearing on organisational practices and here are some thoughts. The current organisational position, if it was to reflect this postmodern moral crisis, would be a place where authority is challenged and where there is an underlying and growing awareness of contestation and ambiguity in relation to how the strategic and tactical development of any organisation is being set or determined.

Strong leadership, leadership from the front, clear and unambiguous structures based on equally clear hierarchies of responsibility are often presented as how organisations can maintain efficiency and effectiveness within a context that is recognised as being fluid, dynamic and characterised by change. Here there is a direct link between hierarchism and efficiency. However, this link can be challenged.

> If there is no good reason to believe that hierarchy leads to efficiency and that the prevalence of hierarchism is ideological rather than 'natural' then there is perhaps no reason to limit our imagination of organisational democracy either.
>
> (Kokkinidis 2012: 238)

More horizontal organisational structures can, in the first instance, be aligned with the collaborative features of information technologies.

> ... non-hierarchical structures guided by participatory management can effectively co-ordinate collective action.
>
> (Kokkinidis 2012: 240)

The practical functionality of emerging digital technologies, the digital environment itself and the nature of the postmodern moral crisis can be aligned here. Essentially, the task is to focus on the collaborative nature and challenges inherent with the postmodern condition and to maximise the collaborative potential of information technologies to allow for the emergence of organisational mechanisms that will facilitate a more participatory identification of the ethics that will guide organisational practice.

- What we are accepting here is the fluidity and dynamism of the organisational context.
- That this context, in its fluidity and dynamism, reflects a postmodern perspective.
- This perspective requires us to recognise that rules, regulations and ultimately ethics will draw their authority from a more local and complex base.
- Contestation will be ever-present and there is a 'leap' to be made in acknowledging that this does not detract from effectiveness.
- To make this work there is a need to create an environment that is capable of an enhanced form of collaboration.
- The digital environment provides a functional platform that would facilitate this level of collaboration.
- Organisations can 'stand' more contestation because of the functionality of the emerging digital environment.

Without foundation

The principles that underpin organisational ethics have an uncertain foundation in the postmodern but must be related to the role and purpose of the organisation. In commercial organisations profit must be balanced with the concept of community good and decision making must be seen as a shared or collaborative activity. The sense of 'other' needs to be embedded in the understanding of what a moral position might be and draws us away from the more neo-liberal agenda that characterised practice in the late twentieth century. What remains constant here is the drive to do, to produce, to create, but not in a way that performs or responds to predetermined criteria.

> What makes the moral self is the urge to do, not the knowledge of what is to be done; the unfulfilled task, not the duty correctly performed.
>
> (Bauman 1988: 80)

These predetermined criteria, these conventions and social norms serve as convenient screens for our actions and they justify our actions. It is how 'things are done around here'.

To give this up, for the uncertainty of postmodern ethical structures, will appear to condemn us to an ever present doubt, where no position can be fully justified or expected to last for long. However,

> It is, ultimately, the lack of self-righteousness, and the self-indignation it breeds, that are morality's most indomitable ramparts.
>
> (Bauman 1988: 81)

What is being suggested here is that within the postmodern organisational context, ethics are rightly to be seen as a contested element of organisational practice. As OL practitioners we then concern ourselves with how and where this contestation might take place. Our role is to ensure that this contestation is in the first instance viewed as making a positive contribution to the progress of the organisation and that the nature of the contestation itself, on the other hand, is as efficient as possible and as equitable as possible. From this we, therefore, have a series of relevant questions:

* Where should this dialogue take place?
* Who should be entitled to contribute to this dialogue?
* Who is to make sense of this dialogue and to transform it into meaningful organisational information?
* How will it be applied by the organisation?

The simple answer to these questions is that they will form part of coherent OLPs that seek to manage the range of dialogues that drive the collective and collaborative learning in the organisation. Ethics, in this sense, is one of the principal dialogues that will define OL practice.

As part of a dialogic process there is embedded, the need to ensure that the 'other' is given due consideration. This is often referred to as 'participating ethics' and has at its core the need to ensure that a sense of decency drives the agenda and that the principle of emancipation is fully embedded. This latter element concerns itself with ensuring participation across all levels or boundaries that might exist and, therefore, can be aligned with the principles associated with OL.

 Pause for thought – ethical behaviour and OL

Is OL fundamentally based upon a specific ethical view?

As a collaborative form of learning there is a requirement for all participants to be perceived as having equal value. Even experienced and well-qualified individuals cannot claim any more authority in relation to OL than even the most junior or least experienced member of staff – or so the theory goes!

In this sense OL can be described as egalitarian. However, in any group dynamic there always exists a naturally forming hierarchy often based on participation. It is often said that the online/digital environment of social media is, as Marshall McLuhan (2001) said, a global village where we all have a voice and where embedded prejudices are less explicit. Nevertheless, the initial absence of cues (often visible cues) that in face-to-face groups helps to form the group dynamic and determine the 'voice' that an individual might have is often replicated in online/digital contexts. For example, trolling is about positioning oneself in relation to others. By looking to wrong foot an individual by misleading them, the troll will highlight that individual's subservient position.

So, non-ethical behaviour is embedded in group dynamics within both face-to-face and online/digital environments and in many respects these different environments are looking more like each other than might initially have been hoped.

Ethics may form a basis for implementing OL programmes. In considering group dynamics it needs to be recognised that unethical behaviour can be regarded as a norm, even within the emerging digital environment.

Ethics are, therefore, an acceptance of the 'other'. Without the presence of another individual ethics cannot exist, it would simply be 'my will'. To an extent ethics forms the basis of the laws that govern us and to an extent determine our behaviour.

However, the significance of ethics to this consideration of OL is directly related to this notion of the 'other'. Specifically, it is the sense of responsibility that one has to the 'other' that forms the basis of moral behaviour. It lays down the sense of obligation that is at the heart of ethical behaviour. This responsibility is impacted upon by its own extension beyond the individual and the singular other. From three and beyond this responsibility is transformed.

> Asymmetry of the moral relationship is all but gone, the partners are now equal, and exchangeable, and replaceable. They have to explain what they do, face the arguments, justify themselves by reference to standards which are not their own. The site is clear for norms, laws, ethical rules and courts of justice.
>
> (Bauman 1988: 114)

The wider social context for ethics (society) is now present and there is a need to either accept the embedded structure, the norms of life or behaviour or to constantly challenge them. On the one hand there is differentiation of status and on the other an absence of status. Bauman (1988) refers to these two states as *societas* and *communitas*. The former drives and moulds the creation of an ethical structure that addresses the inherent autonomy of moral behaviour by presenting instrumental and procedural rationalities. The basis for ethical action is the rationality of the collective goal.

> All social organisation consists therefore in neutralising the disruptive and deregulating impact of moral impulse.
>
> (Bauman 1988: 125)

The emphasis here is on the grounding of ethics and it being located in the purpose and goal set for it by the organisation. Standing outside of the goal of the organisations places the individual in an irrational and unethical position. This begins to unpack and illuminate the condition of the individual in the organisation where they are being asked to separate themselves from their function or role. It is not the individual acting but the employee. This allows for an alignment of behaviour with the rules and regulations that are identified through the ideological machinations of those who are able to exert power within any social context. Morality in this sense is wrestled from the individual, the responsibility to the 'other' is nullified and the individual need only now accept the structure that is being presented. The process of socialisation is partly the process by which the individual is drawn into this structure.

> ... it is rational calculation, rather than non-rational, erratic and uncontrolled moral urge, that orients the action.
>
> (Bauman 1988: 128)

Responsibility is cut free from the individual and in this sense the ethics of modernity can be aligned with those who exert power.

 Pause for thought – postmodern ethics

Bauman's argument up to this point has placed ethics directly in alignment with a Foucauldian form of power. Here individuals relinquish their opportunity to make a moral decision and instead are 'forced' through the dominance of the existing discourse to accept the ethics that best represent the goals of the organisation. This is set up in such a way as to place an individual in opposition to rationality if they fail to align themselves with these goals and ethics.

To what extent do we recognise this as part of organisational practice? Do we find ourselves separating our actions, as individuals and as employees?

Where the individual is 'detached' from the responsibility of their own actions the production of an ethical framework becomes aligned with the purpose of the organisation. The individual enters what Bauman refers to as the 'agentic state' where they become agents of the collective effort and where efficiency in achieving the aims of the collective effort becomes the basis of morality. The individual takes a step 'outside' and within the context of the collective it is not the individual that is focused upon but the traits that represent them.

Sociality and socialisation

The consequences of the agentic state are significant from an ethical perspective. By creating a structure from which an individual loses the responsibility for care that is the basis of the relationship with the 'other' and for this to be aligned with whatever might be discerned as the collective mind. The goals and the purpose of the collective becomes the basis for moral judgement and processes can be put in place to clarify this alignment and to positively work towards the understanding and ultimately the acceptance of the basis for this judgement.

Socialisation is a process through which this judgement is embedded into individual action and through which behaviour will be governed. In other words, this becomes the basis for the 'way we do things round here'. We recognise this as the basis of organisational culture and organisational culture is very much at the heart of organisational learning.

Within a postmodern context there is a challenge to this agentic state. *Sociality*, as opposed to socialisation, is the *autotelic* position that can be presented as opposing this state. Here the emphasis is placed not on being aligned to predetermined structures and patterns where individuals need socialisation as a process to ensure that they understand what is required. Rather, a more open and fluid context is presented:

> Feelings are shared, but they are shared before having been articulated and instead of being spelled out: the sharing itself is foremost amongst the feelings shared – the most overwhelming of feelings, overriding all other feelings, leaving no room or time for the scrutiny of other feelings.
>
> (Bauman 1988: 130)

Sociality concerns itself with the process of sharing and less with what is shared or even how what is shared might inform action and here there is a direct connect with OL, where OL is seen as a mechanism to meet a context of constant change, where individuals need the capabilities associated with being *knowledge-enabled*.

To an extent sociality can be seen as a mechanism to dismantle structure and to reintroduce uncertainty. Structures provide certainty and this certainty is embedded through socialisation, sociality will remove this structure. In doing so it removes endless repetition and, it is argued, re–ignites the creative powers that flow through the dynamic context of change coupled with doubt, uncertainty and unfamiliarity.

> ... modern times were prominent for the ruthless assault of the profane against the sacred, reason against passion, norms against spontaneity, structure against counter-structure, socialisation against sociality.
>
> (Bauman 1988: 135)

In this context ethics are required to be extended into the global reach of organisations, to mirror and reflect the goals and perceived purposes of the organisation and in this lies the dilemma for ethics and for how OL might position itself in relation to ethics. If ethics are to be aligned with the goals of the organisation then there is likely to be a direct connect between the search for efficiency and productivity, which is at the heart of organisational practice, and the ethical structure or moral behaviour of those who form the social collective of the organisation.

> Ethics is different from efficiency but the two are interdependent. Having an ethical sense pushes one to be responsible and to act in the best way for the purposes of efficiency. In turn, efficiency in a business firm is a contribution to the common good. An efficient use of means provides material support to human life and better accessibility to economic goods. Through increasing competitiveness, efficiency also contributes to maintaining jobs, so providing the livelihood of many people.
>
> (Melé 2012: location 116/117 of 4540)

However, this position is difficult to sustain, because there clearly needs to be an opportunity to explore and examine ethics and moral behaviour outside the organisational mission or goal for increased productivity. Efficiency is here linked with the economic well-being of those who form the organisation and this inevitably allows actions to become justifiable from an ethical perspective where they can be said to enhance or just sustain the economic position of the individuals concerned. Here there is no inherent challenge to or apparent engagement with the 'recipients' of this largesse. If the emerging technologically driven and globalised organisational environment removes individuals from a sense of proximity to the actions of the organisation, this can lead to a sense of there being no possible control of or potential contribution to the ethical structure of the organisation or beyond this link between efficiency and ethics. Indeed, this sense might help create and sustain this position. However, technology also sustains a level of connectivity that allows for dialogue to be localised globally. The opportunity afforded by technology can sustain dialogue and this can include the dialogue associated with OL, and embedded within this the dialogue associated with the uncertainty of a postmodern ethical position.

The ethics of organisational learning

To speak of ethics within the context of OL there is a need to marry the characteristics of learning with organisational practice. Here, we learn from our experience and this experience is constantly changing, forming and reforming itself within an environment where the degree of contestation is sustained, welcomed and embraced.

Certainty and the active pursuit of certainty is recognised as both unobtainable and unnecessary. It is only with uncertainty that a level of contestation is sustained and through this contestation a continual review of behaviour can be maintained. Questions will form and re-form themselves.

> Our collective responsibility, much as the moral responsibility of every man and woman among us, swims in the sea of uncertainty.
>
> (Bauman 1988: 222)

Embedded within the OLP, therefore, is a clear ethical imperative. The role of OL is to sustain the capabilities of the organisations to engage in the necessary dialogues that will allow the emergence, re-emergence and sustained engagement with the issues associated with the ethical direction of the organisation. As with learning generally within this collective context, of uncertainty, fluidity and doubt, there is a need to rely, not on imposed certainties that will ossify and restrain practice and behaviour, but to embrace uncertainty. Sustaining dialogue and accepting the need for this rich and sustained dialogue becomes the driver of ethical structures and informs moral behaviour.

Concluding remarks

Ethical structures and moral behaviour, therefore, are central to the actions associated with OL. As we will see, the nature of organisational knowledge, the concept of the LO and the application of key OL tools such as communities of practice, is underpinned by the extent to which the individuals who are being asked to participate (everybody within the organisation) trust those around them. This trust is not an element that needs to be considered and managed effectively, but a prerequisite for all OLP. Ethics, therefore, and the postmodern perspective of ethics that Bauman in particular has outlined for us here, forms a crucial part of the OLP. In our subsequent consideration of the key elements of the OLP, that forms the rest of this text, this view of ethics will be drawn on and reflected upon throughout.

7 Human resource development

Learning outcomes:

1 Understand the emergence of human resource management from welfare officers and personnel managers to the broader HR functions.
2 Be able to define the concept of culture as it relates to an organisation.
3 Understand the nuances associated with different perspectives on critical human resource development.
4 Appreciate the role of leadership as it relates to organisations that are seeking to embed learning programmes.

Introduction

The centrality of the relationship between the individual and the organisation inevitably draws the emerging HR function to the fore. The human resource has become a key component of organisational well-being and the link to concepts such as intellectual capital have emphasised this centrality. It is the people who make up the organisation that will determine its effectiveness and this goes beyond simply how fast they might accomplish tasks or how effectively they approach tasks. Rather, it is their broader engagement with the organisation, their alignment with the goal of the organisation that will 'unlock' the embedded experience of individuals. The HR function has, therefore shifted from the practical issues associated with employment law to the more sociological issues associated with engagement and empowerment.

From human resource management to critical human resource development

It is helpful to provide some background to the emergence of human resource management (HRM), both in the UK and internationally. In the UK, it is possible to trace the development of the concept through a number of stages or traditions. In the nineteenth century, a number of employers, notably Quaker-owned companies, such as Cadbury and Rowntree, appointed 'welfare officers' to look after the needs and interests of their employees. In the twentieth century, the emphasis changed from welfare to 'industrial relations', reflecting the acrimonious climate between employers and trade unions throughout much of the century. By the 1980s, however, the emphasis had changed again, from collective industrial relations to the individual relationship between the employer and individual employees.

During the twentieth century the generic term 'personnel management' was almost universally used in the UK to describe the activities being undertaken by these welfare officers, industrial relations officers and others. The scope of the activity developed and adapted to take account of environmental changes, such as the reduction in trade union power during the 1980s and 1990s, and the increasing importance of employment protection legislation.

It was – and remains – an activity that faces criticism. Welfare officers were never seen as having a managerial orientation. There were conflicts between their activities and those of line managers. Industrial relations officers were seen as playing an intermediary role between trade unions and line management. Frequently, the people engaged in the personnel function were accused of being 'out of touch with the business world', 'people who always say "no"', 'unable to read a balance sheet', 'not able to contribute to organisational strategy'. In brief, in many organisations the personnel activity was unloved, and seen largely as an administrative support function.

Largely as a replacement for the unpopular term 'personnel management' there emerged the term 'human resource management' in the UK. This became increasingly common during the 1980s and 1990s. The problem is that it is difficult to get agreement on exactly what the term means. Some commentators suggest that it is simply a new name for 'personnel', in an attempt to overcome some of the criticisms listed above. Others take different views: that HRM should take a purely managerialist position or that the human resources of an organisation are so important to its success that major HR decisions should be made at the top of the organisation and implemented by line management.

Managers were able to take such an initiative in the latter part of the twentieth century, as the external environment changed: the power of the unions was eroded, unemployment rose and organisations were de-layered and downsized.

In the United States, by contrast, personnel management was a recognised activity before the end of the nineteenth century, which identified closely with the objectives of the organisation. Thus, the transition to 'human resource management' was comparatively smooth.

Human resource management has become embedded within strategic planning to an extent and in ways that personnel management did not. Human resource management therefore:

- is a managerially-focused activity;
- relates to the management of people throughout the organisation, it is not a new label for what has traditionally been called 'personnel management';
- is concerned with the achievement of business strategy.

People management is the responsibility of *all* line managers. It is not solely the responsibility of the organisation's personnel manager or HR manager. Of course, the HR manager will have people management responsibilities – for his or her own staff and potentially for certain aspects of people management of employees engaged in other parts of the organisation. But he or she is not responsible for all aspects of the management of all the other people in the organisation. The finance director is responsible for the management of his or her staff; the production manager is responsible for the management of the people engaged in production and so on.

If the organisation truly espouses the concept of HRM, then the HR manager or director should be at the centre of the organisation, contributing to the development of business strategy and subsequently developing HR strategies that converge with the business strategy.

As a developing field there remains some ambiguity about how HRD relates to the broader field of HRM. Human resource management concerns itself with all of those aspects that relate to the management of the individual and the organisation. This is the practicalities of payroll and ensuring that relevant legislation is properly understood and applied. It is often presented that from within this broad base the role of HRD is emerging.

HRD concerns itself with the role or position of the individual in relation to the organisation. It focuses on the relationships that exist or can be developed within organisations. This in turn is dependent upon the socio-cultural context within which the organisation sits.

> HR practices can only be understood in the context of economic-societal factors that shape or direct these practices.
>
> (Bratton and Gold 2011: 7)

As this organisational landscape has changed, so has the perceived function of HRD. As change itself has come to be recognised as the only constant then so the individual has been drawn back to centre stage in a way and to an extent that transcends both the neo-liberalism of the market economies that emerged in the 1980s and the previous Keynesian doctrine that fore-fronted the processes associated with the management of industrial relations within a planned economy. Here people are neither a resource to be organised nor an element to be reconciled or mediated within a context of conflict and internal competition. Instead, the individual is the recognised source of sustainable advantage, the 'capital' that will, through the identification and application of its embedded knowledge, form the basis of organisational survival and success.

The emergence of 'critical' HRD (Delbridge and Keenoy, 2010) reflects the challenges inherent in HRM practices as they move to reflect the societal shift from modernity to postmodernity. It is this shift that identifies the social nature of the organisation and highlights the need to recognise the ideological basis of organisational policy and practice. It is the ideological position of the organisation that will determine its actions. People managing people in this context becomes a contentious issue and supports the notion that HR is no longer a function of a discrete department within an organisational structure but a reflection of the ideological position of the organisation as a whole.

This will impact upon the way in which basic or traditional HR functions are perceived. In the first instance, their determination through the embedded power structures, become themselves the focus for dialogue. In the postmodern, socially constructed world the HR function is characterised by plurality. Here, efficiency and effectiveness is determined by the extent to which this dialogue is sustained and nurtured. It is driven by the identification of the next relevant question as opposed to the identification of the answer to the current question.

This effectively forms a link between the micro and strategic domains of HRM. Recruitment, training and rewards all emerge from the contested dialogue around the purpose of the organisation and its strategic direction. Embedded as we are (in 2015) in a context that is looking to emerge from the financial crisis that ended the first decade of the twenty-first century, organisational practices are under scrutiny and there is a call for some alternative ways of operating.

It is evident that some of the old ways of doing business will have to change and so too will organisational cultures that encourage irresponsible risk taking; leadership whose behaviour results in low trust; poor practice that gets hushed up; unintended consequences of, for example, company values where at an extreme people end up demonstrating cultish behaviour. There are growing demands for better governance greater transparency and fairness over executive pay, new forms of leadership, greater accountability. And many of these practices fall directly or indirectly within HR's remit.

(Cheung-Judge and Holbeche 2011: loc. 4359 of 7543)

In this sense there begins to emerge the notion that in fact HRD (development as opposed to management) becomes the primary function and that in relation to all of the concerns associated with HRM there is an identifiable HRD perspective. Payroll may remain an operational function of the organisation but it too is embedded within a dialogic and systemic process that places it within the organisational remit of HRD. The embedding of legislation becomes part of the organisational learning processes that sustains a fluid and dynamic engagement with the organisation's environment through the capabilities associated with OL.

In examining the basic functions of HR, therefore, these need to be embedded within a consistent willingness to engage with the characteristics of the emerging context. This, in turn, requires the application of a consistent perspective. OL does impose itself on the organisation, as a particular way of looking at the organisation. It transcends the training and development function often associated with it. In this sense HRD, at present, better represents the HR function within the LO than HRM.

Organisational culture

Human resources concerns itself with key organisational functions, all of which are focused upon and based around the culture of the organisation. Culture is *shared values* and can exist within any social context. We can speak about a national culture, or the characteristics that individuals within a specific nation might be said to share. This can be the national stereotypes we apply to nations, such as the Germans being efficient or the Scots being careful with money. Similarly, we can talk about an organisation having a specific culture or 'the way things are done around here'. We often talk about specific characteristics, a 'hard working' culture, a 'get things done' culture, or embedded practices such as not taking all of your lunch break or your annual leave entitlement and so on. Each of these is indicative of the type of culture that is said to exist within an organisation and, importantly, that there would be a degree of compliance expected from individuals who 'enter' this organisation.

As with national stereotypes we need to consider the extent to which we can justify such characterisations as applicable and meaningful for the organisation. In doing this we need to explore the 'mechanisms' through which such cultural claims are made, what their origins are and how they might be subject to change. Culture is perceived to be a dynamic process with *compliance* at its heart. Culture attempts to clarify and externalise accepted or embedded norms of behaviour and in doing so can alleviate feelings of isolation but can also enhance the feeling of pressure and of control being exerted.

David Kynaston (2009) in his history of modern Britain, *Tales of a New Jerusalem* explores the embedded culture of post-war Britain in the 1950s and describes through the voices of individuals who participated in or studied the sociological environment of the prevailing culture. One of these voices was Margaret Stacey of Banbury:

> 'The techniques of acceptance or rejection are subtle,' she wrote about the frontiers between the classes in a town pervaded by class. 'You must possess appropriate characteristics: occupation, home, residence area, income (suitably spent), manners, and attitudes. You must know or learn the language and the current private "passwords" of the group. You must be introduced. If you fail in these particulars you will simply be "not known". Nothing is said or done. The barrier is one of silence.'
>
> (Kynaston 2009: 136)

This rather chilling description is as true for organisations today as it was for British society in the 1950s. The culture of the organisation is its manners and attitudes and the language that it speaks. Failure to identify or accept these cultural parameters will marginalise an individual, they will *not be known* in the organisation. More than 'how things are done around here' the organisation's culture will determine who is capable of doing anything and will both include and exclude. The extent to which an organisation can continue to accept that this is an inherent part of the organisation, that it is something that just happens or is something that is inevitable and therefore outside of any attempts to change or alter it, becomes problematic within the field of OL.

Many definitions of culture can be presented here. It has been expressed as a metaphor, the organisation as either a machine or an organism. In the industrial era, organisations were often seen as part of the process that they were embedded in, they were structured entities which could be broken down into their key component elements and then down further into its basic operational elements. Culture here was similarly mechanistic and as human social elements became more prominent the machine metaphor began to be replaced by that of the organism. Here the organisation is a living entity, complex and existing within its environment. Inevitably metaphors have their limitations in that something may be like something else but it cannot be exactly like it and may only share some rudimentary characteristics that ultimately tell us little about the organisation.

Alternatively, culture has itself been regarded as an objective entity, a set of behavioural or cognitive characteristics. Schein (1985) talks about the basic assumptions that individuals make and that they are predisposed to act in a specific way. It is obviously important to work with a definition of culture and depending on how culture might be defined the OLP will be analysed and designed in accordance with this definition. In this text culture is a shared set of beliefs that form and re-form around the shifting behaviours and experiences of the individuals who make up the organisation. In considering the development of an OLP, culture can be both a barrier and a key facilitator. Where it is a barrier culture creates a series of questions for the organisation. Why do we think in this way? In doing so, we potentially stall the development of learning from our experiences and delay the development of the OLP. This characteristic, whatever it might be, needs to be identified and challenged.

As we have considered in relation to ethics the values and beliefs of the organisation will reflect the moral code that underpins the actions of the organisation. Openness and honesty are values that become part of the broader belief system of the organisation. Where openness is seen to be effective then it will become embedded within beliefs. Alternatively, if more negative values are perceived to be effective then they too will become embedded. The process of perception here is key. The contestation of values is dependent upon the legitimacy of the 'voices' and this can obscure actions of value that even common sense would suggest are wrong. A bad decision by a powerful individual is often not fully acknowledged. Failure might be put down to 'other' factors and individuals may choose to align themselves with this view as they pragmatically assess their position within the organisation as their priority.

Handy (1985) presented four types of organisational culture:

Power culture: here there is a central source of power, with authority emanating from this central point. There can be a great deal of freedom to get on with specific tasks and this does require trust and empathy to be effective. However, it is reliant upon the 'charisma' of an individual or key individuals and this can be difficult to sustain.

Role culture: here the structure is key. There are clearly defined tasks or roles and these form specialisms that can be focused upon and carried out. It requires a stable environment, where change is certainly not the norm. Highly bureaucratic organisations such as a civil service can fit into this organisational type. It does not look for or encourage individual initiative and can suit those who favour predictability.

Task culture: here the task itself is central and the expertise associated with the defined task is highly regarded. This requires a degree of flexibility to bring divergent talents together to accomplish tasks. Team and group working is favoured in this type of organisation and they favour flexibility and autonomy.

Person culture: here the focus is on the commonality of the overall goal. This will bring professionals together to share and collaborate. Internal organisation is defined by the individuals themselves, based on autonomy and expertise will determine the exercise of power, with different individuals at different times exercising power depending on the circumstances.

A culture can be said to be strong where it is able to provide support and reassurance, but this might be indicative of an over-reliance on the cultural characteristics to provide a means of avoiding uncertainty and doubt. In this case a strong culture can be an impediment. Where there is a context of change and where there is an expectation that high levels of uncertainty are to be regarded not just as the norm but as a defining characteristic of the environment, then the strength of a culture lies in its adaptability, rather than its consistency or longevity.

Organisational culture is an expression of the collective, of the group and the relationship between the individual and the organisation:

> At a collective level the influences of politics and culture are, perhaps, the most important potential inhibitors of organisational learning. Organisational politics can counteract and neutralise individuals' and groups' positive learning initiatives. The political influence of dominant coalitions can also be responsible for rejecting information, however valid, which does not suit their requirements, and refuses to pursue solutions to problems if such solutions threaten to undermine their authority.
>
> (Brown 1998: 101)

OL needs to be able to embrace uncertainty in order to be able to learn from experience and to avoid behaviours that fail to challenge and test the validity of actions. This takes individuals with a high level of confidence and to a large extent the role of the OL practitioner is to build this confidence as an integral part of the culture of the organisation. The purpose or goal is to build the critical capacities of the individuals, to allow them to build an iterative process of continual critical engagement with practice and experience.

Critical human resource development

A traditional and mechanistic view of the learning function, as it has been presented in relation to training and development, is challenged by both HRD and critical HRD (CHRD). A more critical approach is being adopted and more positively promoted and the literature is:

> ...beginning to witness a growing interest in critical perspectives of practice and pedagogy. It has identified tensions between dominant and modernist orthodoxy whose ideological practices are founded upon a measurement and output driven culture and those that espouse humanistic, ethical, empowering and emancipatory practices.
>
> (Armitage 2010: 735)

To an extent, this is a shift of emphasis away from the more explicit identification of value, measured in return on investment (ROI) or a decrease in lost hours through sickness and so on. This moves the emphasis from performance to learning and in doing so focuses on the embedding of critical thinking as a key 'capability' for OL.

This is associated with the earlier work of Wilmott, (1994, 1997) who sought to link critical thinking to management learning and embed a more thorough or rigorous sociological perspective. Inevitably this draws the focus away from economic to more social issues.

> Critical HRD asks questions of the appropriateness of marketing strategies that create new 'needs' for consumer products in a world of diminishing natural resources. Critical HRD helps practitioners explore questions of management as a social, political and economic practice.
>
> (Trehan and Rigg 2011: 280)

This transforms the focus of training as a mechanism to enhance the capabilities of individuals to achieve stated organisational goals, to the capacity of individuals to engage with a process of learning which itself might transform the organisation. Rather than training for a specific purpose, the focus is on learning as a critical transformation of the organisation as it exists within its wider environment.

The OLP within this context is one that is expected to critically engage not only with the management of the organisations, but also with the teaching and learning process that it is forming a part of, and to then relocate the learning process within a less instrumental model. This goes beyond the straight or conventional delivery of content, from teacher or expert to learner. Rather, it is a more collaborative relationship based on open dialogue, mutual respect and a strong ethical sense of the position of the '*other*'.

> Dialogue espouses a value and ethical approach that engenders dignity, honesty and trust built upon equitable personal relationships and offers creative approaches to established common meanings and understandings.
>
> (Armitage 2010: 740)

Clearly, CHRD challenges a positivist perspective and the more quantitative methodological approaches with which positivism is associated. This is often presented as the rational school of thought. Indeed, many schools of thought can now be associated with organisational culture from modern structural theory and systems theory to more ideologically based theories. Our understanding of the dominant discourses within the wider social context can be seen to drive our interpretation of how culture embeds itself within the policies and practices of any given organisation.

If we take a look at examples of each of these theories in turn we can get a sense of just how significant these theoretical frameworks can be for practice.

A rational perspective

There a number of interventionist theories that can be aligned with this perspective and to a large extent they represent the systemic view of the organisation that emerged in the middle to late part of the twentieth century. Here it is recognised that the management of change is an ongoing and iterative process. This type of perspective is characterised by a belief that the organisation is a discrete set of elements that relate to one another in a complex but deterministic way.

Max Weber's (1864–1920) concept of bureaucracy, far from having the negative connotations we today associate with this word, was rather an expression of the rational organisation, one that was governed by specific features:

- A distinct set of rules.
- Hierarchically structured with distinct functions and specialisms.
- A coherent strategy for data and information management.
- Authority based on the formal role that one might hold within the organisation.

Within this framework, organisations came to be viewed as systems, the elements of which could be understood and changed. This change was affected by the intervention strategy which itself developed into a distinct process. Various *intervention strategy models* have been developed, the basic component elements are:

- problem definition
- evaluation
- design
- implementation.

These models have embedded feedback and overall are perceived to be an iterative process with the change initiated by the intervention precipitating another problem requiring definition and so on (see Figure 7.1).

All of these more rationally based processes, not surprisingly, are based on a belief that organisations as systems have identifiable variables that will relate to each other in a determinable manner. There is a clear cause–effect phenomenon at the heart of organisation. If we identify these variables and how they relate to each other then we will be able to predict the outcome of actions.

A Marxist perspective

Karl Marx has added a great deal to our understanding of organisations through his analysis of the socio-political environment of late-nineteenth-century Europe and in particular

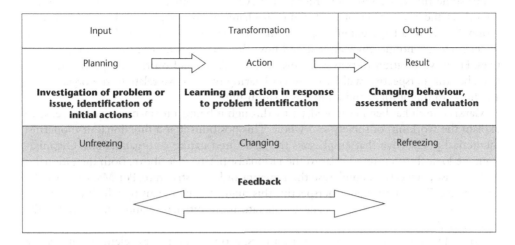

Figure 7.1 Transformation model

Britain. Specifically, Marx highlighted class as the determining feature of a society where there existed different relationships between different groups of individuals to the means of production. Where one group or class controlled the means of production Marx called this a class society.

This became an exploitative society with only one group in a position to accumulate wealth, and at the expense and to the detriment of the other classes. The working class, who carried out the operational functions within this class-based society, were said to be alienated from the labour they performed in that they neither felt any association with the product they were producing nor directly benefited from its production. This became an iterative process of exploitation and entrapment with the ruling class extending their privilege at the expense of those being ruled. As everyone was 'enmeshed' within this system, according to Marx, this made capitalism the highest form of class society. When the means of production are owned and controlled by those who produce the product or deliver the service – the worker, then this will end class conflict and create a socialist or communist model. Exploitation and alienation will inevitably cease.

Marx's views have been the subject of more debate and consideration than any other theory. The notion of a class struggle has been challenged, not least by the numbers who could not be categorised as either part of the capitalist bourgeoisie (ruling middle-class) or the proletariat (exploited working-class). Nevertheless, the element of power and exploitation has been used to help understand the way in which cultural dynamics have emerged in organisations and how one group ensures that they maintain a privileged position over others. For those exploited in this type of system, alienation can be identified as a lack of autonomy, poor pay and conditions or low status.

> Much research has been done to show how attempts were made to gain managerial control over professional work processes in the context of the cultural change under-taken in many of these services, following the Conservative Thatcher government's push to introduce private-sector market values into the public sector.
>
> (Crowther and Green 2004: 106)

For some this was control in order to achieve greater efficiency and effectiveness and for others the imposition of controlling mechanisms that exploit and target a specific group. This is, to a large extent, a debate that still draws on Marx's understanding of the wider socio-economic environment and how this manifests itself in organisational practices. How we position ourselves in this debate will depend on the perspective that we have, but this perspective will have a direct bearing on how we relate to the organisation and how we might form and build this relationship.

Marxism itself has been criticised, partly through it being a meta-narrative that seeks to explain the workings of society as a whole. This positions it as a functional or modernist theoretical perspective that emphasises the structured nature of organisations. Organisations are logical structures, similar to the rationalist perspective above. Both the rationalist and Marxist perspectives emphasise the inherent order or structure. For Marx this can be exploitative. From a rationalist perspective this might be the means by which the organisation can be understood and made to operate more efficiently and effectively for the benefit of all.

Control is clearly central from a Marxist perspective and it is these elements of Marxist theory that have proven more enduring than the more speculative consideration given to the trajectory of a class-based society and the inevitability of the class struggle resulting in global revolution and the triumph of the working class.

A postmodern perspective

The challenge to both Marxist models and models that are based on a modernist perspective of rationality and logic, in turn based on the scientific world view and methods of observation and experimentation, can be identified as postmodern. The postmodern is an elusive term, identified with plurality and local rather than grand or meta-narratives. In many respects the postmodern can be characterised and aligned with theories associated with social constructionism. Here the emphasis is placed not on the identification of a single truth or fact but that there will be multiple truths. What will determine a fact is not its own inherent 'rightness' but the social acceptance of it being right. This shifts the emphasis towards the process through which this 'rightness' is assigned either value or not. This therefore makes the process of *contestation* of particular significance, as it is this process that will determine what is regarded as a truth in any particular instance. Dialogue forms the basis of contestation and asks questions around who can make statements and who will be listened to. Who has legitimacy?

In order to illustrate a less rational perspective and the more critical approach adopted by CHRD, the issue of privacy is being considered here. Privacy is a complex issue.

- Where and how do we draw the boundaries between competing and conflicting interests?
- Does the right to know supersede the right to retain personal privacy?
- Does this depend on the circumstances and if so what circumstances?
- Does an employer have a right to know about your actions and behaviour while at work, in order to manage the information more effectively?
- Can or should we be confident that the use of this information is in our own interests and used not to control us but to protect and, indeed, care for us?
- Are we liberated or controlled by this collection and use of information?

The point about privacy is that it raises hard cases; people want privacy for per-
fectly good reasons, and others want information for equally good reasons. Technology will alter the delicate balance between such people as it evolves.

(O'Hara and Shadbolt 2008: 23)

A particularly significant illustration of the potential of technology to control human
beings rather than liberate them can be seen in the concept of *panopticism*. The term panopticism stems from the work of the critical theorist Michel Foucault, in *Discipline and
Punish* (1991). Foucault's project in this and other works is to trace the relationship
between *knowledge, discourse* and *power* in history. *Discipline and Punish* examines the system
of punishment from the eighteenth century onward, showing how punishment moved
from the *spectacle* of the public execution in the eighteenth century to the nineteenth
century institution of the prison, whose main principle was *discipline* and *control* of those
to be punished.

Foucault's main point in tracing this change in the discourse of power and punishment
was that in order to make the prison, and the system of discipline it is based on, work, the
authorities needed to collect information on people – to keep them under surveillance.
The ideal device to keep people under surveillance was the *panopticon* – invented or con-
ceived by the nineteenth-century English philosopher Jeremy Bentham (1748–1832).

The design of Bentham's circular prison is such that all (*pan-*) prisoners can be kept
permanently under surveillance (*-opticon*) without them being aware of this:

Each individual, in his place, is securely confined to a cell from which he is seen from
the front by the supervisor; but the side walls prevent him from coming into contact
with his companion. He is seen, but does not see; he is the object of information,
never the subject of communication.

(Foucault 1991: 200)

The ultimate aim of the surveillance in the panopticon, therefore, is not just to keep people under surveillance, but to instil in people the fear, or at least awareness, of being
watched so that they will *discipline themselves*:

... the major effect of the Panopticon: to induce in the inmate a state of conscious
and permanent visibility that assures the automatic functioning of power ... the
inmates should be caught up in a power situation of which they themselves are the
bearers ... what matters is that he knows himself to be observed.

(Foucault 1991: 201)

We see here the key features of panopticism. These make it of interest beyond the confines
of the nineteenth-century prison system and capable of being applied to the relationship
between technology and culture in modern societies. If people *believe* they are under constant surveillance, if the technological means for this exist, then they will *discipline themselves* – the state will not need to exert power on them, as individuals will exert power on
themselves:

The Panopticon is a marvellous machine which, whatever use one may wish to put it
to, produces homogeneous effects of power ... He who is subjected to a field of

> visibility, and who knows it, assumes responsibility for the constraints of power; he makes them play spontaneously upon himself; . . . he becomes the principle of his own subjection.
>
> (Foucault 1991: 201–2)

Panopticism, or the principle of the total surveillance society, which Foucault extends beyond the immediate discourse of discipline and punishment, has as its aim the production of an individual who subjects him/herself. We can apply Foucault's ideas to modern technology and its surveillance potential in the following ways.

- First, while the original design of Bentham's panopticon was constrained by space, with the advent of technologies such as the Internet, CCTV and other surveillance mechanisms, the scope of panopticism has been hugely increased without limitations of space.
- Second, whereas in the nineteenth century and early twentieth century the bodies carrying out the surveillance were primarily the state and its apparatus, those involved in contemporary surveillance include a multiplicity of bodies, private and public, which collect information on individuals, and are therefore more difficult to monitor.
- Third, the sophistication of modern technology means that, while using it, we do not *appear* to be under surveillance, but in fact we are. When making an online purchase or just visiting a website, for example, we leave behind an invisible 'trace' of ourselves which can then be monitored and collated by those interested in doing so.

Modern Internet and digital technology arguably extends panopticism beyond its original dream towards the vision, dream or nightmare, of a total panoptic society.

In the workplace, the extended ability of employers to monitor and measure the performance of employees through technology has led some commentators to see in this the extension of the principles of 'Taylorism' or scientific management. 'Taylorism' refers to the principles of F. W. Taylor, which were:

- the division of labour, reducing tasks to the simplest possible actions;
- managers should have complete control of the workplace;
- time-and-motion studies would be used to control costs and efficiency within the workplace.

Robins and Webster (1999) argue that the panoptic potential of technology has enhanced the ability of managers to monitor employees as they can now do this without the employee's awareness. The element of visibility and the continuous nature of the surveillance possible with modern technology correspond to the panoptic principles discussed by Foucault.

Similarly, the increased surveillance in everyday life through our use of the Internet and digital technology (for example, the preponderance of CCTV cameras on the streets and other public places) is seemingly accompanied by a lack of awareness or concern by the public for any lack of privacy or any infringement of human rights which this might entail. As the sociologist David Lyon (2001) suggests, this seems to stem from the fact that the public in some way feel *comforted* by this surveillance, and are therefore willing to go along with it. Lyon argues, we are living in a panoptic surveillance society where the benefits of increased coordination (decreased risks and desire not to miss out on the benefits the information society offers, such as personalized information tailored to our consumption needs) make us willing to put up with this surveillance. The question is whether this constitutes an extension of panopticism or whether we have now moved into a post-panoptic society?

CHRD would be looking to highlight and engage with the significance of any increase in the panoptic effects of technologies in the workplace. It would ask or seek to identify the purpose of the development, how it will impact upon individuals and whether or not its primary aim is to enhance management control over the individual or the well-being of the individual. How capable an organisation might be in addressing or even answering these questions will to an extent reflect their ability to effectively embed an OLP. A key attribute of CHRD is:

> ... the awareness of power relations and the need to shift power from the oppressor to the oppressed to give them voice and freedom.
>
> (Sambrook 2009: 67)

The externalisation of learning process through performance reviews and learning plans will focus on the individual and align themselves with the more humanistic elements associated with HRD, but these cannot necessarily be divorced from organisational mechanisms that seek to 'manage' the performance of the individual. In this sense they constrain the individual rather than liberate them and in doing so they are likely to form a barrier to OL. From a practical perspective the embedding of CHRD will or may have key consequences:

> In the practice arena, these consequences might include: more democratic work production, improved (working/learning) relationships; more effective and relevant learning; enhanced transfer of learning; improved creativity and productivity; and an acceptance of alternative approaches to knowing.
>
> (Sambrook 2009: 68)

A more egalitarian workplace is directly linked here to a form of learning within the organisation. This challenges the organisation, requires it to reflect, constantly, on its own structures and strategies, and ultimately externalise the power dynamics that make it up. The challenge here cannot be underestimated. Many organisations fail to frame the questions that are inherent within CHRD and even when they do so there is a reluctance to fully appreciate the extent to which this is requiring an acceptance of change to the key power dynamics that make up the organisation. In purely OL terms the relationships required to drive OL can be aligned with CHRD in that they help to form the questions that make explicit the key relationships within the organisation. This will inevitably impact upon all of the functions associated with wider HRM, including leadership.

Leadership

In HRD leadership is a crucial element and there is a need to present some details about what leadership has been perceived to be and what it might become within the emerging context. In particular, what type of leadership can best be equated with the emerging knowledge-based environment and the need to embed learning within the organisation?

Leadership itself is often equated with the characteristics of an individual, the charismatic leader, leading from the front and inspiring others. This is devoid of any sense or awareness of context and from an OL perspective largely fails to recognise the value of collaborative dialogue. This style of leadership remains common, if less regarded, today, in favour of specific behavioural characteristics that look to identify the qualities of leadership and approaches that offer more awareness of context as a relevant factor.

Transformational leadership has gained some currency recently and focuses on the key function of leadership as largely strategic in terms of its primary focus. Here, communication of the 'vision', motivating and inspiring those around to greater and more innovative engagement, is central. In contrast to this, leadership needs also to ensure that the operational imperatives of the organisation, the day-to-day routine activities, are carried out and that the cultural values of the organisation are protected and promoted.

Leaders are, therefore, representatives of the organisation, charged with upholding its values and ensuring that it functions. This is done by:

Planning: The planning process is concerned with the development of long- and short-term plans. It looks to set the organisation's goals and objectives. It is concerned, therefore, with strategic planning that will create and implement the policies and procedures that underpin the operation of the organisation. As part of the strategic management function, this is normally associated with strategic managers who tend to make up the senior management team.

Organising: Leaders also carry out vital organising functions that will involve the effective and efficient assignment of tasks and responsibilities. This will also involve a degree of delegation and ultimately ensure that there will be a sound basis for accountability within the organisation. All leaders throughout the organisation are involved with organising, but perhaps more specifically it is the middle, tactical, managers who perform an important liaison role between the strategic and operational levels who are more specifically involved with this function.

Directing: The direction of the organisation is fundamentally based on the leadership it receives. To be effective here leaders will be expected to be efficient communicators; to be creative and inspirational; to positively motivate the staff within the organisation. Again all leaders will direct to some extent, but overall direction is a strategic function and the emphasis at this level should be informing the efforts of operational and tactical leaders.

Controlling: In order to be able to control the various functions of the organisation the leader must observe its operation; be responsive and reactive to the necessary changes; and be willing to make the necessary modifications.

Leadership, therefore, can often be equated with authority, the authority to make decisions, in order to get things done. To do this we get others to follow us and they follow us because we have authority. The question that can be drawn from this is: *where does authority come from*? In organisational terms authority can be embedded within the structural characteristics of the organisation. This might in turn be drawn from the environment within which the organisation operates. For example, a university draws on the embedded value of education that has been socially constructed over many centuries. Within this it will draw on embedded titles and practices that reinforce its own position. The conferring of titles such as professor, dean and chancellor all bring authority to the holder. The ceremonials associated with graduation and even some teaching practices (wearing of gowns and so on) all play a part in sustaining a sense of legitimacy and ultimately authority that most institutions actively seek to maintain or acquire.

The leadership of an organisation that is looking to embed learning is often associated with the transformation leadership style:

> With regards to the style of leadership argued to be necessary to achieve such performance, [organisational learning] as outlined, there is virtual unanimity in the knowledge management literature that transformational leadership is the most appropriate form of leadership. Thus, this literature talks about the importance of leaders who are concerned with long term strategy and vision.
>
> (Hislop 2005: 263)

This appears to contradict the OL literature where it is focused on collaborative models and where the vision of the organisation, for example, is looking to shift from a telling to a co-creating dynamic. The role of the leader in developing an OLP, needs to be inspirational, rather than just transformational – but this responsibility needs to rest upon a broader base of individuals, if not all the individuals who make up the organisation.

Hislop goes on to say:

> ... responsibility for leadership should be the concern of all workers and managers, and that leadership should be dispersed throughout an organisation.
>
> (Hislop 2005: 263)

Where leadership becomes an inspirational function and moves away from the command and control function, then it begins to emerge as part of a programme of relationship building. Rather than imposing a vision it facilitates the creation of a shared vision. This makes authority more of a shared function and the empowerment of individuals within organisations is this sharing or dispersal of responsibility for decision making and ultimately the creation of the strategic vision of the organisation. Authority becomes a more egalitarian concept and in turn has embedded within it an expectation that more individuals are able and willing to accept enhanced responsibility.

To an extent the professionalisation of the workforce is this process in action. Professionalism can be identified by certain characteristics including:

- body of knowledge.

This particular attribute largely defines the professional in terms of their potential contribution to society. In other words they have access to a complex body of knowledge not readily available to others.

- autonomy
- self-regulation
- accountability
- responsibility
- capability
- trust.

These attributes relate specifically to the position that the professional would expect to adopt both within society and within an organisation.

- representation by professional body;
- achieved through recognised academic standards at the higher level.

These final attributes identify and embody the process and recognition achieved by the professional. As mentioned, it is difficult to either suggest that professionals have exclusive claim to these attributes or that professionals represent each in equal measure. Accountability, responsibility and so on are difficult concepts to measure either in terms of their growth or decline.

Professionalism represents an ideal standard, a benchmark of behaviour and service that will be constant, reliable and unquestionable. However, questioning this ideal has been perhaps the only constant. Robert Louis Stevenson in his famous tale of *Dr Jekyll and Mr Hyde* (1886) is studying the contradictory nature of the individual professional man in Victorian Britain. Despite the outward respectability of the good doctor there is in fact a tormented soul hidden beneath. To some extent this is an indictment of respectable Victorian society as a whole and perhaps calls into doubt the efficacy of unquestioned professional trust both as an unreasonable strain on the individual and as a general policy.

Nevertheless, the professionalisation of the workforce draws on this need to embed a more shared understanding of responsibility within the organisation. As a professional and with a professional persona, this acceptance of responsibility becomes more achievable. The body of knowledge is the experience that one is constantly acquiring at all levels within the organisation. The individual will be provided with enough autonomy to stimulate their acquisition of experiential knowledge and will take responsibility for this as an ongoing process. In the first instance they are accountable to themselves, but their enhanced capabilities are based on their acceptance of this responsibility and that others around them will be doing the same. This finally builds the trust that is required for any sustainable OLP.

In terms of leadership, therefore, there is a distinct drift towards participative forms of leadership and management that base themselves on shared responsibility. Leadership becomes a collaborative effort, challenging the concept of authority through the realisation that there is a mutual interdependence between those who make up the group both in terms of their mutual reliance on one another and specifically in relation to their appreciation that their mutual fate is also based on this interdependence.

This raises some issues for leaders and how the 'traditional' view of leadership might be emerging within a predominantly OL context. Here the development of the leader's role needs to be considered. To develop inspirational or transformational leaders is not straightforward but sound communication skills coupled with a sound understanding of key traditional pedagogical skills are necessary. Presentation skills are necessary but these need to be embedded across the organisation and not limited to certain individuals.

The embedding of more egalitarian principles will inevitably challenge many existing power structures and the authority that they represent – the ownership of the functions of leadership. Planning, coordinating and so on, are devolved and dispersed. In Senge's disciplines this is the development of co-creation rather than telling as a key cultural dynamic. The organisation is tasked with creating a shared vision for itself that is created by those who are affected by it – namely all those in the organisation. Rather than this being a logistical nightmare and an idealistic dream that could not be achieved in any 'real' situation, it is a more critical and positive reflection of the panopticism considered above. The opportunity to make visible our explicit knowledge has been enhanced within the technology-rich context that is emerging within the digital age and rather than being used to control it is used to care. The same capability to control is applied in a more open way in order to sustain the dialogues that will realistically drive the development of a genuinely shared vision. Ownership, in this sense, can be realistic rather than idealistic in this emerging environment and ownership can look to become more democratic and more egalitarian. Ownership of the creation of a shared vision builds trust within the organisation.

> ... the creation of a shared vision creates a bridge between the present and the future fostering long-term commitment to organisational effectiveness.
>
> (McGuire 2014: 195)

The process of creating the shared vision is as significant as the vision itself. The process, too, is its own leadership in that there is a shared responsibility for its creation and ultimately its realisation. Leadership in this sense draws on the characteristics that might be associated with a different style of leader. These might be the traits of leadership embedded more widely, along with the behavioural characteristics that identify good leaders and the awareness of the context as a determining factor. Together these may add up to the transformational or inspirational leader.

> Understanding leadership calls for careful consideration of the social context in which processes of leadership take place. Leadership is not just a leader acting and a group of followers responding in a mechanical way, but a complex social process in which the meaning and interpretations of what is said and done are crucial. Leadership then is closely related to culture – at the organisational and other levels.
>
> (Alvesson 2002: 94)

Within any context the language used, the understanding of professionalism and so on, will help to determine the understanding of what the purpose of leadership might be and what is expected of a leader. If OL is based upon genuine collaboration then it will favour a more participative style of leadership. The issue here is that this style is not one that can be embedded simply by the practice of an individual manager as this will tend to grow uncertainty, confusion and anxiety amongst those being led. This is based on their expectations of leadership, on it being expected to provide a direction and where they had detailed instructions as to their role. Participative leadership is, therefore, more to do with the dissemination of responsibilities, rather than the adoption of a style by an individual who happens to be in a prominent position.

> ... leadership is per definition seen as 'cultural', that is leadership must be understood as taking place in a cultural context and all leadership acts have their consequences through the (culturally guided) interpretation of those involved in the social processes in which leaders, followers and leadership acts are expressed.
>
> (Alvesson 2002: 101)

This places the emphasis more fully upon the position of all those involved and leadership as being the ability to identify this common understanding or position. Here, community and open communication forms the basis for leadership, despite this appearing to mean or define the opposite. This is leadership that has democratic and egalitarian characteristics and this has been recognised as a genuine trend.

> Companies on the cutting edge of technological change tend to be forced by their very nature to operate by democratic principles, and those that become bureaucratised and hierarchical usually find themselves quickly upstaged by egalitarian newcomers.
>
> (Bennis 2009: 103)

OL, therefore, is drawing on organisational developments that are challenging many of the key roles and responsibilities. OL requires a more democratic structure in order to form a broader base of responsibility. Individuals will take up this responsibility only where they are assured of their position or where they trust that those around them are also accepting of these new levels of responsibility. Once the OL practitioner has identified this as a key goal and is working to achieve it, then learning at an organisational level can begin to happen.

The organisation, therefore, must support individual learning and harness the learning capabilities of the individuals within the organisation to the maximum advantage of the organisation. Leadership is a significant element here and can impede learning where it negatively impacts upon individual learning activities or outcomes. Friedman (2001) illustrated the way in which individuals can act as agents of change in organisations that emphasises the willingness to challenge existing practices and to actively look for alternative solutions. In the brief cases outlined one individual learner is criticised for attempting to instigate what was seen as a learning opportunity.

> Marc wanted to do something that would cut through the game playing, but he knew that his intervention was touching on very sensitive and threatening issues for all the parties concerned. Under these conditions it would have required considerable work simply to arrive at a common definition of the problem, much less its cause and possible solutions.
>
> (Friedman 2001: 406)

This case highlights the social nature of the organisation and how an individual must, to some extent, be in a position to apply their individual learning within and in accordance with the social parameters that exist within the organisation. Individual learning in this instance is not simply about what one person might believe to be an answer but how the organisation itself is prepared to adopt or accept this answer or solution. Assessing this preparedness becomes a vital part of managing the learning that will take place within any organisation.

The charismatic leader presents an inspirational persona designed to instil trust in followers who will be led and take the clear directions of the leader. Richard Branson and Steve Jobs can be defined in this way. They represent or embody the values of Virgin and Apple respectively and inspire loyalty and even affection in those who 'follow' them. However, where an organisation is looking to learn from the embedded experience of all the members of that organisation then charismatic leadership, or autocratic leadership from the front becomes less viable. An organisation capable of learning needs to draw its understanding of leadership close to its collaborative cultural objective. Trust here is founded upon the relationship these individuals have and leadership styles must be aligned with this.

How able, ready or prepared an organisation might be to take on board the implications of participative or a collaborative form of leadership, where responsibility is dispersed, is the 'call' of the OL practitioner.

Many organisations claim to be LO that embrace the inherently democratic character-istics that have been outlined. Happy is such an organisation.

> Imagine a workplace where people are energised and motivated by being in control of the work they do. Imagine they are trusted and given freedom, within clear guidelines, to decide how to achieve their results. Imagine they are able to get the life balance they want. Imagine they are valued according to the work they do, rather than the number of hours they spend at their desk.
>
> (Stewart 2012: loc. 73 of 1957)

In *The Happy Manifesto* (Stewart, 2012) the organisation that is being described will look to ensure that individuals are given the opportunity to do what they are best at. They will be supported in identifying what this might be and the role of managers will be to avoid stifling this. This can build confidence and it can help to ensure that positive aspects of actions and behaviours are focused upon. A direction is no less necessary, but beyond this there can and should be freedom to act and to take ownership of what it is you are being asked to do. Where there is transparency and this transparency does not amount to surveil-lance then it becomes a part of the open dialogue that will characterise the organisation. This will include both good and bad news! The individuals making up the organisation should be recruited based on their 'fit' with the ethos of the organisation. The journey to, through and out of the organisation should be positive.

Positive might reflect the 'happy' that names this organisation. The premise is that indi-viduals who are happy will be more effective and efficient, they will work better and harder. The organisation can support individuals by recognising their inherent value and willingly supporting them when necessary. It can create systems rather than rules where each individual is entitled to suggest how the system can be improved rather than being seen to challenge existing rules. This creates more dynamic change mechanisms that seek to draw individuals into the process through which change is initiated. This in turn allows the manager to step back, to observe rather than impose, and to allow the process of man-agement to become more about creating and participating in dialogue.

The Happy environment is important, creating a strong sense of belonging and looking to achieve a level of self-actualisation where individuals feel that their contribution is valued. This places the emphasis upon the position of individuals as responsible contribu-tors able to make decisions for themselves and to see where these decisions support the aims of the organisation. This responsibility creates a stronger sense of job or task owner-ship and it is therefore important that individuals are able to value the organisation's aims. This in turn requires a level of visibility and openness in order to ensure that each indi-vidual can be confident that they are informed enough to justify taking on responsibility for their work. Not all information here can be good, and it is necessary for hard and difficult information to be made available too.

Building this relationship should ensure that even individuals who leave, will leave with a positive view of the organisation, based on a perception of it as a mutually beneficial expe-rience. This is often related to the important issue of work–life balance. Individuals should not be expected to be working at all times, and the benefit of having time to pursue other interests can enhance performance. Flexible working can support this but the need should be to prioritise the benefit to the individual – in order to be beneficial to the organisation.

In all of these areas it is important to have managers in place who can sustain this crucial relationship and see the management of people as their primary role. Decision making might be regarded as the principal function of managers, but there is an equal need for them to be supportive and empathetic. It cannot be assumed that a good decision maker is also empathetic.

> The role of managers is to help people perform at their best. Their job is to support, coach and challenge. We all know from personal experience that some managers are great at this, and others are not.
>
> (Stewart 2012: loc. 1766 of 1957)

All of these elements are focused on the relationship between the individual and the organisation. They may appear to be idealistic and ultimately unrealistic for large global-ised organisations, but they help to raise the type of question that is relevant for organisa-tions that are looking to engage with the knowledge-economy and to embed social learning. Where individuals are self-motivated, where it is assumed that they want to do a good job and to take or accept the responsibility for ensuring that their learning becomes an asset for everyone, there can be said to be a sound basis of trust within the organisation. Trust forms the relationship that will facilitate learning within the organisation.

Leadership within the LO is a shared experience and forms part of the iterative expe-riential learning process that drives OL. The shift is towards more democratic and egali-tarian models which are certainly regarded as positive and often supported, if only in principle. They are also, often, regarded as inefficient and ultimately ineffective, as Bennis again has said:

> There are probably few men of affairs in America who have not at some time nour-ished in their hearts the blasphemous thought that life would go much more smoothly if democracy could be relegated to some kind of Sunday morning devotion.
>
> (Bennis 2009: 105)

The organisational context within which democratic principles appear to work best is becoming more common place. Indeed it is defined by the concepts embedded within the knowledge-economy.

Concluding remarks

The basic functions of HRD concern themselves with the culture of the organisation and the leadership of that organisation. Both of these elements can represent the relationship between individuals and the organisation. A sharing, collaborative culture requires to be led in a way that will not contradict this culture. Leadership and culture need to be aligned and it needs to be recognised that one will shape and influence the other. The LO, there-fore, will have a collaborative culture which cannot be led non-collaboratively.

8 Knowledge as an organisational asset

Learning outcomes:

1   Identify the elements within the tacit to explicit model.
2   Understand the concept of the knowledge-economy.
3   Identify the characteristics associated with both scientific and socially constructed knowledge.
4   Identify the key elements associated with knowledge organisation, acquisition, mapping, and transfer and sharing.

Introduction

Any consideration of knowledge management (KM) can either focus on knowledge or on management before looking to blend these two concepts into a coherent strategy or discipline. Knowledge is resented as the asset that will drive the emerging economic environment, relying on what we know about what we do, rather than on any more tangible assets such as raw materials or even finances. Jashapara (2004) presents the different elements that make up KM as a tree with its roots in anthropology, sociology, economics, HR, management science, computer science and so on. It has branches that grow from a strategic management trunk covering organisational learning, change management, KM systems and tools, and producing dialogue and discussion around the tacit and explicit knowledge that is created.

KM can be regarded as having this multi-disciplinary base and having created a series of related disciplines of which organisational learning can be regarded as one. The centrality of organisational learning is emphasised when knowledge is presented or defined in a specific way. When it is defined as a specific entity and aligned with a more instrumental or positivist perspective then the technologies associated with KM systems can be ascribed more significance. This view can be countered by a perspective more sympathetic to social constructionism, where knowledge is less regarded as a discrete entity and more akin to a process – a learning process. OL inevitably favours this latter view of KM and it tends to focus on specific elements of the key KM models. It is the definition of knowledge itself that determines the validity of the perspective being applied and it is this that will be considered here.

Tacit to explicit: the key KM model

KM can be regarded as an extension of the discipline of information management (IM) which concerns itself with ensuring that individuals and organisations are able to exploit as effectively and efficiently as possible the inherent value of the information asset. There are key principles that support this, not least our ability to create the necessary taxonomies through the applications of the skills associated with classification, cataloguing or knowledge organisation. These skills ensure that what we know can be accessed by as many individuals as possible and represents one element of the key KM model – the *tacit to explicit* (Nonaka and Takeuchi, 1995) model.

IM can be associated with a key element in this tacit to explicit model:

- The management of explicit knowledge.

This is the knowledge that has been externalised and can therefore be codified and embedded in the elements that make up the information system. These are the systems that store information in databases and data-warehouses. They move this information around through networks and manipulate and present this information through data-mining, decision-support systems and expert systems.

> If lessons are being learned from many projects, for example, from retrospects and after action reviews, then these lessons need to be collected within an IT system that stores them, classifies them, and routes them to the person who needs to act on them.
>
> (Knoco 2015)

Here, IM concerns itself with the management of explicit knowledge and can draw on the technologies associated with knowledge-based information systems – essentially the storage capacity and connectivity that has enhanced organisational practices over the last few decades.

However, the management of explicit knowledge represents just one of the three elements that make up the tacit to explicit model. The other two are:

- The creation of tacit knowledge.
- The transformation of tacit knowledge to an explicit form.

The creation of tacit knowledge is a key issue for OL. The ability of an individual to learn is perhaps less contentious than any attempt to explain how they learn, but the ability of an organisation to learn is somewhat more contentious. An organisation may be presented anthropomorphically and claims may be made that, like an individual, an organisation will learn, but in considering the ability of an individual to assess and reflect on their experience, as a basis for their knowledge, raises questions around the capability of the organisation to do this. Rather, OL aligns itself more with the notion that organisations learn via the willingness of those individuals who make up the organisation to use their learning on behalf of the organisation. This then raises the question of where, when and under what circumstances will individuals willingly apply their learning for the benefit of the organisation? Addressing this question is central to OL. Why would an individual use their acquired knowledge for the benefit of the organisation?

This question can be broken down in two ways:

- Why would an individual not want to use their knowledge for the benefit of the organisation?
- What might the organisation do to encourage an individual to make their knowledge available?

These questions cannot be taken for granted. In the first instance, we can expect that individuals will create tacit knowledge simply by going about their daily experiences but we cannot assume that they will be aware of this or fully appreciate the extent to which they are acquiring this knowledge. Unless they do so, then tacit knowledge will remain 'hidden' even, to an extent, from the individual as well as the organisation. Second, even when an individual is aware of their growing and developing knowledge base there can be no assumption made about their willingness to share this knowledge. An individual for many and varied reasons will 'fail' to make their knowledge available to the organisation. For example, the individual may perceive their environment as a competitive one and that in their own interests they need to deploy parts of their knowledge base to support their own individual position rather than that of the organisation. If we recognise organisations as competitive environments then we are acknowledging this barrier. This forms a series of questions around this competitive environment:

- How embedded is this sense of competition?
- Is this, as a cultural characteristic, supported and nurtured by organisational practice?
- What is the alternative?

A simpler but more difficult question would be:

- How do we know whether or not this organisation has embedded and entrenched competition?

Equally, the individual may be willing to share their knowledge but not have the skills to do so. We can certainly not take for granted that individuals will be able to effectively and efficiently share knowledge.

 Pause for thought – Knowing what you know

Not knowing what you know is a key barrier to the use of knowledge as an individual and an organisational asset. Think about any time where you were involved with a specific task, this might be studying as a student or in your first job or even as a parent.

With the latter we often learn as we go along, commenting that there are no manuals that specifically apply to us. However, we get along, we become adept at a range of things, but (for those who have more than one child) we often experience the need to re-learn or rediscover what we have learnt if we are asked to do this again. How to hold a baby properly in a bath, to support the head when carrying a baby and so on? At school we often claim that 'cramming' for examinations is ulti-mately limited in that we often forget what we needed to 'know' for an examination shortly after we have sat it. The perceived purpose of the knowledge has passed and the need to retain it has also passed.

There is little or no externalisation of what we know or what we have learnt in this type of context and, therefore, we can experience the need to re-learn. Unless there are specific opportunities to reflect on the learning that is embedded in your experience it will be lost.

Try to remember an instance where you had to re-learn something or where you felt you had known something but that it was now largely 'gone'.

The creation of knowledge may be ongoing but this needs to be recognised. Equally, there needs to be a willingness to engage with a series of activities that will ultimately make this knowledge explicit. On top of this there is the need to support and enhance the process of knowledge creation itself. KM looks to combine these three elements in a coordinated discipline that draws a series of actions together and which can all be regarded as the OL process. It is all based on the value of knowledge as an organisa-tional asset. This has been extended to the emergence of the concept of the *knowledge-economy*.

The concept of the knowledge-economy (Drucker, 1969) has focused attention on what creates value for organisations and obviously settles on the ability of the organisation to create knowledge and to sustain this knowledge creation. The knowledge-economy is characterised by the centrality of knowledge in relation to economic processes. Rather than raw materials, including financial resources, knowledge takes a step back and acknowl-edges the process by which these raw materials or financial assets might be deployed. The acumen associated with the deployment of the other resources that an organisation has is, from this perspective, the key to organisational success. Competitiveness, driven by the ability to be innovative through the application of knowledge sustains and nurtures the organisation.

In recent years many people in management and information work have talked about KM. This suggests that it is of relevance to both groups. In fact it is – it involves both groups, working together. Interest in knowledge and information management is a sign of the times. Powerful forces are reshaping the economy of the world. There are funda-mental shifts in how organisations use information in their strategic planning and market-ing. This reveals itself in new ways of working and new organisational structures. These changes have come in many forms: globalisation, complexity, new technologies, increased competition, changing customer demands and expectations, and changing economic and political structures.

The key tacit to explicit model is made up of three elements and it is the last of these that is directly associated with IM. The other two are more associated with KM. The first is the creation of tacit knowledge and the second is the process through which this tacit knowledge is made explicit. This section will look at some of the sociological origins of knowledge as an organisational asset, the philosophy and strategy associated with KM within the concept of the knowledge-economy and focus on the 'generations' of KM.

As knowledge is central to our understanding of OL it is necessary to explore what we might mean by knowledge. In order to tackle this substantial question, two basic positions will be described here, with a view to more consistently focusing on one rather than the other as a basis for this text. In the first instance, scientific knowledge will be described and explored and then more socially constructed forms of knowledge will be considered.

The position of scientific knowledge

Scientific knowledge largely rests upon a sense of knowledge as contributing to a process that ultimately, through continual progress, leads to the fulfilment of a social purpose.

> The idea that knowledge progressed was readily extended to the claim that the entire course of human history represented a more or less continuous forward movement.
>
> (Callinicos 1999: 13)

The trajectory of scientific knowledge might be traced to the Enlightenment, a period in European history beginning in the mid-seventeenth century and also referred to as the *Age of Reason*. It was an age of reason rather than an age based on faith. It was hoped that through the observation of the natural world and ultimately the application of the scientific method, that an understanding would emerge that would be objective and therefore form the basis for statements of *truth*. Instead of relying on the doctrines of faith associated with major religions, there would be a new basis for truth, a new narrative that would ultimately explain everything. The trajectory was a search for truth, for knowledge, and it is one that resonates today more than 400 years later.

> It would be absurd to deny the validity of a theoretical system such as quantum mechanics, to which we owe our stock of nuclear weapons. Who would doubt the credibility of Mendelian genetics, now completely confirmed at the molecular level by the deciphering of the genetic code? At least some of the knowledge that has been acquired 'scientifically' is as reliable as it could possibly be.
>
> (Ziman 1978: 9)

Enlightenment principles represented an axis shift in relation to knowledge by attempting to base a true belief upon experiment and observation. Knowledge, previously, had been regarded as being founded upon mythological principles, the legitimacy of which was inevitably open to doubt. This doubt emerged during the period of the scientific revolution and replaced a mythological grand narrative with a scientific grand narrative. The knowledge to understand the world around us would now emerge from the application of the scientific method.

> The conviction of the progress of human knowledge, rationality, wealth, civilisation and control over nature with which the eighteenth century was deeply imbued, the 'Enlightenment', drew its strength primarily from the evident progress of production, trade, and the economic and scientific rationality believed to be associated inevitably with both.
>
> (Hobsbawm 1973: 34)

This technologically led and biologically based assault upon the knowledge discourse ultimately shifted legitimacy from mythologically based knowledge to scientifically based knowledge. This manifested itself in a physical struggle and is reflected in the medieval inquisition and the persecution of such figures as Copernicus and Galileo for their scientific endeavours. The church did not fear scientific endeavour itself, and was indeed at the forefront of scientific discovery and inquiry; they were not 'flat-earthers' and this perception was imposed at a much later date. It was, however, the separation of scientific activity from the church that precipitated a reactionary and oppressive response from the church. The Enlightenment could therefore, be seen as a radical shift in relation to the power/knowledge discourse – it did represent a revolutionary ideology.

> It is more accurate to call the 'enlightenment' a revolutionary ideology, in spite of the political caution and moderation of many of its continental champions, most of whom – until the 1780s – put their faith in enlightened absolute monarchy. For illuminism implied the abolition of the prevailing society and political order in most of Europe.
>
> (Hobsbawm 1973: 35)

The 'illuminism' that Hobsbawm refers to can very much be seen as a process that creates the fluidity within the knowledge discourse by challenging and undermining the 'mortar' that holds the existing discourse in place. Fuelled by a humanistic belief in the power of reason to unfetter and set *free* the individual and the talent and potential that they hold was a powerful shift in the knowledge discourse. The object importantly, is not to destroy the edifice but to replace the way in which it is held together. Thus the apparent contradictory nature of conservative continental champions of Enlightenment principles and the radical impact of these principles can be reconciled.

The triumph of this rational and scientifically based shift in the knowledge discourse saw the decline of knowledge based on religious faith and belief and its replacement with knowledge based upon *objective* scientific observation. This view of legitimate knowledge has been sustained by its adoption of, and association with, the emergence of the modernist principle of sustained human progress within the wider knowledge discourse. Science was presented as the means by which human progress would be achieved and the products and achievements of the industrial age have come to embody this sense of progress.

> For the first time in human history, the shackles were taken off the productive power of human societies, which henceforth became capable of the constant, rapid and up until the present limitless multiplication of men, goods and services. This is now technically known to the economists as the 'take-off into self sustained growth'.
>
> (Hobsbawm 1973: 43)

 Pause for thought – scientific knowledge

Consider your own attitude to scientific knowledge and identify ways in which the basic principles associated with the scientific methodology manifests themselves in everyday life. Think of examples of how we order and package our understanding in a way that mirrors the belief that a truth can be determined through empirical means.

For example, the current tendency to constructs list on both television and through social media – Britain's best building, Top 100 favourite adverts and so on. Do these indicate anything about our underlying understanding of knowledge?

Challenging scientific knowledge

Attempts to deny or challenge the legitimacy of scientific knowledge, based upon human progress, can be identified in the work of Friedrich Nietzsche (1844–1900). Nietzsche was critical of the objectivity of scientific knowledge and placed a strong emphasis upon the creativity of the individual and ultimately the emergence of an individual personality that was capable of transcending the limitations inherent within the modernist concept of humanity. These early challenges to the emerging modernist position were further enhanced with the disillusionment that followed the Second World War and the excesses of Nazi Germany and the Soviet Union. The Frankfurt School, a group of critical social theorists who studied social phenomena in the decades around the Second World War, including figures such as Theodor W. Adorno (1903–1969) and Max Horkheimer (1895–1973), at once sought to present limitations in relation to this scientific view of legitimate knowledge and to an extent precipitated a crucial split within the wider knowledge discourse. Jürgen Habermas (b. 1929) has attempted to sustain a view of modernism that represents this Enlightenment view of human progress, while poststructuralists/postmodernists have presented a challenge to the legitimacy of modernity and the knowledge that emerges from it.

> Even as Nietzsche and Dostoyevsky said that if God is dead, everything is permitted, so these thinkers [deconstructive postmodernists] are saying that since knowledge is a human invention, humans are free to redefine it continuously.
>
> (Gill 2000: 5)

The limitations of scientific knowledge and in particular the extent to which it began to draw on a general theory of biological evolution was most forcefully presented by Nietzsche. Important in the development of his position is his opposition to 'naturalism' where human action is seen as having a direct relationship with nature. For Nietzsche, nature is subjectivised.

> The human subject is naturalized, reduced to an incoherent cluster of biological drives, while nature is subjectivized, since all aspects of the physical as well as the social world are expressions of the will to power.
>
> (Callinicos 1999: 115)

This 'will to power' is central to Nietzsche's view of human action, and importantly it is deeply embedded within a sense not of individual empowerment but of an individual's full participation within social domains that exert their own power on individual action.

The human world as well as the interactions of physical bodies and the development of living organisms – is thus the continuous process of transformation arising from the endless struggle among a multiplicity of rival centres of power.

(Callinicos 1999: 119)

These centres of power can be seen to represent the social context within which the knowledge discourse is conducted. Knowledge in this sense is relative to and reflective of the interests of those within the discourse. This, to an extent, helps to explain the apparently opposing interpretations or applications of Nietzsche's views. On the one hand the Nazis could see this as a context whereby the strongest will, will prevail, while on the other hand poststructuralists and individuals such as Michel Foucault (1926–1984) could see this as a more subtle interplay of power dynamics.

However, the importance of Nietzsche is in his challenge to modernity as it was presenting itself in the late nineteenth and early twentieth century. This challenge focused upon modernity and its grand narrative, based upon the belief that scientific knowledge will ultimately present a single Truth, once we are capable of understanding the world around us sufficiently. Our ability to understand is the faith upon which this grand narrative is based and the mechanism through which it will be achieved is through the waves of technologically based progress that we have witnessed over the last few centuries.

It is Nietzsche who presents knowledge as an expression that emerges from a contested context and 'will to power' can very much be seen as a precursor to Foucault's views on power/knowledge and the wider emergence of the socially constructed nature of knowledge. In this way Nietzsche challenges the hegemonic position of scientific knowledge, presents the ideological foundation of scientific knowledge that would be taken up by Jürgen Habermas (1986a,b; 1992) and others, and ultimately can be seen to be the catalyst for much of what is now regarded as a postmodern perspective.

Criticism of 'truth' in this form is often presented as a counter to those characteristics founded upon a scientific rationality and is associated with arguments based upon social constructionism, where there is perceived to be no definitive truths other than those agreed amongst ourselves within a social context.

...true' is merely a compliment we pay to statements we find good to believe.

(Goldman 1999: 10)

The debate that emerges here concerns the nature of truth and is an unwieldy, complex and ongoing debate. Primarily this centres upon the Aristotelian notion of 'justified true belief' and both foundationalists and anti-foundationalists have argued over the extent to which a claim to legitimate truth can be made. Rationality has been presented as the basis for claiming this legitimacy in truth statements but Wittgenstein (1889–1951) can be seen to challenge elements of this when he presents his notion of 'language games' where the acceptance of a truth claim as a form of legitimate knowledge is dependent upon social interaction and complex nuances within the language that is used.

The understatement that language is a set of convenient symbols used according to the conventional rules of a 'language game' originates in the tradition of nominalism, which teaches that general terms are merely names designating certain collections of objects – a doctrine which … is accepted today by most writers in England and America, in abhorrence of its metaphysical alternatives.

(Polanyi 1963: 113)

Inevitably, this argument for the socially constructed nature of knowledge elevates the process by which a truth claim can be legitimately made to centre stage. It focuses on the process of contestation and how, within a social context, we reach an agreement.

The social position of knowledge

The *sociology of knowledge* is deeply embedded within this debate and essentially concerns itself with attempting to reveal the nature of knowledge within the social. It has challenged, to varying extents, the relationship that can exist between objective and subjective forms of knowledge and the very existence of these forms of knowledge.

> The task of the sociologist of knowledge was to define the nature and functioning of the subjective beliefs of social life so as to facilitate the acquisition of objective knowledge in the social sciences.
>
> (Hekman 1986: 15)

The emergence of objective forms of knowledge as a result of Enlightenment forms of thinking is challenged by a growing awareness of the position of subjective forms of knowledge. The relationship between the two is realigned and to a large extent this can be seen as part of the mechanism that creates fluidity within the knowledge discourse. Criticising, challenging and contesting the dominant form of knowledge within the wider discourse opens up the opportunities to acquire legitimacy within the discourse.

> The sociology of knowledge in the nineteenth and twentieth centuries is characterised by practitioners who define a larger and larger role for subjective knowledge.
>
> (Hekman 1986: 16)

However, in repositioning subjective knowledge in relation to objective knowledge there is an inevitable acceptance of this as a valid distinction. More significantly there is an acceptance of objective forms of knowledge. To a large extent the debate associated with the *Methodenstreit* at the end of the nineteenth and beginning of the twentieth centuries can be seen as a continuation of this attempt to re-present a view of knowledge within the social. On the one hand positivists maintained the Enlightenment tradition of the natural sciences and objective knowledge and that this could and should be extended to the emerging social sciences. On the other hand humanists attempted, initially, to argue for a quite distinct form of knowledge within the social. In doing so they were again not rejecting scientific or 'pure' knowledge, but what they were doing was inevitably undermining the legitimacy of scientific knowledge within the wider discourse. Max Scheler (1874–1928) can perhaps be identified as the first to begin to seriously challenge this hegemony.

> Unlike the positivists, Scheler argues that the scientific world view is not the only true and absolute representation of 'absolute things' … Rather, it is only one of a number of different types of knowledge.
>
> (Hekman 1986: 25)

In attempting to develop the implications of Scheler's early work there was a need to address the relativism inherent within his position. Here Husserlian (E. G. A. Husserl, 1859–1938) phenomenology played a significant part by presenting a methodology based on a 'common-sense' view of reality where meaning or knowledge emerges from intentional acts of the individual ego. By placing knowledge production in close proximity to the individual there is a denial of the socially constructed nature of knowledge. Social phenomenologists of this type therefore rely very much on psychological explanation.

Jürgen Habermas (1986a, 1986b, 1992) attempted to reconcile the positivist tendencies inherent within the sociology of knowledge and the difficulty that it was having in establishing the relationship between objective forms of knowledge. He presented an 'objective framework' within which social action was constituted.

> It is his [Habermas'] assertion of an objective framework of social action that commits Habermas to an approach to the social sciences that, although clearly not positivist, is yet consistent with the Enlightenment distinction between pure and impure knowledge. To put it simply, for Habermas there is a position outside socially constructed reality by which that reality can be assessed.
>
> (Hekman 1986: 37)

The nature of knowledge in this sense is dependent upon the framework within which it sits. This forms a significant school of thought within the sociology of knowledge but the social nature of knowledge itself and the implications of this are taken further by those who sought to dispense with the notion that knowledge was based on any foundational theory or grand narrative. Habermas in this sense can be aligned with the Enlightenment tradition as he presents an objective view of knowledge within the social sciences, although clearly there is some distance between Habermas and the positivists.

This position reflects that of the 'realists' within the sociology of knowledge who attempted to present an ontological position where society is seen to exist before social action.

> Social actors' concepts do not produce society, but, rather, it exists independently of their conceptualisations. And, although all beliefs are socially determined and thus epistemological relativism is correct, ontological relativism does not follow because society predates socially determined beliefs.
>
> (Hekman 1986: 44)

One important consequence of the realist position was the re-engagement of what had been objective and subjective forms of knowledge. All knowledge sits within the realm of interpretation and it is this that defines all knowledge as hermeneutic. In relation to the discourse of knowledge realists were reasserting the scientific character of all knowledge, rather than its hermeneutic characteristics. This provides some insight into the nature of the discourse where residual reflections of, in this case, foundational principles can re-emerge to support what appears to be a form of knowledge that is being fundamentally undermined.

Knowledge is, therefore, what we know, rather than what I know.

> You may have personal knowledge that you value, but in order to make knowledge socially useful and socially accepted, it must be recognized as legitimate by social actors and institutions.
>
> (Styre 2003: 36)

Essentially, there is an emphasis upon the justifiable and verifiable nature of a truth. As with Mendelian genetics there are bases upon which a truth can be claimed that do not depend upon any social context. It draws on the success of a statement that in turn has drawn on its establishment as true through repeated experience. In other words, it is justified upon this basis. However, rather than there being two opposing epistemological camps, on the one hand social constructionists and on the other those who align themselves with an empirical or scientific view of knowledge, it is possible to be accepting of scientific knowledge and that the social context will have an impact upon this knowledge. This impact will not necessarily undermine the claim to truth, it may remain valid. However, the imposition of the social may alter the significance of any piece of knowledge by determining its positional location in relation to the social itself.

Human action is determined by and within this social context. It is an ongoing and cyclical process through which our individual actions are normally reconciled to and embedded within the existing social structures. This is a 'task' for individuals within the social and it relates to the knowledge that we acquire, use and apply within our every-day existence. In other words, there are no inherent orders or laws that govern our social conduct. We must decide these for ourselves. Recognising the necessity of doing so very much defines the context of knowledge creation that is social interaction and existence.

> Social order is not part of the 'nature of things', and it cannot be derived from the 'laws of nature'. Social order exists only as a product of human activity. No other ontological status may be ascribed to it without hopelessly obfuscating its empirical manifestations.
>
> (Berger and Luckmann 1971: 70)

Knowledge as social action

Knowledge is, therefore, a social statement and as such it is contested, it never ceases to be contested and similarly the agents that can claim some legitimacy within this contested environment are fluid and dynamic. These agents, or what Karl Mannheim (1893–1947) referred to as 'living forces', within this contested environment are the institutions that represent and make up our social world. This might be any two individuals who come together (face-to-face or through social media) and create a shared understanding, or it might be a global institution that can claim historically significant legitimacy in terms of its own knowledge statements.

> The living forces and actual attitudes which underlie the theoretical ones are by no means merely of an individual nature, i.e. they do not have their origin in the first place in the individual's becoming aware of his own interest in the course of his thinking. Rather, they arise out of the collective purpose of a group which underlie the thought of the individual, and in the prescribed outlook of which he merely par-ticipates.
>
> (Mannheim 1936: 240–1)

For Berger and Luckmann (1971) this legitimacy is based upon the *typification of habitu-alised action*. This is the embedding of accepted social knowledge and its creation of institutional forms of social behaviour and action. Being based on the recurring 'facticity' of this knowledge provides it with legitimacy but does not render it exempt from contestation. However, to contest it requires an assault to be made on something that has become accepted, through social practice, and has, through an iterative process, become embedded in accepted patterns and norms. It is difficult to challenge knowledge with such legitimacy:

> The institutions, as historical and objective facticities, confront the individual as undeniable facts. The institutions are there, external to him, persistent in their reality, whether he likes it or not. He cannot wish them away. They resist his attempts to change or evade them. They have coercive power over him, both in themselves, by the sheer force of their facticity, and through the control mechanisms that are usually attached to the most important of them.
>
> (Berger and Luckmann 1971)

One of the main implications for knowledge of this process of institutionalisation via the typification of habitualised action is that they become self-justifying and create a legitimacy through this institutionalising process. Knowledge of the institution is derived primarily from its own habitualised nature:

> Since this knowledge is socially objectivated as knowledge, that is, as a body of generally valid truths about reality, any radical deviance from the institutional order appears as a departure from reality.
>
> (Berger and Luckmann 1971: 83)

 Pause for thought – socially constructed knowledge

Consider this view of knowledge emerging from social dynamics and describe some examples from your own experience. This might include some awareness you have of social dynamics within group working situations where the presence of an individual or a group of individuals has resulted in one course of action being taken, rather than another.

Knowledge, in this sense, is presented as little more than a series of socially accepted and deeply embedded norms that through a process of trial and error has appeared to justify a legitimate claim to being a truth. Through this process of typification knowledge becomes embedded and associated with institutional forms. This, to a large extent, reflects Hans-Georg Gadamer's (2004) presentation of the need to reposition our attitude towards the notion of prejudice. The marginalisation of the centrality of individual prejudice, or the unique positioning of individuals in relation to a knowledge statement, has largely been lost as a result of the Enlightenment's presentation of objective knowledge and its 'discreditation' of prejudice.

> If we want to do justice to man's finite, historical mode of being, it is necessary to fundamentally rehabilitate the concept of prejudice and acknowledge the fact that there are legitimate prejudices. Thus we can formulate the fundamental epistemological question for a truly historical hermeneutics as follows: what is the ground of the legitimacy of prejudices? What distinguishes legitimate prejudices from the countless others which it is the undeniable task of critical reason to overcome?
>
> (Gadamer 2004: 278)

Prejudice here can be associated with the contestation that is necessary and ongoing within the knowledge discourse and indicative of the nature of this contestation. In particular, it is concerned with the social characteristics of this contestation as a process of individual self-reflection and the externalisation of one's understanding of one's own position. This philosophical position is the basis of Gadamer's definition of hermeneutics and draws any discussion of understanding inevitably towards an ontological position rather than an epistemological one. Hermeneutics, for Gadamer, is the study of being.

> The understanding and the interpretation of texts is not merely a concern of science, but obviously belongs to human experience of the world in general.
>
> (Gadamer 2004: xx)

This forms the basis of a challenge to the legitimacy of scientific knowledge claims.

> The human sciences are connected to modes of experience that lie outside science: with the experience of philosophy, of art and of history itself. These are all modes of experience in which a truth is communicated that cannot be verified by the methodological means proper to science.
>
> (Gadamer 2004: xxvi)

Science is, therefore, not the basis upon which any legitimate knowledge claims can be based. Rather, it is to language that we must look for the means by which we are able to communicate our understanding of the social world.

> Humans live within language. Every encounter with reality presupposes linguisticality, the linguistic constitution of understanding. Human reason cannot hold a position outside of language and then translate that position into language. Even reason is constituted linguistically.
>
> (Johnson 2000: 57–8)

Truth, reality, understanding and knowledge are all constituted through language and it is the dialogic process that will ultimately determine the nature of the knowledge that we accept. Knowledge is, therefore, based upon a series of dialogues, a series of opportunities to discuss our own engagement with the environment around us and our own identity in relation to this environment.

For Gadamer (1900–2002) and for Jean-Francois Lyotard (1924–1998) the developments associated with information and communication technologies (ICT) can be associated with the need-creation and the consumer-stimulation required to sustain a productive capacity that is its own purpose.

> Gadamer says that this relationship of science to technology in modern life has obscured concern for if and how work actually benefits people and for whether or not the achievements of technology actually serve life.
>
> (Johnson 2000: 68)

Language and the social dialogue that it represents is the mechanism by which knowledge emerges. The institutionalisation of knowledge claims within the knowledge-economy place an emphasis upon the language or the rhetoric of language that is used within the organisation. How we use language within institutions helps to form knowledge and these formations appear to be more prevalent, substantial and formative.

The legitimacy of knowledge claims, therefore, that these institutional forms can make is enhanced and this can be to the point where any challenge to it can place one outside of the perceived reality or normality as it is contemporarily understood. Michel Foucault in his analyses of sexuality and sanity explores these power dynamics behind this socially based knowledge context.

> Power must be analysed as something which circulates, or rather as something which only functions in the form of a chain. It is never localised here and there, never in anybody's hands, never appropriated as a commodity or piece of wealth. Power is employed and exercised through a net-like organisation. And not only do individuals circulate between its threads; they are always in the position of simultaneously undergoing and exercising this power. They are not only its inert or consenting target; they are always also the elements of its articulation. In other words, individuals are the vehicles of power, not its point of application.
>
> (Foucault 1980: 98)

Although the vehicles of power, individuals exercise this power as part of established social formations. It is the institutions and organisations within the social that make up the wider knowledge discourse. This discourse is a power discourse that is intricately related to the creation and dissemination of knowledge. The context within which this discourse operates is fluid and dynamic. The 'chain' and the 'net' are these social formations and individuals engage with this dynamic process of knowledge creation and dissemination but in association with the mechanisms inherent within these social formations.

The knowledge discourse is, therefore, a representation of this process of the typification of habitualised action. This, itself, primarily emphasises the socially constructed nature of knowledge. It emphasises our experience of phenomena and the negotiated nature of knowledge within the social. Beyond an individual level, in other words within the social, knowledge is formed, but although it may form itself into an apparently solid truth, the contested nature of knowledge identifies the inability to ultimately accept any truth as absolute or objective.

However, the contesting of a truth in this way itself represents a significant positioning of both the individual and groups within the social. For individuals this is a potentially dangerous and subversive activity, primarily because the opportunity to claim legitimacy within the knowledge discourse is one that is related very closely to power and authority within the social. For example, the knowledge claim of a university has been substantial. An individual academic standing in front of a class of undergraduate students draws legitimacy from the position of the university within the knowledge discourse. From its own history and from the contemporary legislative and policy frameworks within education, the university is able to present itself as having a legitimate claim to the knowledge that it is making available through its teaching and research. The individual academic is supported by the legitimacy of the institution and their association with it.

No individual or group is excluded from this discourse, but it is the legitimacy of their knowledge claims that will determine the extent of their authority (legitimacy) within the knowledge discourse. The dynamics within the different elements within the knowledge discourse and the relationship between the different elements, will determine the positioning of legitimacy within the knowledge discourse. Far from being a monolithic structure this knowledge discourse is now seen as being a fluid and dynamic series of interactions and it is postmodernity that has most effectively presented this fluid context by challenging the objectivity of scientific knowledge and the overwhelming claim to legitimacy that it has presented within a modern industrial context.

Returning to the knowledge-economy

The knowledge-economy sits within this fluid and dynamic context. In identifying the value of knowledge as an organisational asset, it has become necessary to engage with this asset and to understand it more effectively. From the perspective presented above, knowledge has specific characteristics. Not least the creation of knowledge is dependent upon the mechanisms that allow it to emerge. This is the knowledge discourse and the 'voices' within this discourse need to acquire the necessary legitimacy if they are to have any credibility within the social group or collective – the organisation. Not all voices are equal, therefore not all knowledge statements will have the same value. Knowledge that has no value will not be perceived as an asset for the organisation and will be marginalized, at best.

Nevertheless, there have been a series of shifts that have placed the emphasis upon knowledge rather than the production of tangible goods. Even within the production process, where tangible goods are produced, the role of knowledge is now seen as being of the highest significance. We need to know not just how we produce goods but also why we produced these goods. In asking these questions we are looking to understand our markets through our customers and how best to manage this understanding. Armed with this we are then able to modify and adapt our products or services to ensure that they remain profitable both in terms of maintaining the financial viability of the organisation or that it achieves the objectives that it has set for itself.

In doing this an emphasis has been placed on the role of ICT, beyond these simply being mechanisms to store and retrieve, manipulate and move increasingly complex data and information sources. Rather, they are being asked to directly address the key questions of how to manage knowledge, which in turn forms the questions around why we do things in the way we do things and how best to apply our knowledge of this to sustain our competitive edge. A network in this sense is not simply a channel of communication but a medium that can directly impact upon the social and cultural dynamics within the organisation.

The concept of the knowledge-economy to a large extent can be seen as a direct extension of the Information Age. The Information Age (Levinson, 1997; Davis and Meyer, 1998;

Castells, 2001; Van Dijk, 2006) and the revolution that is associated with it have, through their recognition of the centrality of information and knowledge to the production process, assisted in the emergence of the concept of the knowledge-economy. This is a concept and a context or environment that is characterised by the need to respond to constant change, and it is only knowledge that appears to be able to sustain any operational viability.

> The competitiveness of a firm is more than anything a function of what it knows, how it uses what it knows, and how fast it can know something new.
>
> (Davis and Meyer 1998: 199)

In accepting the relationship between organisational well-being and knowledge, and placing such an emphasis upon the importance of knowledge, is the distinguishing characteristic of organisational knowledge as it emerges within the Information Age and helps to forge our understanding of the knowledge-economy.

> Explicitly recognising knowledge as a corporate asset is new, however, as is understanding the need to manage and invest it with the same care paid to getting value from other, more tangible assets. The need to make the most of organisational knowledge, to get as much value as possible from it, is greater now than in the past.
>
> (Davenport and Prusak 1998: 12)

The emergence of the concept of the knowledge-economy raises the awareness of knowledge and begins to place upon it the characteristics that align it with the aims and objectives of the organisation. If knowledge is a key organisational asset then those characteristics of knowledge that specifically relate to this will inevitably be emphasised and focused upon. This, essentially, is the concept of organisational knowledge that is being considered here. One key characteristic is the ability to respond to the perception of change inherent within the notion of sustaining competitiveness.

> The modern world is swept by change. New technologies emerge constantly, new markets are opening up. There are new competitors but also great new opportunities.
>
> (Blair 1998: foreword)

Change of this nature and on this scale appears to present a very clear course of action.

> Our success depends on how well we exploit our most valuable assets: our knowledge, skills, and creativity. These are the key to designing high-value goods and services and advanced business practices. They are at the heart of a modern, knowledge-driven economy.
>
> (Blair 1998: foreword)

The survival of the organisation depends upon the underlying fluidity within its environment. The organisation requires responsiveness, agility and flexibility.

> To survive in the new competitive environment, no enterprise can afford to stand still. All have to be open to new ideas, new ways of working, new tools and equipment, and be able to absorb and benefit from them.
>
> (Commission of the European Communities 2000: 5)

To be responsive, agile and flexible in the ways that organisations now appear to need to be places an emphasis upon the nature of the importance of knowledge to the organisation. It is its use of knowledge that will determine its success or failure within the knowledge-economy. Central to the organisation's engagement with knowledge is the development and presentation of an epistemological position and to a large extent this focuses on learning.

> The new, knowledge-based economy is becoming a striking feature of life in all advanced economies. Increasingly, economic success and prosperity are coming to depend on learning, the creation of knowledge and its application, and businesses working smarter and not harder.
>
> (McLeish 2001: foreword)

By focusing on learning the organisation engages with the existing knowledge discourse making one of the challenges inherent within the Information Age and the knowledge-economy directly related to the position of education (teaching and learning) in relation to knowledge. More specifically, this appears to call for a critical re-examination of the knowledge discourse itself. Who has legitimacy within this discourse and can this position be sustained within the changing climate or context that is beginning to emerge and is characterised by the notion of the knowledge-economy?

> New media create new information, which in turn requires new modes of acquisition.
>
> (Levinson 1997: 31)

These modes of acquisition reflect the changing relationship between teacher and learner. If knowledge and information are emerging legitimately from more diverse sources then the implication is that pedagogical processes will also be emerging in different and more varied contexts and forms. The knowledge-economy and the Information Age more generally, recognises that pedagogy as a process is no longer exclusive to children or young adults at school, college or university.

> Learning has become too important to be left to educational institutions and in-house training departments.
>
> (Boud and Garrick 1999: 5)

This changing perspective on learning has resulted in a greater acceptance of a more diverse pedagogical context. As a result of this the role of educational institutions is being reconsidered and realigned in accordance with the emerging principles of the knowledge-economy.

> In the long term, the importance of the knowledge factor must be taught in EU Member State schools. University and school lessons must be harmonised and adjusted accordingly as a precondition for scientific integration in Europe and improved mobility for scientists.
>
> (Commission of the European Communities 2000: 9)

The university itself is changing in response to the massification process that has emerged. But also, the purpose of these universities has been more fully and more comprehensively aligned to the performative characteristics of organisational knowledge which essentially aligns knowledge with practice, through experience. This in turn mirrors the recognition that information and knowledge represents the most significant organisational resource for the twenty-first century.

> It is a defining fact about organisations in the Information Age: Knowledge and information take on their own reality, which can be detached from the physical movement of goods and services. From this divergence come at least two important implications. First, knowledge and the assets that create and distribute it can be managed, just as physical and financial assets can be. Indeed, intellectual and physical-financial assets can be managed separately from one another; they can be managed together; they can be managed in relation to one another. Second: If knowledge is the greatest source of wealth, then individuals, companies and nations should invest in the assets that produce and process knowledge.
>
> (Stewart 1997: 31)

As Bell (1974) has pointed out, the post-industrial context (often identified with the emergence of the Information Age) is characterised by the need to sustain competitiveness, rather than dominance through conflict. Applying the concept of structural differentiation organisations in the contemporary context have specialised and this in turn has led to an increasing pace of innovation and change:

> These two concepts – the pace of change and the change of scale – are the organizing ideas for the discussion of the central structural components of the post-industrial society, the dimensions of knowledge and technology.
>
> (Bell 1974: 174)

Knowledge has therefore, become important for practical organisational development and indeed, survival to an extent that has not previously been recognised.

> With the shift in business focus and the increased emphasis on knowledge, organisations need to adapt to the changing markets and tap new opportunities. This affects the organisation's structure and forces it to be more flexible and effective in terms of management, employees, and infrastructure.
>
> (Al-Hawambeh 2003: 9)

This inevitably means that the move from information to knowledge-rich organisations will subject the knowledge discourse to different and more diverse pressures than might have been placed upon it when it was, largely, seen to be more settled within the domain of the university or wider education system. Questions are inevitably asked concerning the relevance and usefulness of knowledge and specifically the legitimacy of the university to represent the position that it has done in relation to knowledge statements. This is the practical expediency we associate with the commercial sector.

Education becomes rooted within day-to-day operational activities and more than asking questions around know-what, the deeper implications of know-how (capability to do something) and know-who (who knows what and the extent to which individual areas of expertise are known to others) are emphasised.

Access to expertise through key social relationships is the nature of learning within organisations and this is very different from learning in a traditional context. So, the way to manage in this type of environment is distinctly different from managing in the 'traditional' sense.

The SECI model (Nonaka, Toyama and Konno, 2002) is perhaps the most recognised of models that look to exploit the knowledge generated through the tacit to explicit model. The SECI model has four elements (see Figure 8.1):

Socialisation
> Here knowledge is acquired through social processes. It is recognised that tacit knowledge is place and time specific, making it a fluid and dynamic resource. The need would appear to be to ensure that the ability or opportunity to acquire or create it is present within the learning environment.

Externalisation
> Here tacit knowledge is made explicit. Some piece of knowledge is put into a form that can be made accessible to all. Given the limitations of tacit knowledge that were mentioned above it must be that the type of tacit knowledge being referred to does not fall into the category of that that is time and place specific!

Combination
> When tacit knowledge is made explicit it must then be fully exploited by the organisation. This can be done through ensuring that it is accessibly stored, effectively moved and creatively manipulated by the organisation. Information systems can play an important part in this particular element of the process.

Internalisation
> Explicit knowledge and its effective use should form the basis of the creation of tacit knowledge. In turn this will begin the process all over again in what has been described as the knowledge spiral. This stage of the process is essentially a reflective process.

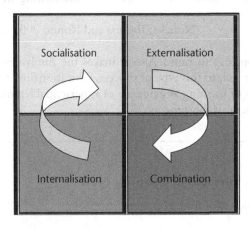

Figure 8.1 SECI model

The processes associated with the SECI model, therefore, identify this virtuous spiral of knowledge creation through the effective application and management of this knowledge spiral. Essentially, each part of the process is associated with the following:

Socialisation	Tacit to tacit	Empathising
Externalisation	Tacit to explicit	Articulating
Combination	Explicit to explicit	Connecting
Internalisation	Explicit to tacit	Embodying

This process is inclusive and comprehensive. It should be allowed to grow from an individual level to a level beyond the organisation to that encompassing the environment within which the organisation operates. This requires us to consider the key relationship between the individual and the organisation. Argyris (1993) refers to this as the 'organisational dilemma' and Senge (1993) unpacks this with the disciplines embedded in *The Fifth Discipline*. For example, the organisation might need to address mental models, the development of a shared vision or the prevalence of a blame culture. These types of issues are closely associated with what Nonaka, Toyama and Konno refer to as 'ba':

> *Ba* is the context shared by those who interact with each other, and through such interactions, those who participate in *ba* and the context itself evolve through self-transcendence to create knowledge.
>
> (Nonaka, Toyama and Konno 2002: 49)

Nonaka and others have presented a challenging picture of the knowledge creation process. It is essentially one that attempts to identify collective learning activities, but often relies too heavily on the assumption that there is an overwhelming willingness to share what knowledge one has. This leaves only the challenge of storing it, moving it and manipulating it – the classic information management tasks. The need for a trusting environment is, however, highlighted:

> As knowledge needs to be shared to be created and exploited, it is important for leaders to create an atmosphere in which organisation members feel safe sharing their knowledge.
>
> (Nonaka, Toyama and Konno 2002: 62)

Easier said than done is the phrase that springs to mind. Also it makes the fundamental assumption that it is the role of the leader to lead this type of process. Educationalists, too, tend to focus on the practical expressions of learning as evidence of experiential learning and have little to say about the management of this process.

 Pause for thought –Kolb's experiential learning cycle

The experiential learning cycle is made up of four key elements:

1. **Concrete experience** – where we experience being involved with something new.

2. **Reflective observation** – where we watch and observe or we reflect on our own experience and how this might be altered by observing others.
3. **Abstract conceptualisation** – where we build our understanding upon our ongoing engagement with practice.
4. **Active experimentation** – where we use our developing understanding to inform our action.

Identify from your own experience where an opportunity to reflect on current practice has been embedded in organisational processes.

Managing in the knowledge-economy

Knowledge management (KM) as a discipline covers a range of different areas and perspectives. Earl (2001) identified seven Cs that represent this diversity:

1   codification
2   connectivity
3   capability
4   commercialisation
5   collaboration
6   contactivity
7   consciousness.

The first three express the *technocratic* view of KM that equates closely to the management of explicit knowledge and the discipline of information management, with a strong role for technologies. The fourth, is the *economic* view that underpins the commercial imperative and represents the need to link the business and the knowledge strategy to ensure that the intangible asset of knowledge creates value for the organisation. The last three, are *behavioural* elements that look to build communities and are more closely related to the processes of learning within the organisation.

These views, the technocratic, the economic and the behavioural, then translate into specific sub-disciplines that cover key knowledge processes. These include:

• knowledge acquisition
• knowledge mapping
• knowledge organisation
• knowledge transfer and sharing.

A *knowledge strategy* becomes a key organisational imperative to begin the process of embedding knowledge practices within the organisation. This will reflect the unique characteristics of the particular organisation where different types of knowledge are being emphasised. For example, KM can be used to accelerate innovation, it can be used to enhance professional skills or to improve customer relationships. Which type of knowledge is prioritised is part of this knowledge strategy and has over recent years resulted in KM being associated with a variety of different themes, including *total quality management* (TQM), *business process re-engineering* (BPR) and the LO.

Each of these concepts stresses the importance of learning. This in turn helps managers to form the questions that need to be addressed if the organisation is to positively engage with the management of the knowledge asset.

Knowledge acquisition

The acquisition of knowledge is central to the development of the organisational knowledge base. This will include knowledge of products, markets, technologies and the organisational environment. It will be an integral part of the organisation and will ultimately add value to the organisation.

As part of the knowledge strategy there is a need to identify where the knowledge asset will add value to the organisation. This might be to *enhance organisational relationships* with external customers, suppliers or stakeholders, or internal groups and individuals. In looking to enhance relationships the crucial element of building trust is supported and this in turn will enhance the opportunity to improve internal commitment and *minimise the loss of expertise* and maximise its retention.

Organisations can actively seek expertise. They can locate it in *recognised experts* who can either be attracted to the organisation or be contracted to the organisation. Again the knowledge strategy will look to embed this and make explicit the range and type of expertise that is important to or significant for the organisation. Increasingly there are opportunities to create *networks* that draw together organisations that can collaborate and share expertise. Social media such as Facebook, LinkedIn and Twitter can all be used to create knowledge-based networks that enhance individual performance through the embedded sharing of information.

Customers can also be a useful way to acquire knowledge through customer relationship management (CRM). Again social media can be used to acquire this knowledge. The case of American Airlines (AA: 2015) illustrates this:

> Each contact with their customer is regarded as an opportunity and through the creation of advocates and the use of social media, including Twitter and flyertalk (a frequent flyers forum) AA looks to identify the relevant comments. Employees track all public comments and will actively look to identify an individual who has a high number of followers or if a specific issue has come up regularly or where an individual might be either aggressive or distinctive in terms of their own profile, perhaps a celebrity or someone with specific health issues. These 'connects' create Customer Relationship (CR) files that in turn will add to the knowledge base of the organization as will the ongoing exchange that each CR initiates. The team handling these relationships is referred to as the Social Defense team and it is their role to make contact with customers and where necessary to respond, in this case, by crediting air miles. Any positive responses, the customer was then tweeted.

The engagement with customers can shift from being responsive to more proactive through the use of the advocates. They can ensure more positive messaging through social media, publicise the rapidity of positive responses to issues and indeed advocates themselves can be drawn from the bloggers on the most prominent social sites. Cultivating an active and positive body of advocates through social media creates a more collaborative approach to the building of customer relationships, provides more direct opportunities to understand the needs of customers and thereby becoming more agile and able to make changes in an informed way. Getting to know communities, building advocates, being constantly vigilant and proactively looking to engage with customers are the key priorities for CRM.

Knowledge is acquired both externally as well as internally. External reports, conference papers, journal publications, textbooks, legislation and so on are all relevant sources of knowledge. Similarly, the less formal conversations and email exchanges can all be of value. The organisation allowing or facilitating these types of knowledge acquisition, both formal and informal, will be making a positive contribution to the accumulation of the competitive intelligence required by the organisation in order for it to maintain or sustain its own competitive position within whichever market it might operate. This of course applies equally well within the service sector where, it might be argued, there has been a history of cooperation and the sharing of information and knowledge. The culture of the organisation is important here and it requires an open style that encourages sharing and transparency in relation to ideas and thoughts.

A variety of methods can be used to acquire knowledge:

- Conduct interviews and ask targeted questions.
- Observe the work in progress.
- Obtain the network traffic logs.
- Explore the common and individual file structures.
- Gather policy documents, organisational charts, process documentation.
- Concentrate on formal and informal gatherings, communication and activities.
- Move across multiple levels (individual, group, department, organisation).

Once captured the aim is to:

- Record promising best practices.
- Explore reuse opportunities.
- Look for learning points, natural knowledge stewards, gatekeepers, isolated islands and narrow communication channels.
- Map, flows, sequences and dependencies.
- Check for network patterns, critical nodes, high traffic and highly valuable information.

All acquired knowledge, from whatever source, needs to be managed. The construction of a knowledge-base, such as a Lessons Learned Database, needs to be *organised, elicited* and *tested.*

Organising requires *domain experts* to articulate their knowledge and *knowledge engineers* to apply their technical skills.

The domain expert:

- Will know the domain − he or she will be experienced in the domain and will have formal as well as informal qualifications backed up by learned experience based on-the-job. They will have an understanding of the tasks involved and the relationships which exist within the domain between individuals, sources and flows of information.
- Should be a confident communicator and be able to express the knowledge and experience associated with their expertise and provide suitable contexts within which theory can be tested.
- Will be patient.

Clearly, the domain expert is a key individual in the knowledge acquisition process. These domain experts might be senior engineers, IT specialists, HR professionals, doctors and so on. Their selection as experts will be based on experience and perceived expertise, often coming from their reputation within the organisation and may not necessarily be based on academic qualifications or seniority. Difficulties arise in relation to these experts where there is more than one expert identified. This is further compounded when there are differences between the experts. To some extent this highlights the need for there to be an intermediary within the process and it is indeed one of the roles of the knowledge engineer to deal with these types of difficulties.

The knowledge engineer:

- Will have a sound understanding of the technology supporting knowledge-based information systems. This will include modelling techniques and appropriate methodologies.
- Will have good interpersonal skills and will possess a formal or informal interest in areas such as psychology or cognitive science.
- Needs to be able to learn quickly.
- Must ensure that the domain expert is encouraged to participate and contribute to the process and regards it as a positive process.

The role of these two individuals is crucial to the success of the knowledge acquisition process and the skills required by both are quite different. One is responsible for the content, the other for the elicitation of that content and the subsequent representation of it in an appropriate way. The view that each has of the process can be quite different, for example the expert view of how well they are able to explain the knowledge that they hold often is quite different from the view of the knowledge engineer. The domain expert often believes that they are able to express themselves well, but the knowledge engineer often sees the expert's skills in this respect as often far from adequate.

For each knowledge asset that is identified it is necessary to identify whether or not there are mechanisms by which that asset can be captured and used, this is part of the *elicitation* process:

Developed – can this asset be added to or enhanced?
Preserved – how is it to be captured and where will it go?
Updated – how will its currency be ensured?
Used – who needs it?
Transferred – how will those who need it, get it?
Transformed – how will changes and adaptations to it be handled?
Assessed – what value does it have, how useful is it?

Content and availability of the asset is the first priority. Content refers to its domain, type and quality, in other words where has it come from, is it explicit, how complete it is and how up-to-date is it? Availability refers to the form that it takes, whether or not it is available at a particular time and at a particular location.

It is the role of the knowledge engineer to skilfully question and interrogate the domain expert in order to produce a series of generalised examples. Based on the collection of these examples it is possible to use *inductive generalisation algorithms* that are computer representations of these examples that can subsequently be applied to comparable problems within the same domain. An algorithm is simply a mathematical representation of a rule ($E = mc^2$). They are designed largely to transform the operational knowledge of the domain expert into heuristic rules for making inferences (this process is often referred to as *case-based reasoning*). The skilled knowledge engineer should aim to gain the respect of the domain expert in order to elicit the knowledge data. This might require learning elements of the domain, the basics of the jargon and acronyms used. Some of the techniques involve software and can be automated – some programs can now engage the domain expert in a conversation or dialogue. Tests have shown that individuals can be much less inhibited when it comes to communicating with a computer than in face-to-face encounters.

Once the knowledge base has been represented and captured within a suitable program it will be *tested*. To do this it will pass through a series of stages to ensure that it operates in the expected way. These processes will include *verification* that will both consider the technical accuracy and the intellectual accuracy, the latter is carried out with the assistance of the domain expert and the former the knowledge engineer. Both will *validate* their efforts in relation to the user specifications or management objectives in relation to the initial project proposals and ensure that the end product meets these specifications.

Knowledge mapping

A knowledge map is:

- A visual display of captured information and relationships.
- A navigation aid to explicit (codified) information and tacit knowledge, showing the importance and the relationships between knowledge stores and dynamics.
- An outcome of synthesis, portraying the sources, flows, constraints and sinks (losses or stopping points) of knowledge within an organisation.
- Used to enable communication and learning of knowledge by observers with differing backgrounds at multiple levels of detail.
- Able to include texts, stories, graphics, models and so on.
- A link to more detailed knowledge.

A knowledge map aims to track the acquisition and loss of information and knowledge. It will explore personal and group competencies and proficiencies and it will attempt to 'map' how knowledge flows throughout an organisation.

Knowledge mapping helps an organisation to appreciate how the loss of a particular member of staff might influence the knowledge base. It might also look to:

- assist with the selection of teams;
- match technology to knowledge needs and processes.

The map should highlight islands of expertise and it should suggest ways to build bridges to increase knowledge sharing. Also, it provides an inventory and evaluation of intellectual and intangible assets.

Knowledge mapping can be used to recognise and locate knowledge in a wide variety of forms:

- tacit and explicit
- formal and informal

- codified and personalised
- internal and external
- short life cycle and permanent.

It should locate knowledge in processes, relationships, policies, people, documents, conversations, suppliers, competitors and customers.

A knowledge map should minimise the amount of information directly contained in it. The directly visible map of information should be limited to that required for high-availability, high-value browsing and queries. The vast majority of information should be made available to users through links to the original, maintained sources.

There are a number of benefits associated with knowledge mapping:

- Organisations must be able to capture relevant knowledge as it evolves (thus saving them from recreating it from scratch).
- Capturing knowledge in all sorts of forms (text, pictures, stories, data and models).
- Making this knowledge accessible.

Once knowledge has been captured it is essential that it can be used or exploited fully. It must, therefore, attempt to identify evidence for use and record promising best practices. It should seek to encourage opportunities for the reuse of identified knowledge and to look for learning points, natural knowledge stewards, gatekeepers, isolated islands and narrow communication channels. The relationships that exist between these knowledge elements within the knowledge base should be mapped, indicating where appropriate the associated flows, sequences and dependencies. Also, there needs to be some check for network patterns, critical nodes, high traffic and highly valuable information.

Mind mapping techniques can be used to create knowledge maps for the organisation. These can be drawn by hand, but the more complex maps can be supported by a range of tools that can help create more effective results. For example, Smart Draw (www.smartdraw.com/) offers opportunities to create various types of diagrams, including mind maps.

As with any diagram or table the goal is to more effectively represent complex information. Mind maps themselves were popularized by Tony Buzan (b. 1942) an educational psychologist who has promoted the use of mind maps (http://thinkbuzan.com/). The basic techniques are as follows:

- Begin at the centre with a graphical representation of the topic.
- Use codes, symbols and images throughout.
- Identify key words.
- Each entry (word or image) should sit alone on its own line.
- Connect lines from the centre, getting progressively slimmer.
- Lines should mirror the length of the word or image.
- Use colours throughout for visual effect and coding.
- Develop a personal style to show associations.
- Keep the map clear.

Knowledge organisation: thesaural construction

Acquiring knowledge inevitably requires the skills and capabilities to ensure that the individual knowledge assets can be used and applied as effectively as possible. The principles of knowledge organisation (KO) seek to ensure that embedded knowledge is made available. Through indexing and the construction of thesauri, access to specific bodies of knowledge should be made more effective and efficient. Essentially, a thesaurus is a tool that can be used to access knowledge stored in a knowledge base. It is not enough to simply acquire knowledge, it needs to be organised too.

The development of thesauri for information and knowledge retrieval represents a significant step towards the creation of highly structured approaches to vocabulary control. Indeed thesauri are becoming the key tool for dealing with the growing size and importance of websites and intranets.

Thesauri use *preferred terms* to build a controlled vocabulary that seeks to ensure that all sought concepts are located using the same terms.

Conceptually, a typical thesaurus is made of the following elements:

Descriptors (preferred terms): words or expressions which denote in an unambiguous manner the concepts of the subject area covered by the thesaurus, e.g. IMPLEMENTATION OF THE LAW.

Non-descriptors (non-preferred terms): words or expressions which are synonyms to the descriptor APPLICATION OF THE LAW or equivalent concepts ENFORCEMENT OF THE LAW, VALIDITY OF A LAW.

Semantic relationships: relationships based on meaning, first between descriptors and non-descriptors (equivalence relationship) and second between the descriptors themselves (hierarchical and associative relationships).

A typical thesaurus entry includes the elements listed above plus a range of abbreviations denoting the status of terms within a network of relationships (synonymy, hierarchical and associated).

The abbreviations are:

UF   used for another synonym
USE use the preferred term
SN   scope note clarifies the usage of the preferred term
BT   broader term
NT   narrower term
RT   related term

Thesaurus entry: CAT:

UF   moggy, feline, puss
SN   cats considered as domestic animals
BT   pets
NT   Burmese, Norwegian cat, Ragdoll (belonging to the short hair category)
NT   Persian, Manx, Angora (belonging to the long hair category)
RT   dogs, hamsters, rabbits
RT   cat HIV
RT   veterinary care, breeding, showing
RT   cattery, Crufts Show
RT   veterinary surgeon, owner-dotting, RSPCA

Thesaurus entry for the entity CAT in the context of a domain dealing with pet care.

The BTs and NTs form a hierarchy and the RTs refer to concepts that are deemed to be in some way associated with the entity DOMESTIC CAT, namely DOGS, HAMSTER, RABBIT, CAT HIV, actions/processes: VETERINARY CARE, BREEDING, SHOWING, location/event: CATTERY, CRUFTS SHOW, people and group of people: VETERINARY SURGEON, RSPCA.

The thesaurus' dual purpose of assisting both indexer and user has numerous applications for knowledge organisation, particularly in supporting the abstracting and indexing of electronic bibliographic and full text databases. This might also be a Lessons Learned Database (LLD) that represents the conversations and dialogues that drive OL.

Furthermore, the thesaurus can be used for computer based techniques like automatic classification of documents, automatic indexing, and for automatic query expansion. The hierarchical structure of the thesaurus may also be used as the basis for the classification of an organisation (e.g. a corporate taxonomy).

A thesaurus is constructed as follows (see Figure 8.2):

1   *Identify and conceptualise the knowledge domain*
    Unlike a typical bibliographic classification scheme, the thesaurus is not a universal knowledge organisation system. It works best when it is applied to a small area of knowledge to serve a highly specialised subject-specific collection. It is therefore important to isolate the core as well as the peripheral concepts in order to determine the parameters of the thesaurus. Equally, the relationships between them should be identified to establish the semantic structure. It may be the case that the chosen knowledge field is interdisciplinary in nature and that the resulting meanings arise from different areas of discourse.

2   *Identify the users and their information needs*
    Once user groups have been identified, the thesaurus compiler should seek their opinion and cooperation at all stages of the compilation in order to create a tool which will be useful to them, whether they are indexers or searchers.

3   *Collect the 'raw' vocabulary*
    The next logical step in building the thesaurus is to collect words which represent, as near as possible, single concepts. This can be achieved by consulting a wide range of the specialised published literature: encyclopaedias, indexes, glossaries and dictionaries in print and in electronic format. Specialised portals and gateways are a good source of current information.

4   *Select preferred terms*
    Then groups of synonyms are identified, i.e. words representing the same concept. This reflects an evolutionary approach to determining the list of words which form the basis of the thesaurus – each word becomes a candidate for inclusion as preferred term (or descriptor). The criteria for selecting words as preferred terms will vary depending on: i) the type of thesaurus being developed (in particular it will depend on the specialist vocabulary which has been established in a particular subject area) and ii) the type of vocabulary used by the group of users.

5   *Standardise form of preferred terms*
    The form of the preferred term should be controlled whether this involves grammatical form, spelling, singular and plural form, abbreviations or compound forms of the term. The meaning of the preferred term is deliberately restricted to fit the purpose of the thesaurus. The restriction can be indicated in a scope note, a definition and qualifying phrase to clarify the usage of homonyms.

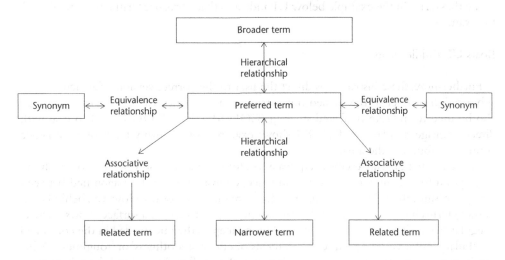

Figure 8.2 Visual representation of the network of relationships between terms in a typical thesaurus entry
Adapted from Rosenfeld and Morville, 2015.

6   *Establish relationships between terms*
Clustering of terms (as identifiers of concepts) to indicate relationships between them is critically important in thesaurus construction. This is best achieved by applying classification techniques to provide an overall picture of the subject field. In this way it should be able to identify accurate and meaningful relationships between the terms.

7   *Create thesaurus entries*

There are three basic thesaural relationships: equivalence, hierarchical and associative.

Equivalence

In the context of a monolingual thesaurus, equivalence is the relationship between a pair of synonyms or quasi-synonyms. The relationship is directional (i.e. not reciprocal), linking terms of unequal status. One of them has been designated 'preferred term' or 'descriptor' while the other(s) is considered as 'non-preferred term', 'non-descriptor' or 'lead-in term'. Here are two typical thesaurus entries showing equivalence relationships:

Watercrafts **USE** Boats   Boats **UF** Watercrafts

The function of this relationship is to guide the user to the term that is preferred for both indexing and searching. The instruction USE tells the indexer and the searcher to use the term 'boats' instead of 'watercrafts'. The corresponding abbreviation UF means 'used for' and indicates the term to be used in preference to 'watercrafts'.

A good thesaurus should provide a wide range of entry terms and a good set of references to the preferred term which ensures that the user has a fair chance of finding the right words on which to base their search.

The instructions USE and USE FOR not only help to control synonyms and quasi-synonyms but they can also help to deal with specific terms which do not have an entry in the thesaurus. In the example below UF indicates that a broader term has been selected, for example,

Boats **UF** Paddle-boats

Furthermore, these instructions direct the user to the correct version of an acronym or abbreviation or refer to the spelled out version of abbreviations as appropriate. They can also be used to indicate preferred spelling (COLOR UF COLOUR), and to deal with direct language translations. Table 8.1 shows examples of the many types of equivalence commonly found in thesauri.

Indexers will normally establish equivalences for pragmatic reasons which do not always correspond to semantic accuracy. For instance, equivalence may be established between terms like 'smoothness' and 'roughness', which are direct opposites. However, behind each of these terms lies the concept of describing the degree to which a surface shows physical irregularities such as bumps and hollows. This concept is the one needed in the controlled vocabulary and it could be expressed in terms of either 'smoothness' or 'roughness'. Arbitrarily, one of these two terms may be chosen as the 'preferred term' and the other one as the 'non-preferred term'.

The example of concepts subsumed in a broader concept shows how equivalence may be established between terms of differing levels of specificity. A user interested in the concept of 'sweetness' needs to be informed, first, that this term is not valid for searching this particular database and, second, that the most appropriate search term is 'flavour'. Thus, an equivalence relationship is established between two terms that could hardly be considered synonymous. This practice is often known as 'upward posting' and is certainly not recommended as it does not allow identifying the presence of possible hierarchical relationships between terms.

Hierarchical

A hierarchical relationship is assigned to a pair of terms when the scope of one of the terms totally includes (i.e. is broader than) the scope of the other. The broader term is assigned the code BT and the narrower term NT.

Table 8.1 Examples of types of equivalence among concepts

Equivalence type	Examples
Common/scientific names	Mad cow disease/bovine spongiform encephalopathy
Non-proprietary/trade names	Vacuum cleaner/Hoover/Dyson
Standard names/slang	Supplementary earnings/perks
Abbreviations, acronyms	SARS/severe acute respiratory syndrome
Inverted entries	Electric cables/cables, electric
Terms from different cultures, sharing a common language	Pavements/sidewalks
Competing terms for emerging concepts or technologies	Laptop computers/notebooks computers
Irregular plural	Mouse/mice
Quasi-synonyms	Perfume/eau de cologne
Specific concept subsumed in a broader concept	Flavour/bitterness/sweetness
Opposites	Smoothness/roughness

Therefore, we can interpret these codes as:

BT (broader term) between a specific descriptor and a more generic descriptor
NT (narrower term) between a generic descriptor and a more specific descriptor

Below is an example showing how hierarchical relationships are displayed in a thesaurus entry:

hospitals
    NT cottage hospitals
    NT isolation hospitals
    NT teaching hospitals
cottage hospitals
    BT hospitals
isolation hospitals
    BT hospitals
teaching hospitals
    BT hospitals

Hierarchical relationships have two major functions:

1   To alert the searcher to alternative terms that may be used to convey the same concept, but at a different level of specificity. A search at one level could fail to retrieve relevant documents which would have been indexed either at the broader level or at a narrower level.
2   To clarify scope. Knowing that 'cottage hospitals' is narrower than the concept 'hospitals' will avoid confusion with a potential synonym or even homonym (not that this is the case here).

It is important to remember that relationships between broader and narrower terms are dependent on the conceptual hierarchies that may have been established for a particular subject area. Furthermore, they may arise out of three types of hierarchical subdivisions:

1   generic
2   partitive
3   instantial.

THE GENERIC RELATIONSHIP

This type of relationship occurs between a thing and its members or species. As such, it is also called genus–species relationship. For example:

internal combustion engines	**thinking**
dual-fuel engine	contemplating
gas engine	divergent thinking
petrol engine	lateral thinking
spark ignition engine	reasoning

In such cases, the broader term names a class or category, and each of the narrower terms names a subset of that class, but not an individual instance of it. It is said that narrower terms inherit the attributes of the broader term. All engines listed below the broader term 'internal combustion engines' are all internal combustion engines. However, in order to be correct at the conceptual level, members of a generic relationship should belong to the same conceptual hierarchy (i.e. each member of hierarchy belonging to either 'things', 'actions' or 'people' categories etc.).

In some thesauri, such relationships are denoted as BTG/NTG (generic broader term and generic narrower term).

THE PARTITIVE RELATIONSHIP

The most common partitive relationships (or whole–part relationships) occur among geographic entities, parts of the body, disciplines of study and social structures. Below are examples of each type:

United Kingdom	ear
England and Wales	external ear
Northern Ireland	labyrinth
Scotland	middle ear
	acoustic nerve

Social Sciences	Roman Catholic clergy
anthropology	cardinal
economics	archbishop
sociology	bishop
politics	priest

Parts of machines, buildings, or networks are sometimes listed as related terms (see below). This type of relationship can be denoted by using BTP (partitive broader term) and NTP (partitive narrower term).

THE INSTANCE RELATIONSHIP

In this case, the relationship occurs between a general category of things or events and a unique instance of that category which is represented by a proper noun. For example:

Mountain regions	Treaties
Alps	Treaty of Vienna
Andes	Treaty of Versailles
Himalayas	Treaty of Rome
Rocky Mountains	Maastricht Treaty

When a term represents the combination of two concepts, it is likely to have been placed in two distinct hierarchies during the building of the classification that supports the thesaurus. This is a polyhierarchical relationship where a term has more than one BT. For example, the term 'acoustic nerve' can have two BT because of the following structure

ear	nerves
external ear	sciatic nerve
labyrinth	optic nerve
middle ear	skin nerve
acoustic nerve	**acoustic nerve**

We have:

acoustic nerve
BT ear
BT nerves

Associative

Associative relationships (also called affinitive) are probably the most difficult type of thesaural relationship to deal with because they are very loosely defined and closely linked to local context, hence the comparison with syntactic relationships. In this respect the guidance given by the British Standard BS5723 (1987) helps in stating what associate terms are not:

> [...] where terms are not equivalents nor do they form a hierarchy [...] yet they are mentally associated to such an extent that the link between them should be made explicit.

It is clear that the main function of these relationships is to suggest alternative terms for indexing or retrieval, namely to alert the user to terms that they may wish to use instead of or as well as the term they first thought of. These relationships are usually denoted by the abbreviation RT, standing for 'related term'. Reciprocal entries must always be provided, as demonstrated below:

trains
    RT railway transport
    RT railways
railway transport
    RT trains
    RT railways
railways
    RT trains
    RT railway transport

As can be seen from the above example, it is not clear in what sense the terms are related to each other. It may even be reasonable to consider these terms as being hierarchically linked rather than associatively.

Therefore, the decision to include related terms in a thesaurus entry depends more on the compiler's feel for what will be useful to the community of users than on precise semantic analysis. However, to avoid too great subjectivity, it may be advisable to consult guidelines such as those proposed by thesaurus compilers (see Table 8.2).

Attempts to be consistent and comprehensive in applying semantic rules can lead to lists of RTs that are so long that they can actually impede finding the related terms that are really needed.

It is worth noting that standard guidelines are not always consistently applied, as many thesaurus compilers interpret them liberally, often because they have to accommodate particular user groups with established traditions and subject-specific needs.

Knowledge organisation is, therefore, an important element in the management of the knowledge asset. As the conversations and the dialogues that define the OLP provide an

Table 8.2 Criteria for associating terms via the RT relationship

Kinds of association	Examples
Siblings with overlapping meanings	Boats RT ships
Familial/derivational	Children RT parents
Discipline and object of study	Zoology RT animals
Operation/process and its agent/instrument	Heating RT furnaces
Thing and its counter agent	Plants RT herbicides
Action and its product	Weaving RT cloth
Action and its target	Harvesting RT crops
Concepts and their unique properties	Perception RT acuity
Concepts related to their origins	Dutch RT The Netherlands
Concepts linked by causal dependence	Bereavement RT death
Concept and its unit of measurement	Length RT metre
Phrases in which the noun is not a true broader term	Heart RT artificial hearts

Source: Aitchison, Gilchrist and Bawden (2000).

ever-increasing amount of data and information, it the role of KO to ensure that the storage of this data and information will enable it to be aligned with the characteristics of 'good' information, and that it can be found at the right time and in the right form, by those who need it.

Knowledge transfer and sharing

The transfer of knowledge across the organisation is made possible when it is identified and after it has been embedded into the systems that will constitute the knowledge-based information system. This is all dependent upon the willingness and the ability of individuals to share their knowledge on an ongoing basis. To an extent this willingness has been taken for granted, it was assumed that ...

> ... people would be willing to share their knowledge, and as a consequence neglected to adequately look at how human and socio-cultural factors can influence knowledge sharing attitudes and behaviours.
>
> (Hislop 2009: 147)

This assumption cannot be justified. Instead it should be acknowledged that individuals will rarely participate in knowledge sharing activities where there is no perceived benefit for them to do so. Individuals may have concerns about where or how their knowledge may be used, whether or not it will treated appropriately and given the respect it is felt it deserves.

Organisational sensitivity to these feelings needs to be allowed to drive the development of the relationship between the individual and the organisation. This might involve an active consideration of the key conflict points within an organisation. In the first instance there is a need to acknowledge that conflict exists within the organisation and that if knowledge is to be shared freely these conflicts need to be addressed. This is not the same as disagreement or the willingness of individuals to contest meaning. Rather, conflict in this sense is the absence of trust and an embedded sense that individual knowledge will not be respected.

Trust is, therefore, at the heart of the knowledge sharing process and needs to embed itself in all of the key relationships, between individuals, between individuals and groups, between groups and across organisations. Certain individuals may be more willing to share than others simply based on their personality type, but fostering an open and supportive environment will positively encourage knowledge sharing and hopefully create a virtuous cycle of sharing based on growing trust.

As this environment is built and developed, different types of knowledge can be shared effectively. Nancy Dixon (2000) has identified five key types: serial, near, far, strategic and expert.

1 Serial transfer: 'The Serial Transfer System involves transferring the knowledge a team has learned from doing its task in one setting to the next time that team does the task in a different setting. The repeated action of the knowledge gained from each action happened in a serial fashion.'

One of the best known examples of techniques used to support serial transfer is the After Action Review (AAR). After Action Reviews have been used to great effect by the American Army, to evaluate their performance after specific missions.

Is short, an AAR is a method of capturing specific learning points which may then be used subsequently by a team. These learning points may include:

- What action the individual team member took.
- How the team member's actions impacted on the outcome.
- What the team member noted about the actions that other team members took.
- How the team member was impacted by the actions of the other team members.
- How the actions of the other team members impacted on the outcome.
- What occurred in the environment (both expected and unexpected).
- The impact of the environment on the team member and on other team members.

2 Near transfer: 'Near Transfer is applicable when a team has learned something from its experience that the organization would like to replicate in other teams that are doing very similar work.'

3 Far transfer: 'Far Transfer is applicable when a team has learned something from its experience that the organization would like to make available to other teams that are doing similar work.'

4 Strategic transfer: 'The pieces are in place for Strategic Transfer when a team has taken on a task that happens only infrequently – a one-off project – and wants to benefit from the experience of others, in other parts of the organization, that have done a similar task.'

5 Expert transfer: 'Expert Transfer is applicable when teams facing an unusual technical problem beyond the scope of their own knowledge seek the expertise of others in the organization to help them address it. Typically, the knowledge that is requested is not found in a manual or in standard documentation.'

(List source: Dixon, 2000)

Knowledge transfer and sharing represents a shift in terms of how individuals are expected to relate to one another. The technical infrastructure will not answer the questions centred on the willingness of individuals to share, even if they do address the practical opportunities to do so. This type of shift, therefore, has drawn the operational activities of IT and HR departments more closely together and, for example, places an emphasis upon networks rather than hierarchies. This fundamentally impacts upon the power dynamics within organisations and the political and ideological structures that characterise it socially and culturally.

The concept of the knowledge-economy, therefore, can ultimately be seen to raise important questions for managers within organisations. These questions are embedded within the drawing of knowledge to centre stage as the key organisational resource or asset. It can be said to raise the professional profile of the organisation and in turn to uphold a greater degree of individual autonomy and responsibility, backed up by higher levels of education, facilitated, in turn by the informed application of ICTs. This will ensure that the organisation enhances its ability to be flexible and adaptable within a perceived context of change where the need for continuous learning is paramount.

Concluding remarks

KM can be regarded as the management of explicit knowledge. Here knowledge has been externalised, it is a captured asset and can be embedded within the knowledge-based information system. It looks to identify where knowledge is being generated within the organisation, makes this explicit through the mapping of organisational knowledge and then organises it in such a way as to ensure its use is maximised. The transfer and sharing of knowledge bridge this practical management of an explicit asset and the processes that are associated with organisational learning. Knowledge management will identify the ways in which transfer and sharing is happening without necessarily looking at the cultural or other characteristics that will address the 'why' questions.

Part 2: key points

- Organisations are collections of individuals and the relationship between these individuals will determine the extent to which collaborative forms of learning, based on individual experience, can be transformed into an organisational asset.
- This relationship is founded upon the trust that is embedded in the ethical structure of the organisation.
- The HR function will manage the development of the appropriate relationship between the individual and the organisation.
- KM drives the acknowledgement of knowledge based on individual experience as the key asset for organisations.
- To use or manage knowledge as an organisational asset we need to understand learning as an organisational process.

These points lead us towards a more comprehensive view of organisational learning. Both HR and KM prepare the ground for the development of a pedagogical model based on collaborative learning that draws on experience.

- Unlike traditional pedagogical models organisational learning is collaborative in nature.
- Social relationships, therefore, are at the heart of collaborative learning.

• These relationships are determined and fashioned by the prevailing power dynamics within the organisation, which can both sustain and undermine the process of collaborative learning.
• Managing knowledge requires a sustainable pedagogy that can be built upon the characteristics of experiential learning.

Part 3

Developing organisational learning programmes

This part will consider the development of the OLP by first looking at learning and the specific characteristics associated with experiential and social learning – not least the need to develop the relationship between the individual and the organisation. It will focus on making explicit the performance of individuals and teams, through key learning practice, including action learning and appreciative inquiry.

The OLP will function as an information system and will be made up of key elements that will support or sustain an experiential learning cycle. The learning management system (LMS) or virtual learning environment (VLE) is the key component of this system, but there will also be other tools and techniques that will support key functions, and the imperative for OL practitioners is to have a sound awareness of the options available. This might be referred to as 'digital literacy' and will include basic design skills as well as a sound awareness of the tools that are being developed.

OL practitioners require a range of capabilities, they need to have both technical skills and awareness, as well as a sound knowledge of pedagogy and in particular a pedagogy that is drawn from experiential learning and embedded within a contemporary technical environment.

Part 3
Developing organisational learning programmes

9 Learning and development

Social and collaborative learning

Learning outcomes:

1 Identify the elements associated with the management of learning in organisations.
2 Understand the nature and significance of different learning styles.
3 Identify the characteristics of experiential and work-based learning.
4 Identify the key methods used to embed learning and development in organisations.

Introduction

In the age of 'super-complexity', learning has left the confines of the classroom and of structured formal education and become a more integral part of our diverse social and economic lives. The contexts and institutions, through which learning takes place, are seeking to meet the challenges within this 'moorland' of learning. Lifelong learning as a concept has perhaps grown to encompass or reflect more fully this complex picture. In particular, it has focused attention on the learner and the experience of learning. There is a need to identify the nature, or part of the nature, of this complexity by examining the learning experience beyond the context of traditional educational institutions. In doing so, there will be a focus on the characteristics of learning and in particular self-direction and autonomy within learning and the exploitation of information and knowledge as a learning resource. By considering learning within the 'learning organisation' we can also look to identify the characteristics of learning within this context and by doing so begin to illustrate some of the characteristics of learning within 'super-complexity'. Each organisation faces the challenge of this complexity and to some extent approaches it from their own perspective.

For organisations, learning has clearly been an important component for a number of years. In particular, continuing professional development (CPD), training, and learning and development (L&D) programmes have represented the recognition of the need to ensure that individual employees develop their skills for the greater good of the organisation. This has included the support of employees in undertaking academic qualifications and there has therefore been an established relationship between the goals of the employer and the perceived growth in vocational education. Equally, it has led to the development of professional accrediting bodies seeking to underpin, through formal educational channels, the skills base that represents a specific profession, for example the Chartered Institute of Personnel and Development (CIPD; www.cipd.co.uk).

This chapter will specifically consider the role of learning in the knowledge-economy and the management of learning and talent development in an organisational setting, both nationally and internationally. It will explore the need to identify learner needs and the design and evaluation of innovative solutions to these needs. Learning and talent development strategies will also be considered along with professionalism and the learning commitment of the developing professional.

Learning

Many definitions of learning can be presented, but within the context of organisational learning it can be related to the changing of behaviour as a result of experience. This experience can be varied and complex but it is appropriate to talk about the concept of the learning organisation (LO) and means that we can identify forms of learning that are specifically collective and embedded within organisations. This is not to deny that we also recognise that it is only individuals who can learn. There is no fundamental contradiction here. However, the context of learning within the knowledge-economy is no longer confined to the classroom and the mantra of knowledge-based organisations is to learn faster than their competitors. Donald Schön (1967) wrote that the ability to experiment and to attempt to embed new activities was often regarded as a threat to the stability of the organisation. It undermined the sense of the organisation but when faced with fluidity and periods of transition it becomes essential to be able to adapt and to challenge current practices. This was written at a time when there was a belief that we had gone through a period of unprecedented change. From our perspective we are tempted to say '*you ain't seen nothin' yet!*' Perhaps we might also fall victim to this in twenty years and perhaps in the future we will have learnt to be more circumspect when it comes to exclaiming the extent of the change that it has been our lot to endure.

Schön raises for us this crucial element within OL, that is, the element of change and we need to identify this as the basis for our study of OL. It is through learning that we acquire the ability to deal with change. Both KM and OL are largely about the need to constantly adapt and if we are to survive, the argument goes, in a context of increasing change then we need to be good at it. It will be the individuals within the organisation that will drive this and this draws in the crucial HRD, or CHRD, functions.

As we have explored aspects of culture, as we have considered the concept of what is modern and wrestled with the idea of fluidity and postmodernity we are also considering this need to adapt through understanding. We have considered the nature of organisational knowledge – we need to return to this debate. What is knowledge and how do we become knowledgeable? In order to be knowledgeable we need to learn and be good learners. Within an organisational context we need to promote good organisational learning. It is this that we will begin to consider here, by first making some general comments about learning and what it is.

We all learn and we all do it in a number of different ways and in a number of different contexts. We learn formally through schools, colleges and universities or informally through conversation and other forms of social interaction. We learn at work and from our own experience.

Where school might be seen as a structured context of learning, the goal of a university might be to encourage a less structured approach and to support depth in learning. This will emphasise personal input, reflection and interpretation. As we continue to learn outside the formal bounds of education we must also ask the extent to which we might be learning strategically (for limited objectives) or are we pursuing deep learning (for understanding).

Let's consider the distinction here more closely:

Deep learning: In the deep approach to learning there is implied an aim on the part of the learner to transform knowledge. The learner would seek a personal understanding of the material presented which will make this meaningful learning.

Strategic learning: By contrast the strategic approach to learning is more associated with the need to achieve certain aims. This might be the production of a report or ultimately the achievement of a specified goal. There is no real attempt to understand necessarily, just to achieve what is necessary in order to meet individual or organisational expectations.

In examining learning we can highlight in particular within our context the need for this to be based upon both experience and upon the important aspect of reflection. Kolb and Fry's (1975) model of experiential learning (the *experiential learning cycle*) identifies the process through which concrete experience passes through a process of reflection. This then, in turn, creates new abstract conceptualisations with which individuals or groups can experiment and it is this that will potentially form the next concrete experience that starts the whole cycle off again. The most important element in this is the realisation or belief that learning perpetuates itself and the learning organisation is largely about attempting to ensure that this type of iterative and virtuous cycle of learning is established and maintained.

How individuals learn is a question that educationalists have considered for some time and during this time a number of different schools of thought and more specific characteristics of learning have been put forward, for example behaviourism, cognitive and social learning.

Behaviourism

In this school of thought it is believed that learning is an observable and measurable process. It would claim that very complex behaviour can be reduced to smaller component elements and has become connected with *associationist* theories and such techniques as *programmed learning*. This type of learning is highly structured. An unconditioned reflex is a form of learning where there is an automatic response, such as blinking to protect an eye. Pavlov's (1927) famous experiments with a dog salivating over food and the ringing of a bell, illustrated that an *unconditioned reflex* can be elicited by the ringing of the bell rather than the presentation of food. The bell becomes associated with food and creates a reaction. The salivation in response to the ringing of the bell would be described as a *conditioned reflex*. There is a clear link between stimulus and response and it is most often applied to learning contexts where the content can be clearly broken down into discrete elements. Many computer-based techniques have applied this approach to learning and in the development of training.

Training programmes in organisations have drawn on the work of Robert Gagné (1985) and applied instructional techniques, such as *instructional systems design* (ISD) that breaks down complex tasks into a series of smaller units that are then sequentially engaged with. Each unit needs to be learnt before the whole will be fully understood or appreciated. The issue here is the underlying assumption that all complex tasks can be broken down in this way, that they represent discrete elements and that they do so in a consistent and a predictable way. Nevertheless, the opportunity to apply technology-based solutions to this type of approach to learning has been and remains popular. Many theories based on more constructionist principles are often just what appear to be, or are presented as, more 'complex' versions of this 'basic' behavioural model.

Cognitive

Contrary to the behaviourist school of thought is the cognitive school primarily associated with Jean Piaget (1896–1980). This is based upon the premise that as individuals our learning is based around our ability to create internal representations of things – *schemas*. Learning is the acquisition and modification of these schemas. It tends to believe that there are not normally radical alterations to these schema but that it is a more organic process, happening over time and relatively slowly and with only small gradual changes. As such, it emphasises *active learning* approaches where there is positive involvement by the learner in the process.

Social learning

Social learning theories (Brown and Duguid, 1991; Marsick, 1994; Scarborough, 1998) can be said to draw on both of these schools of thought in that they recognise that behavioural learning occurs within a specific context or environment. The social context will have a significant input into what is learnt and what can be learnt. Bandura (1977, 1986) is associated with the presentation of social learning theory based on the individual, the collective or the group and the environment. The stimuli within this context are:

- observation
- retention
- reproduction
- motivation.

Based on these stimuli, social cognitive theory is based on how individuals will observe others, retain elements of what they have observed and that this *may* become a characteristic of their own behaviour. Where an individual is positively motivated to adopt this behaviour then it is more likely that they will reproduce it in their own behaviour. Vicarious experience, therefore, forms a significant part of social learning theory and in OL the creation of rich dialogues that explore experience through active reflection creates the learning environment that can be aligned with the LO models. To an extent this can be seen to blend the individual as a learner and the learner as an element of collective, social or organisational learning. The organisation itself might not be said to be learning but the learning of the individual is woven into the behaviour and practices of the individuals who make up that organisation.

Learning within a LO, therefore, is learning with quite specific characteristics. In terms of context there is a question concerning the motivation and purpose of learning for the individual within this context. You, in your current context might be learning for yourselves and/or for your career development. This might be supported by your employer, but you might not necessarily regard the learning that you are doing as directly related to your current employment. At the same time there is a question raised about the different contexts of learning. Within an organisational context we share knowledge and we learn from this sharing. However, this might not be shared in a conventional teaching sense. It might be informal, but no less effective for this informality. There are also more opportunities to learn as a collective or as a team. For many people, the learning experience has been a largely independent one and not a particularly social one.

Similarly, we can consider the nature of the experience that is forming a large part of the knowledge that we consider important to learn. Who has this experience and how well do they share it? How willing are we to be recipients of this knowledge? Within these types of questions are important issues for the LO. They touch on fundamental issues about the practical nature of teaching and learning. However, before this it is necessary to expand on some of the characteristics associated with learning within the OL context.

Identity and adult learning

Perhaps in the first instance we can identify the fact that the learners who are learning within organisational contexts are adults. The characteristics of adult learning, as established by Malcolm Knowles (1913–1997), remain contentious to some extent and his distinction between *pedagogy* (the teaching of children) and *andragogy* (the teaching of adults) has been controversial since it was first made in the early 1960s. However, the central characteristics associated with adult learning are *self-direction* and *autonomy*.

It encourages more of a partnership, with the learner having choices in terms of not only how they learn but ultimately what they learn. Given this it becomes important for the learner to be able, as well as inclined, to direct their learning. What has come to be known as *self-directed learning* (SDL) is an individual process which is independent but not necessarily isolated. Rather, SDL is seen as being an important element in relation to the development of learning within the workplace. This underpins the concept of *action learning* and its emphasis on the process of reflection. This in turn has been based on the models associated with the experiential learning cycle. At the heart of this cycle is a method for professional and personal development that has informed the development of the LO.

There is need here to reconcile the self-motivated and directed individual, seeking some control over the learning process and the need of a collaborative or social learning context – the LO. This is related to the need of organisations to both embrace the fluidity of their context or environment and the diversity or individuals that will make up the organisation itself. Within this diversity is the talent and creativity that will allow the organisation to positively engage with its fluid and ever-changing environment. Yet, organisations are often reluctant to embrace this diversity, even when the fluid nature of their environment is acknowledged.

As organisations shift away from more traditional patterns of working life, as they seek to embrace the benefits of technologies that allow them to operate beyond strict nine-to-five routines or enhance their expectations of a professionalised workforce, the pressure this places on the work–life balance of individuals is considerable. On both the organisational and individual levels the diversity inherent in the emerging relationship between the individual and the organisation is problematic. For the organisation it seeks to challenge rather than align itself with identifiable elements of the organisational culture and creates an instability which only enhances anxiety for individuals. For the individual the need to maintain a healthy work–life balance is challenged by their enhanced presentation as professionals which raises expectations and can open them to harassment and even bullying.

Diversity training has been presented as a discrete activity that seeks to address some of the issues associated with this fluidity and complexity. Gender, race and sexuality can be presented as the key and perhaps most obvious elements of a diverse workforce, but there is an equal need to view diversity in terms of the differing cultural traits that might exist between any individual and the groups that form within the organisation. Individual identity is, therefore, the principal focus of diversity training.

> Various type of sources can inform the self: the activities individuals develop, the roles they perform in different contexts, and the groups they interact with.
>
> (Child and Rodrigues 2011: 307)

This will form the basis of the social identity that will drive their engagement with organisational learning. However, group identification can create a barrier to wider OL, where it might be perceived as a threat to existing practices. Similarly, any attempt to blend knowledge bases across diverse groups will create some conflict in terms of how or what priorities are applied in the management of the collected resource, with each favouring a vocabulary and a taxonomy that better reflects their own group understanding or language.

Groups may be more than willing to share knowledge within the group but across groups is more difficult. Broadening the base of identification across an organisation is a considerable challenge. A bridge needs to be built between these groups, and a common frame of reference found. This will be the first part of a process that will build an organisational identity and will help create a more positive relationship between the individuals (and groups) and the organisation.

> The alignment of group identities with organisational identity will be inhibited in circumstances where radical change is introduced in a purely top-down manner.
>
> (Child and Rodrigues 2011: 312)

Where change is imposed from the top then the impetus for this change is more likely to be perceived as a form of control as opposed to a collaborative and caring move. To effectively manage change in this respect there needs to be a genuine and transparent sensitivity to the social identities that will be impacted upon by the change. Differences that relate to social identity need to be constructively reconciled and this is the role of the OL practitioner.

Building social networks within organisations is one way in which this reconciliation might be achieved. Increasingly, within diverse organisational contexts, this is the building of online or e-learning networks. The democratic potential of these social networks are often presented as their key advantage and that this can be aligned with the self-directed element of adult learning.

However, in mimicking some of the characteristics of social media such as Facebook, this can be seen as an attempt to embed these networking forms within organisational practice, but the ideological impetus here needs to be considered and questioned.

> The corporate Internet needs for its existence both playbour and toil, fun and misery, bio-political power and disciplinary power, self-control and surveillance.
>
> (Fuchs 2013: 121)

The use of social media itself does not determine a more social and collaborative way of working. The democratic potential of social media may be celebrated, but where this is opposed by the less democratic ideological position that drives its use and adoption, then these collaborative principles will be valueless.

 Pause for thought: the case of Google

Using a 'political economy' theoretical perspective it is possible to paint a particular view of Google. This would be described, in the UK, as a left-wing view that interprets actions from a largely Marxist perspective:

> The PageRank algorithm arguably enhanced the searching capacity of the Google search engine and distinguished it from the many text-based engines or early virtual libraries. Google has become a verb, 'to google' meaning to search for information on the Internet. The company has become one of the world's largest companies with a conservative market value of around £150 billion. Its profit margins have proved remarkably robust, partially due to the detailed data it can provide for advertising clients. Clicking on an advertisement on Google is a visible act – it is a form of economic user surveillance.

> The profits that are generated by Google are owned by the directors. It generates income by marshalling the data that passes through its various components or services and selling it to advertising agencies. Google, to an extent, generates profit from the use of data that it collects from the content that is uploaded by users to the web or through their use of Gmail, Blogger, Google Earth or YouTube. PageRank (a secret algorithm) generates income through the surveillance of users.

> The management of Google presents characteristics of the LO. For example, Google employees are encouraged to spend some of their time on their own 'personal' projects while at work – often referred to as '20 per cent time'. Along with extensive leisure facilities made available to staff, such as hairdressers, swimming pools and so on, there is a mix of work and play which is aimed at enhancing worker efficiency. Working hour restrictions are largely non-existent, but a culture of working long hours is embedded. There is autonomy, play, networking and so on.

> Google's stated vision is to make the world knowable, based on a 'faith' that has the power of the Internet at its heart. This is referred to as 'technological solutionism' which certainly draws on a positivist view of knowledge which favours knowledge as a 'thing' rather than its socially constructed nature. This aligns itself with what Karl Marx referred to as 'fetishism'.

> A different theoretical perspective can alter this view of an organisation but from this perspective Google exhibits interesting characteristics that raise some questions for us in relation to OL. The playful, networked organisation can be about control, as much as it can be about care. An organisation can have a culture that might appear to be dedicated and aligned entirely with organisational goals, but might also be seen as exploitative.

> Google either represents a new form of organisation, using new patterns of working that liberate individuals from long established and oppressive practices or it is using new technologies and an awareness of the wider social trends embedded within social networking technologies to sustain these oppressive practices. The political economy view is more aligned to this latter position, but is it valid and what might the implications be for the development of OL?
>
> It is not so much what an organisation does but why it does it that will determine whether or not it is actually driving collaborative learning.
>
> (Drawn from Fuchs, 2013)

The need to embed creativity and innovation as a mechanism to maintain competitiveness is based on the recognition that this is creating what appears to be new organisational forms that are capable of operating within the emerging environment. However, this might be the deconstruction of existing organisational practice, resulting in higher levels of anxiety or a more enhanced form of organisational control that will also result in higher levels of individual pressure and anxiety. Organisational learning needs to ensure that these levels of anxiety are minimised and that the process of learning itself is a positive element in the development of an individual's identity. Where an individual fails to identify with the organisation then the relationship can be said to be failing and this will certainly undermine the development of trust and ultimately the development of the OLP.

Talent and performance

The need to identify and fill knowledge gaps (the *war for talent*) has long been recognised as a crucial part of organisational practice. Training and development functions have always been an element within this practice. The *six stage training cycle* seeks to identify the parameters for a positive engagement with training initiatives:

1   establishing the partnership;
2   integrating planning and evaluation;
3   identifying training and learning needs;
4   agreeing learning principles and strategy;
5   designing and delivering training;
6   monitoring and evaluating outcomes.

This has extended itself to *learning and development, learning and talent development* and *performance management* (Harrison, 2009; Stewart and Rigg, 2011). The premise is the value of organisational knowledge. In order to be able to maximise the knowledge embedded in the experience of the individuals in the organisation there need to be mechanisms in place that will support the transfer of this experience across the organisation and, in particular, the relevant experience to the relevant individuals.

The principles of good IM are to get the right information to the right individuals at the right time and in the right form. Information loses its value if it is not received in a timely manner (getting information about the possibility of an event after it has occurred has little value), or where it is expressed in such a way as to make it incomprehensible (use of jargon or technical language). Good information has characteristics beyond the explicit piece of information itself and the goal needs to be to ensure that the information and knowledge asset is used and applied as effectively as possible.

> Experience at work creates its own knowledge. And as most work is a collective, co-operative venture, so most dispositional knowledge is intriguingly collective – less held by individuals than shared by work groups.
>
> (Little, Quintas and Ray 2002: 24)

This clearly identifies the social nature of knowledge within this context. It is both personal, within the mind of the knower but also of value only when it has been put into a form that can be understood and applied by more than the individual – the group and ultimately the organisation.

Experience is at the heart of this process and at the heart of experience is the developing talent of individuals. Like knowledge, talent can be regarded as representative of the value that individuals bring to an organisation. It is their insight, their ability to quickly assess an issue or problem, their ability to apply their own growing and developing knowledge base and, of course, their willingness to apply it.

Willingness requires an individual who has a positive view of the organisation, who is motivated to apply their talents. The talent of an individual is a reflection of the depth of their experience. The training function, in moving towards talent and performance management is recognising the complexity of embedding learning as a sharing of experience. This should have as its goal the need to value the *process* as much as the explicit knowledge or information that it may be transferring. The process of transference is as important as the knowledge being transferred.

Because of this, the social context is of central significance and within this the relationship between the individual and the organisation is crucial. The basic question that is being presented relates to why individuals would choose to work in the first place. What motivates individuals to accept the contract that will come with employment?

Like any market individuals choose to work and they make this choice based on criteria that will highlight the return that they get for the input that they give. For organisations the cost of this labour often represents the single most expensive operating cost. So, there is a balance to be struck here. Within a competitive market theory model, individuals are trying to sell their input to the highest bidder, while the employer is trying to minimise the cost of this input.

Within any 'systemic' view of the organisation this is a model that is far too simplistic. Individuals are motivated by a range of different factors and organisations will respond to various stimuli within their environment or context. For example, high unemployment rates which might offer an organisational opportunity to reduce costs are socially and politically unacceptable in many respects and conversely high wage demands when labour is short can fuel inflation which is equally socially and politically unacceptable. All of this will impact upon the relationship between the individual and the organisation.

For individuals motivation to work is complex and may include one or more of the following factors:

* opportunity to control;
* opportunity to use talents;
* motivation through goals and challenges;
* opportunity for variety;
* 'environmental clarity';

- availability of money;
- physical security;
- social contact;
- status.

The more *social* approaches to employment tend to favour what are referred to as the *'social market'* models where the focus is on the Internal market in relation to recruitment. This supports the *'commitment'* concept and helps to foster a more positive relationship between the individual and the organisation. As organisations face significant demographic changes the social market models become more rather than less relevant and partly help us to understand why OL has emerged as such a significant organisational factor over the last few decades. The main factors here include:

- The populations of developed countries are stabilising or declining – people are living longer and remaining healthy. Birth rates are in decline.
- Developing countries are experiencing rapid population growth. In some cases this is partially offset by emigration but population pressure will remain for some decades before stability is achieved.
- Population balance between developed and developing will change significantly. Eventually the developed world will decline in importance in line with the reduced working population.

So, we have emerging HR models that at least seek to focus on the individual as a valued asset for the organisation. This has had an impact upon how the organisation responds to the needs of the individual and again there is evidence to suggest that softer or more social approaches are becoming embedded in practice.

Managing performance

Individuals, their experience and their ability/willingness to share the knowledge that is embedded within this experience will drive the ability of the organisation to learn. How well this might be happening, how well individuals are acquiring relevant knowledge and how effective they are at transforming this into an organisational asset will reflect the nature of the relationship an individual has with the organisation. It is the assessment of this relationship that will illustrate how effectively the organisation is functioning in terms of organisational learning.

Performance management looks to identify and evaluate just how effective individuals and teams have been. This is an ongoing process but one that needs to be cognisant of the growing complexities associated with the ability to identify what might measure effectiveness. However, in order to nurture the individual as an asset there is a need to support and enhance the performance of individuals. This will partly recognise the value of individuals to the organisation and provide explicit support as the relationship develops. Four key elements of the performance management cycle have been identified (Harrison, 2009: 162):

- induction
- job related training
- appraisal
- personal development.

Embedded within this cycle is the ongoing building of the relationship between the individual and the organisation. Starting with the induction process, the individual is introduced to the organisation. Ideally, induction will produce a plan for personal development that further embeds the individual within the organisation and identifies the key skills that need to be developed. This can be done through coaching and mentoring programmes, short training events or more substantial educational programmes. Appraisal forms an important part of the reflective process and aims to motivate and build both commitment and trust.

> . . . it is fruitless to try to introduce a developmental appraisal process into an organisation that has a rigid, divisive role structure and a controlling management style that discourages openness, the use of individual discretion and the development of potential.
>
> (Harrison 2009: 164)

Maintaining processes such as this that are not limited by organisational standardisation, is a challenge. Nevertheless, managing performance requires the opportunity to reflect upon this performance and to identify development needs. Methods used to drive this process include *coaching* and *mentoring*. Coaching and mentoring are sometimes confused with each other as they use similar development processes. Both rely on the individual's learning being aided and supported by another more senior member of the organisation (in the case of mentoring this can occasionally be a senior member of another organisation).

Coaching is a relatively informal approach to development where the coach (usually the individual's immediate manager) helps develop the individual by guiding them through an increasing range of activities. This may be in the form of specifically allocated tasks or duties or simply through the coach's day-to-day observations of the individual. Progress is reviewed on a regular basis to determine how the individual has performed. The coach will ask searching questions, outcomes and learning points are discussed, feedback on performance is given and where improvements can be made, plans are established and encouragement given.

For the process to be effective there must be a good working relationship between the coach and the individual. The coach must also have the necessary coaching skills and a genuine interest in developing people. As the *senior* partner in a coaching relationship it is often more experienced individuals who will be coaches. They may be tactical or strategic managers within the organisation. They will certainly have experience, but will need to be able and willing to take on this coaching role and it is this that must not be taken for granted. The manager needs to identify this as a positive development from their own perspective and they must have the skills or capabilities to be effective as a coach. This can be challenging for a manager as it requires them to acquire key skills and to approach OL in a particular way.

To coach there needs to be a clear recognition of the value of learning and managers who will be successful coaches will themselves be successful learners. Just how managers learn is, therefore, a significant question here. Much of a manager's learning occurs naturally through the experiences they encounter during their day-to-day managerial tasks and, in part, self-development can be seen as a conscious effort to gain the most from that natural learning. Although a number of managers are natural self-developers who constantly analyse and improve on their daily actions and decisions, it has been recognised that others are not as aware of the process and are increasingly being encouraged to do so.

Training in self-development comes most usually from two sources. First, through self-development courses which assist individual managers in analysing their strengths and weaknesses, understanding how they learn and how to plan to bring about that learning when they are back on the job. Second, through the feedback they receive from their coach or mentor who, having identified with them an area for performance improvement or a learning opportunity, then encourages the individual to set some learning objectives and develop a development plan to achieve those objectives.

In many cases self-developing managers are encouraged to set up a 'learning log' in which they keep a record of activities from which they have learned, what it was they learned and how they intend to use that learning in the future. Many of the professional institutions require evidence, through learning logs, of an individual's continuing development before allowing that individual to progress through the various grades of membership. In addition some organisations are beginning to use an assessment of learning logs to inform a selection or promotion decision.

 Pause for thought: the concept of managerial competencies

Although in recent years there have been some debates on a number of areas of management development, one which has perhaps created most controversy has been the question of managerial competencies. Through the Management Charter Initiative (MCI) the development of managers is being more firmly focused on job related training aimed at managers developing job competencies to specific predefined standards. Boyatzis (1982) defines competency as:

> ... an underlying characteristic of a person which results in effective and/or superior performance in a job.

The MCI function has been incorporated into the Management Standards Centre (www.management-standards.org/) which also attempts to present a set of standards for managers at the operational, tactical and strategic levels. These standards are based on key competencies which have been identified from analyses carried out on the various job functions of managers where the function is sub-divided into a series of elements or units. The key example is the National Occupational Standards which currently cover six key areas:

1   managing self and personal skills
2   providing direction
3   facilitating change
4   working with people
5   using resources
6   achieving results.

Each of these areas can be applied to OL and each can be approached from an OL perspective. Take some time to look in detail at these areas and identify relevant OL functions.

For many managers people are seen either as an asset or a nuisance (*Theory Y* or *Theory X*), the catalyst for change or an obstacle to be tackled in achieving organisational strategic aims. From an OL perspective, based as it is on the need to embed collaborative learning within the organisation, it is clearly inappropriate to *view* individuals as an impediment or obstacle. This does not mean that individuals will not be obstacles or impediments but it is a requirement of the organisation to understand this behaviour as it will impact negatively on the development of the OLP.

The management of individuals as significant knowledge assets and the talent development functions forming around this can clearly be seen as having an impact upon organisational performance, key barriers can be:

Organisational: performance can be determined by the structures, policies and operational routines that are embedded in the organisation itself.

Political: ideological considerations will look to determine 'favoured' action and individuals and groups will look to identify and to respond to this.

Interpersonal: as a process, performance management will impact upon other mechanisms that support the relationship between groups and individuals.

Performance management must observe and it must ultimately judge. This should not detract from the development and building of the relationships that are necessary for OL and this makes the question of who should carry out the appraisal of performance a crucial question. The process of *360-degree feedback* is appraisal that is carried out by an individual's supervisor, peers and other stakeholders, such as customers or users. This is often led by the supervisor who will have a legitimate view of the individual, but that is often limited. They may not, for example, be in direct contact for much of the time. *Peers* do have this proximity and can express an honest, if personal, view of another individual's performance. However, this too is limited by key social dynamics. Is there personal antipathy, is this based on an underlying competitiveness? Also, the impact of poor feedback can be de-motivating and needs to be balanced with a clear view of why performance might be dropping. Is this identifying a training need, is the individual being asked to perform tasks that they are not capable of doing, are there personal issues that are impacting upon performance?

Performance can also be judged by the *self*. *Self-development* is essentially a learner-centred activity with the developing individual taking responsibility for his/her own development, often referred to as self-reflective learning:

> This is the kind of learning that leads individuals to develop new patterns of understanding, thinking and behaving. It is needed when people have to operate in ways that are unfamiliar to them.
>
> (Harrison 2009: 167)

Because of this unfamiliarity it is necessary for individuals to be confident enough to accept that errors are positive – from a learning perspective. This cannot be successful unless there is a high degree of trust embedded within the individual/organisational relationship.

When used in a more qualitative way and within an environment that is actively looking to embed trust and mutual respect, it is possible to regard self-assessment as a formal part of this process. Rather than relying on specific matrices to measure performance, a *performance statement* can be made to indicate the experience of individuals in relation to the tasks they have been asked to perform. This aligns itself with key elements of the LO and the development of key dialogues around existing mental models, shared vision and so on.

Narrative essays can be used to present a qualitative statement about an individual's performance. This will require the storyteller to have well-developed storytelling skills and this should not be taken for granted. Difficult as it might be to then rate the performance based on a narrative essay this nevertheless will provide a valuable insight into the performance of an individual, even when part of self-assessment.

Team or community performance will look to assess both the group and the individuals making it up. Individuals will be assessed in relation to the function or purpose of the group. Communities of practice will carry out assessments of the coordinators and champions associated with the group, along with the community members both individually and as a group. These will look to identify or comment on:

- Outcome – the extent to which individual and collective aims are being achieved.
- Behaviour – the contribution made by individuals to the group.
- Competency – the effectiveness of the group.

The purpose of the assessment will relate to:

- Development – the extent to which the appraisal will support development.
- Evaluation – the use of the appraisal to establish the usefulness of the group.
- Self-regulation – the use of the appraisal to help individuals manage their contribution.

This is a process of externalisation and therefore can form part of the experiential-learning cycle. It is also reflective, but needs to be conducted within a context of trust and mutual respect. All those involved need to perceive of this appraisal as part of an ongoing process supporting other efforts to encourage the externalisation of key aspects relating to the acquisition of relevant organisational experience. Here, this can be linked directly to both the SECI model (at least the element of externalisation) and to the models of the LO in particular to the dialogue around team learning, personal mastery and mental models.

Action learning

Action learning attempts to embed pedagogical principles into organisational practice. To be effective at doing this there is a need to ensure that there is a clear understanding of what these principles are. In building an OLP there is a need to ensure that there is clarity in relation to what will be achieved and how. What will be the specific outcomes and benefits from both the organisational and individual perspectives?

Action learning was developed in the early 1970s from work carried out by R. W. Revans (1907–2003) the then professor of management at The Manchester Business School. The approach is centred on Revans' belief that for managers there is a need to solve problems.

It is simply based on arranging secondments or exchanges whereby managers from one organisation are planted into another organisation to solve a particular problem or set of problems. They may work on the problem for a period of months and during that time they will have regular dialogue with a peer group of managers similarly placed in other organisations working on similarly challenging problems.

The learning stems from the process of problem solving in that they will need to develop ideas, seek out or research information, establish possible solutions and test them. This fits in with Kolb's (1984) theory of learning where he argues for the merging of the more passive characteristics associated with a traditional pedagogical model with a more active problem-solving model, where the characteristics of learning are more active. In addressing a problem there is a more explicit need to know, rather than attempting to absorb something that someone else believes to be important or necessary.

Modified versions of Revans' approach are used fairly extensively in some organisations in the form of *action learning sets* or *project teams* where groups of managers from different specialisms or parts of the organisation are brought together to solve a particular problem or deliver a specific piece of work. The learning process is essentially the same and the organisation derives two benefits in that those involved will be developed through their participation and they get the problem solved or the work done. However, there are alternatives to this problem-oriented approach.

Appreciative inquiry

The *appreciative inquiry* (AI) model starts not with a problem but with a strength. It then focuses on how to improve or enhance this strength. It looks to recognise what is done well and to use this to drive development. This is a change-management model that fits well into the postmodern perspective of the organisation where the focus is not on the identification of a solution but on the continuing process of engagement that is embedded within the iterative processes of experiential learning. As we learn from our experience this then forms part of our experience from which we then learn. What we learn is almost secondary to our ability to ensure that we are able to drive this experiential-learning cycle.

> ... the focus of Appreciative Inquiry is on co-constructing new theory based on our experiences. We explore our experiences together as we tell each other our stories, giving subjectivity priority over objectivity.
>
> (Lewis, Passmore and Cantore 2011: loc 948 of 4939)

It is this focus on the process rather than the specific issue, task or problem that might drive a project team that distinguishes this type of approach from the more traditionally based model of learning, where there is a perceived goal to be achieved and a belief that there is an explicit solution to be found. Instead it is recognised that there may be many possible outcomes and that these outcomes themselves need to generate further engagement – an iterative or cyclical process of learning.

The AI model is based on four Ds:

- discovery
- dream
- design
- destiny.

Language, discourse and stories are central to AI and it is often presented as a *conversation based change process*. As with any change-management process there is a need to identify the focus of the inquiry, but with AI this needs to be stated as a positive rather than a negative. For example, the problem of low morale becomes the need to enhance motivational factors.

At the *discovery* stage of this model there would be a need to identify where there are good practices in relation to motivation. Why should we be motivated by what we do? Where do we find positive examples of motivation? Is it embedded in the purpose of the organisation or in the practices of individual leaders or in group/peer support? To acquire this 'view' of the organisation there is a need to initiate a series of conversations. This might apply to interviewing skills in order to conduct these conversations.

- What is being considered (the focus)?
- What are individual expectations (what can be achieved by this inquiry)?
- What examples might there be of a positive engagement with the focus of the inquiry?
- What made a difference?

This will generate relevant data around the key focus, which needs then to be collated and organised into a meaningful resource for further consideration. What themes are emerging and how do these relate to the focus of the inquiry?

The *dream* phase is looking to identify what aspirations individuals and groups might have for their future as part of the organisation. This equates with the consideration of personal mastery that is part of Senge's (1993) five disciplines. Again, however, the emphasis in AI is on the positive presentation of experience.

> The Appreciative Inquiry process seeks to make use of the human tendency for dialogue. It seeks to create a positive belief in the future through the discovery of past successes. As we do so, this recognizing of past success in turn facilitates a belief in our future potential.
>
> (Lewis, Passmore and Cantore 2011: loc. 1300 of 4939)

Again, this will employ small group activities that seek to equate or reconnect the discovery phase outcomes with the future dreams.

- Where are the 'connects'?
- How might we get there?
- What will it look like?

In sharing dreams of the future again key themes can be identified, discussed and refined.

The *design* phase identifies action that will support the agreed common future dream. Small and large group discussions can be used to identify and prioritise the decisions that need to be made. This can be presented as a design statement. By the end of this stage of the process there should be a 'connect' between the understanding or appreciation of the strengths of the organisation, what it can become and how this might be achieved.

The final *destiny* stage is about implementing the final design statement. Action groups can be formed that will drive these changes. Group activity here can be self-organising around the key elements within the design statement and will allow individuals to focus on the elements that excite and engage them.

Throughout this process there has been a need to embed group working as a mechanism for reflective learning. The capabilities required to drive this form of inquiry, therefore, are based upon a sound understanding of the pedagogical principles associated with group working. This will focus more on *teaching* rather than learning. What is the nature of teaching in this experiential context? To a large extent it is the facilitation skills of the teacher that are important and here there is a need to consider what it is attempting to do in terms of the *functions* of teaching, the *variables* within teaching and the *methods* of teaching.

It is important to consider these processes within a practical context, not least the *planning* of a teaching event. In particular, there is a need to identify the strengths and weaknesses of different methods of teaching.

The nature of teaching

In Squires' (1999) Micro Model three aspects of teaching are identified:

1   the functions
2   the variables
3   the methods.

Functions of teaching

- **Motivate:** stimulate, get and keep attention, arouse interest, enthuse, energise, excite.
- **Audit:** diagnose, assess needs, pre-test, identify baseline knowledge and skills, explore initial perceptions and expectations.
- **Orientate:** guide, cue, map out, give a sense of direction, negotiate an agenda, establish a framework, set objectives.
- **Inform:** transmit, impart input, put across, tell, show, demonstrate, enact.
- **Explain:** go through, go over, interpret, clarify, relate, amplify.
- **Explore:** open up, respond, engage in dialogue, brainstorm, discuss, debate.
- **Develop:** encourage problem-solving, critical thinking, learning to learn, autonomy, growth, maturity.
- **Exercise:** drill, rehearse, set tasks, practice, engage, try out, carry out, experiment, activate.
- **Appraise:** feedback, comment, criticise, react, assess, de-brief, act as a sounding board.
- **Reinforce:** emphasise, underline, reward, encourage, praise, value.

Variables of teaching

- WHY
  Rationale: why are you doing what you are doing and what will be the outcomes? These objectives are often split into three domains:

  - **Cognitive** (knowledge, thinking).
  - **Affective** (attitudes, values, feelings).
  - **psycho-motor** (routinisable physical or other skills).

- WHAT

  - **Content**: subject matter, themes, topics and areas.

- o   **Process**: procedures, methods, techniques, approaches and strategies – the way of doing the subject, the kind of thinking or action involved.
- o   **Level**: ability and potential, amount of scope and content.

- WHO

    - o   **Group**: group dynamics, role distribution, group behaviour.
    - o   **Individual**: awareness of learners as individuals is essential in order to fine tune teaching and learning.
    - o   **Self**: need to think of ourselves – accessible, friendly, imaginative, responsible, enthusiastic, organised.

- WHERE

    - o   **Physical setting**: actual teaching space, facilities, furniture, acoustics, lighting, heating.
    - o   **Organisational setting**: the teaching or training room may reflect the wider ethos of the organisation.
    - o   **Social setting**: social, economic and cultural setting.

Methods of teaching

- project
- assignment
- placement
- supervision
- practical
- simulation
- discussion
- question and answers
- demonstration
- presentation.

Appreciative Inquiry focuses on the key teaching methods, both in small and large group discussion.

Small groups: discussion/tutorials

When working with small groups the aim is normally to:

- clarify
- elaborate
- consolidate.

There is a tendency for these types of session to be tutor centred with a reluctance to participate on the part of the learner. They are also a means to follow-up material previously presented and can benefit from being more informal. This might reflect itself in the seating arrangements which might be in a horseshoe shape or some other shape less formal than rows in front of the facilitator. There is therefore more management required and there is also a need to be aware that this type of session can create anxiety for some learners and also that there is always a need to deal with the 'talkers'.

Large groups: presentations/lectures

This particular teaching method represents what a lot of learners consider to be the standard means of learning. Ironically it has very limited objectives and is not a very good way to learn. It is, however, a good way to reach a lot of learners at one time. What does a presentation attempt to do?

In most presentations it is recognised that learner attention span is very short. It has been estimated that after about the first 15 minutes of a presentation the attention of learners actual falls sharply only to recover modestly towards the end when there is an expectation of the presentation ending. This alone ensures that when presenting information through this method the expectations on the part of the presenter should be modest.

The aim of the presentation is largely context setting. It tries to:

- orientate the learner
- provide motivation
- clarify some area
- use signposting techniques.

It is easy to try to do too much in a presentation. The points that are made should be supported with handouts and where possible variety should be included to sustain attention. From the learners point of view it is generally a passive experience within which they are not expected to participate actively and can be quite demotivating.

Planning a teaching event

We have seen the characteristics often associated with a formal teaching event. However, there is a quite different learning context within the LO – a less formal context. Nevertheless, to understand and manage OL there remains a need to appreciate the purpose of teaching as an element in the transferring of organisational knowledge. Teaching is, therefore, a form of knowledge transfer, it is fundamentally about getting knowledge from one individual to another.

Different teaching methods produce different results and the implication is that less formal teaching methods will also have different results. For example, bearing in mind the fundamental limitations of the presentation and the limited nature of the aims associated with it, when it comes to planning presentations these considerations should be carefully reflected. Prior to delivery the aims and objectives should be clearly identified. The presenter should have in place some means by which the learning outcomes can be both achieved and also seen to be achieved. In terms of structure the introduction should include an overview, which clearly highlights the purpose and content of the presentation – this should act as a means of orientating and motivating the learner. If there are no formal presentations within an informal learning context, where and how is this need to motivate and orientate achieved? This, to some extent, highlights one of the limitations of this area, namely the fact that we often consider only how tacit knowledge is transferred but not how that tacit knowledge was created in the first place.

Mainstream thinking focuses attention on this process of translation but does not explain how new tacit knowledge comes to arise in individual heads. The explanation starts from the point where some individual already possesses important tacit knowledge. For an approach claiming to explain the creation of knowledge, this is a major limitation.

(Stacey 2001: 18)

As previously mentioned, in relation to learning styles, in the cognitive school, learning is the acquisition and modification of schema and emphasises *active learning* approaches. The condition by which these schema might be modified is often described as the *optimum conditions for learning* and, again referring to the Squires model, the optimum conditions for learning have been identified. These are broken down into the four main characteristics:

- person
- process
- information
- environment.

In order for teaching and learning to be effective:

The *person* must have a positive self-image, with an open mind, with ability and be able to prioritise.

The *process* should be active (learning by doing); reflective (able to consider material independently); involve an element of processing (goes in and then comes out); informative.

The *information* itself should be patterned (chaotic or random looking information can be difficult to learn); meaningful (relating to our own world or perceptions); embedded (identifiable within practice or procedures – relates to knowing what is expected); embodied (represented by a particular person).

The *environment* should be a rewarding one and this raises some interesting issues related to pain and pleasure principles. Might you learn better if you were given a cash prize at the end for a good or best performance? Might you learn better if you were told that you would be punished if you did not perform well? It has been shown that people tend not to learn effectively if they are punished, discouraged or criticised.

A formal presentation, therefore, is largely about orientation and motivation, rather than about the delivery of explicit content or context knowledge. Small groups need to avoid being led or dominated by either the facilitator or individuals within the group. These are issues that any experienced teacher will recognise. They are now key capabilities that need to be embedded within the OLP. In order to effectively present the knowledge that is being acquired through experience the appropriate tools and techniques need to be applied. The conversations embedded within AI themselves need to be managed effectively. Not least the data generated by the four Ds as part of the AI process need to be made available and to align themselves with the principles associated with good information.

Concluding remarks

Organisations are seeking to embed a pedagogical model that is aligned with the recognition that the knowledge asset of that organisation is based upon the experience of individuals. It is personal, it is fluid and it requires the organisation to reassess the key relationship between the individual and the organisation. It is essential for the individual to engage appropriately with the type of learning that will allow them to externalise their experience. They can only do this in an environment based on trust and mutual respect. Shifting learning from individual experience to collective resource requires a collaborative model of learning. This is the social basis of learning from experience and any social context is founded upon a relationship between those within the social context. The willingness to actively and openly share experience needs to be achieved and in doing so it will change or add to that experience and ultimately create an iterative process that itself is central to the OLP. This can be referred to as a sustainable pedagogy, based upon experiential learning.

10 Knowledge-based information systems

A technical infrastructure for learning

Learning outcomes:

1 Identify the elements associated with systems.
2 Understand the distinction between different types of information systems.
3 Identify the elements of the systems development life cycle.

Introduction

Emphasis is being placed on the need to be innovative and competitive and to sustain an increasing pace in relation to these. Achieving this relies on the availability of accurate, confidential, realistic information; the kinds of information which organisations have about their products and services, their processes and human resources, their competitors and environment. Such information may be embedded in information systems, like databases and corporate intranets, a payroll or inventory system, an extranet or a website. It may be available to everyone in the company and even those outside such as customers and stakeholders, or reserved only for privileged insiders because it is critical for decision making. Having such information takes time and effort, and the cost–benefit of having and using it are important factors in an organisation's performance. These issues are often described as 'information management'. It has many variations – it may be business systems integration, content providers, Internet service providers, information design, information analysis, IT management, ICT (information and communications technology) implementation. Many of the most successful 'knowledge players' – providers and customers – define themselves as information specialists. Certainly, when we think of the hard systems which need to be developed and put in place to embody OL, we find ourselves talking to information managers and reading about information management. Knowledge-based information systems are the systems that seek to do more than store, move and manipulate explicit data and information. They seek also to support the learning that underpins the production of the knowledge that will ultimately produce the data and information.

This chapter will consider information systems that specifically support knowledge cycles within organisations and how these can be used to inform management decision making. Methods for the sharing of knowledge and the construction of social networks will be explored.

Information systems

The purpose of an information system (IS) is to manage the information asset and to support the decision-making process that drives organisations. The basic functions of the IS are to collect, store, process and disseminate information. Where an IS is able to include and integrate the explicit knowledge that is being generated by the learning within the organisation it can be said to be a knowledge-based information system (KBIS). However, the KBIS recognises that this system will not be defined by the technologies that make it up and will attempt to encompass all of the elements within the tacit to explicit model. It is not enough to simply store information that might emerge from a lessons learned database (LLD), there is also a need to ensure that this information is 'good' information and that it can be applied for the benefit of the organisation as a whole. Equally, there is a need to ensure that any of the technical applications not only support but also engage the individuals being asked to generate the knowledge asset.

In developing an IS, we are concerned with the way in which disparate elements, including hardware and software, organisational structures and personal attitudes, will operate together. This is the notion of the system:

> ... systems relate to each other and they themselves consist of sub-systems.
>
> (Avison and Fitzgerald 1995: 39)

An information system, like any other system, will have certain characteristics normally referred to as *elements*. The elements within an IS are:

- system boundaries
- system environment
- sub-systems
- control system.

The elements within any system will sit within the system's boundary and the boundary in turn will sit inside that system's environment. For example, a political system will have elements such as the electorate and political parties. The system boundaries will be those of the area in which one wants to define the political process – perhaps in the UK, or on a larger scale, within Europe, or on a smaller scale, within local authority areas. The environment will include all the areas within which the system operates. If the system boundary were a parliamentary constituency within the UK, then the environment within which it operates would be the UK. A sub-system might be the political parties. If political parties were considered as the system, then it would have elements such as different political parties (in the UK this would be, Conservative, Labour, Liberal Democrat and so on). Differences in scale and focus change the denotations of the terms. The control system in this example would be the legislation governing the operations of the parties.

Another example would be a *university library*:

- university: environment
- university library: boundary.

The university library as a system would be made up of several elements, the users, the staff and the library management system (LMS). If the LMS were regarded as a system the elements could be defined as:

- cataloguing
- circulation
- acquisition.

Systems are, therefore, organised assemblies of parts, in which each part has a particular role. If one of those parts was removed, the whole would be affected. Rules dictate the way in which the parts operate, and thus express the interconnectedness that exists amongst the features which make up any system. If we consider the game of chess as a system, for example, the removal of any rule would at least change the game considerably, and potentially render it unplayable.

Transformation process: input–process–output

The idea of input–process–output is common to all systems. Information systems are concerned with how information flows through a system, and how that flow is regulated. Let's take a domestic central-heating system as a simple example. Its components are a boiler, radiators and a thermostat. The thermostat is a control sub-system. Its inputs are a temperature setting, perhaps from a dial, and temperature readings from sensors. If the ambient temperature drops below the minimum setting, the thermostat supplies more power to the boiler, to heat more water, which will raise the temperature of the radiators. When the ambient temperature reaches a predetermined limit, the thermostat switches the boiler off again.

This *input–process–output* is referred to as a *transformation process*, as some input is transformed to create an output. This can be applied to many operational activities within information services. For example, the issue and discharging of textbooks from a library takes as an input the identifiers of the material (barcode or other indicator on the textbook itself) being loaned and the user (the reader's unique number on their library card) and transforms the status of the textbook (from *available to borrow* to *on loan*) and the user (now with another loan attributed to them).

Systems are also referred to as being open or closed, depending on their relationship with their environment. A closed system is not affected by the environment, whereas an open system will be. In most cases, information services are heavily influenced by their environment, and are therefore considered open systems.

Types of information systems

Although the classification that follows cannot be regarded as being entirely accurate there are nevertheless basic characteristics of information systems in relation to the level of management activity that is being supported. So far, consideration has been given to systems at the operational and tactical levels where there is a degree of structure to the processes involved. However, at the strategic level there is a greater reliance upon judgement and experience that makes these decisions less structured.

Transactional processing systems

The main purpose of the transactional processing system (TPS) is to *capture data* generated by *operational* processes. This data will be almost exclusively *internal* and will be highly *structured*. At the operational level, the information needs of managers can often be met by routine administrative data-processing activities. An example might be financial statements – are the budgets being applied appropriately? Essentially, the questions or issues here refer to whether or not the operations of the service are being carried out as efficiently as possible.

Any adjustments or alterations are intended to make these operational processes more effective. An instance might be the introduction of barcode scanners, or their more modern analogue, the radio frequency identification (RFID) system. Comparatively recently, many information services used barcode reading pens which were physically drawn across the barcodes that identify the item and the customer or user. It was found that this tended to damage the barcode, so that time was wasted, either in keying in the barcode number, or, ultimately, replacing the barcode. Moving to a hand-held scanner protected the barcode, saved time and effort and can be seen as a small operational improvement. The data involved are entirely internal to the organisation, and, in this instance, might relate to the number of barcodes being replaced, the staff time spent in carrying this out, and so on. The data are generated by the activities and *transactions* of the organisation.

With a bank we would be likely to think of transactions as being the deposit or withdrawal of money. In the past, this has been done by the customer filling in an appropriate form and taking it to the teller. With the advent of automated teller machines (ATMs) these face-to-face transactions have largely been replaced. In libraries the transactions might be the issue and return of loan materials, and many library management systems have automated these transactions, in the same way that banks have automated cash withdrawal, and supermarkets have introduced self-service checkouts, which are also linked to stock control.

In all cases, the user or customer can accomplish what they need to do more quickly and conveniently, and from the organisation's point of view, the transaction has been carried out more efficiently, saving staff time and costs, and engendering customer satisfaction. The effectiveness of these services has been enhanced.

Transactional processing systems, therefore, represent one of the earliest types of computerised IS. They were intended to carry out the basic transactions of the organisation by recording the transactions, processing them once they were recorded, then validating the data before finally storing them, thus enabling future retrieval and use. This was in itself an important development, because TPS thereby provided a previously non-existent source of data, which could then be used to influence decisions on marketing, production, or other organisational management functions.

Very 'rich' data can easily be collected – not just the day you borrow or purchase items, but the time, the identity of the item, and so on. Not just the amount you take from an ATM, but the time, place, and frequency with which you do so. Not only your 'spend' at the supermarket, but all the above, plus did you buy any special offers, and so on.

Transactional processing systems are, therefore, the backbone of an organisation's IS. They are responsible for the input and processing of fundamental data relating to the organisation's operation. They will provide operational managers with routine statistics to aid in decision making. For example, data about times of peak usage can be used to justify plans for extra staffing at those times. They provide the data that indicate either that the organisation's operations are going according to plan, or that they may be operating differently from the expected standard, thus highlighting the need to make alterations.

Management information systems

The main purpose of the management information system (MIS) is to generate *reports* that will support *semi-structured, tactical* decision making. The data used to create these report will almost exclusively be *internal*. Information systems mostly use internal information, they are dependent on rapid processing and retrieval, and their principal focus is on making efficient use of organisational data. At the operational level the function of the IS is almost entirely related to developing more efficient processes. The ATM makes the process of withdrawing money more efficient from the point of view of both the bank and the customer. The issuing of a library book from a self-service terminal eliminates queues and frees up staff time. This is the key advantage of the TPS. However, the one key thing that the TPS will also do, as well as allow the more efficient execution of operations processes, it will also *record* these transactions. The significance of this is that valuable data are created that can be used to help or assist in the management of the business or service. For example, in supermarkets a record is kept of what is being sold through the checkouts. How many items of soap or cereal each day, week, month, year or years? The value of this is further enhanced where it is possible to identify who was purchasing these items and this has led to the introduction of loyalty cards. Now a supermarket can identify what has gone out and to whom. Effort has now gone in to the proactive creation of data, specifically for the purposes of supporting decision making, rather than simply to make operational processes more efficient.

The purpose of the MIS is, therefore, to help managers at operational and tactical levels of the organisation to make decisions. They do this by providing a more informed view of what is happening in relation to the key organisational processes. The basis of this is the quality and reliability of data and information that is being processed through the IS. This might be the TPS.

The goal of MIS was to get the correct information resource to the appropriate manager at the right time, to monitor and control internal operations within the organisation, and to help middle or tactical managers to make decisions and assess the impact of daily operations on longer-term aims. At this point data becomes a valuable asset for the organisation and, as it is used to inform management decision making, it can be regarded as information. As an asset with a purpose it has qualities beyond its own content. Information, if it is to be useful has other characteristics that make it valuable, these are:

- *Timely*: provided at the time when it is most useful for the purpose intended.
- *Appropriate*: in relation to the type of task so if it were a public library, decisions about overdue procedures and actions will not rest on Mrs Johnstone having an overdue book but that piece of information will be relevant to the individual responsible for recovery procedures. The former group would want information related to overdue patterns and so on.
- *Understandable*: often information is provided which is not understandable, and perhaps this represents the specialism character within a bureaucratic organisation – baffle them with jargon and they will think you know something and you get promoted. Statistical tables are another form of baffling information – often overlooked and avoided.
- *Accurate*: appropriateness, too much detail is bad.
- *Directed*: allow for immediate action.
- *Novel*: address and highlight the unusual patterns or events rather than the things which are running smoothly.

Information is 'good information' where it has the above characteristics and it is the role of the IS and the information manager to ensure that there is an information management strategy that in the first instance will identify and gather the required data and information and then ensure that it is made available to the right person, at the right time and in the right form.

A key goal of the MIS is, therefore, to produce meaningful reports. For example, the data collected by a TPS remains as data, or basic statistics (number of items borrowed or sold, for example) until they are specifically used to interpret the trends within the organisation's operation. This largely involves the integration of data to create information. This process of integration is iterative and aims to create a range of different reports, for example a management reporting system (often an integrated element into specific management systems) might produce:

- *Summary report* – this might be issues statistics for a library by the hour, or the number of times a specific website was viewed over a specified period.
- *Exception report* – this might look to identify where there are deviations from a 'normal' trend. Perhaps a spike in sales or an unexpected downturn in demand, when previously it had been high.
- *Detail report* – this might be burrowing down into the data to get specific information perhaps relating to a specific brand of good or sales over a very specific period of time.

Each of these reports allows managers to make decisions from a more informed position. How they might interpret the report and what solution they might choose to apply is not defined by the report itself. Nevertheless with MIS there is the crucial recognition of the value inherent in the data that is being produced by the organisation through its day-to-day operations. To an extent the operational experience of the organisation is being recognised and the role of information management is to maximise the value of the information asset.

Intelligent support systems

The main purpose of the intelligent support system (ISS) is to assist largely *unstructured, strategic-level* decision making. The data used here will draw on both *internal* and *external* sources. Information systems at the strategic level, therefore, are attempting to support complex decision making. They will be attempting to support decision making that will employ all types of information both internal and external. A number of systems attempt to do this including:

- decision support systems
- executive information systems
- expert systems
- social network analysis.

Decision support system

> ... a set of well integrated, user friendly, computer-based tools that combine data with various decision-making models ... to solve semi-structured and unstructured problems.
>
> (Gupta 1996: 288)

The decision support system (DSS) is generally made up of the database management system and models.

DATABASE MANAGEMENT SYSTEMS

The database management system (DBMS) represents a significant development in the application of database technology. Essentially the database can be described as an integrated repository of related data. The database management system acts as the interface between the application and the database itself.

The DBMS provides access to data. It should also allow the merger of data from different sources. The DSS summarises the data within the organisational databases and has separate extraction software, which will also store existing data in a required form. This is usually combined with other data, perhaps related to goals and is the beginning of the process that will structure and manage data.

Advantages of databases: There are a number of advantages to electronic databases. In the first instance, unlike simple paper based databases like the telephone directory there is no need necessarily to know a particular field within the record in order to extract information (surname in the case of the telephone directory). So, rather than being *field dependent*, electronic database can largely be *field independent*, allowing greater degrees of access to the information within the database. This impacts upon the complexity of the information that is being handled, making it far less complex and also enhances the flexibility of dissemination.

Relational databases: Relational databases such as Microsoft Access have been particularly significant here. These databases relate data in one 'table' to data in another 'table' thereby facilitating the sharing of data through the sharing of common attributes, the *key field*. This might be where different departments might hold customer or supplier details. These could be shared rather than each holding a separate file of the same details.

MODELS

Models are essentially a representation of reality. They can be:

Predictive: These are used for predicting the future and used for planning. One of the most famous models is Newton's model of the laws of motion. If you drop an object from a height, its velocity at any moment can be represented as:

velocity of a dropped object (v) = acceleration due to gravity (g) $\times$ time (t)

Normative: These are optimising models which aim to suggest the best action to be taken in a given situation.

Descriptive: Descriptive models should provide a deeper understanding of the situation through that description – this model uses the classic input–process–output concepts, along with systems boundary and environment. For example, data flow diagrams are descriptive models.

Problem oriented: These allow the user to change the definition of one or more of the variables in a model.

'What would be the effects on profit if we were subjected to a 3 per cent material cost rise?'

Within this particular scenario you would need a model of the company's profit making and how the different variables impact upon it in order to be able to estimate a rise in material costs.

... material cost are ...?
...wage costs are...?
... other costs...?

This allows the user to find the value of a variable in order to achieve a certain goal:

... in order to increase profit over the next financial years we might:
increase productivity by...
reduce staff costs by...

The *database* and the *model* make up the DSS. The DSS supports choice in decision making by organising information and modelling outcomes. In order for these systems to be effective they follow an activities model with the following elements:

Intelligence: Looking for the areas where decisions need to be made – problem identification.
Design: Consider approaches and possible alternatives.
Choice: Select course of action.
Implementation: Monitoring success and considering improvement.

In order to successfully exploit the DSS, therefore, the manager would need to have some knowledge of models and be confident and able to exploit the computer interface. Perhaps more than both of these there would be a need for time in terms of becoming able to fully exploit this system. At this level of management it is often seen that time is not readily available to the manager who must often make decisions quickly.

Executive information systems

Executive information systems (EIS) attempt to address some of the difficulties in terms of time and in particular in terms of the way managers at strategic levels operate. The user friendliness of the system, through such things as graphical interfaces and so on, assists in making the system more accessible to the strategic manager.

 Pause for thought – Deep Blue

On 10 February 1996 a chess playing computer, Deep Blue, defeated the chess grandmaster Garry Kasparov. In a re-match in 1997 Deep Blue defeated him more comprehensively. Chess is a highly structured activity with explicit rules for each of the pieces and with a very clear goal – checkmate. Deep Blue was able to embed these rules and, using its power as a processor, to calculate the 'best' move to make in relation to the goal.

> Deep Blue, as a DSS, is able to provide and process information about the next move, based on the game that is currently being played. An EIS will also include a profile of the specific opponent, psychological data, based on time of day and so on and a history of previous meetings. An EIS will summarise complex data and customise it in a form that supports and facilitates easy and quick use.

Where there are defined goals and definable rules then there is an expectation that these systems will be able to 'take' increasingly complex decisions. Think about, for example, a lawyer drawing on case law or a car mechanic looking to identify the problem with a car. Each of these has a definable goal and a set of rules to follow, precedence in the case of the lawyer and the working of the internal combustion engine in the case of the car mechanic.

It is often quite difficult to identify an organisational or professional role that cannot define a goal and be said to follow explicit rules. Does this mean that there can be a reasonable expectation all organisational decisions can or will be taken by our KBIS?

Executive information systems are criticised because they are incompatible with management styles and do not accommodate 'soft' information. Is this justified?

Some of the characteristics of the information need of strategic mangers might be defined in the following way:

- timely and in an appropriate form;
- accommodate personal preference;
- allow the manager to locate the information behind the information and the data behind the information;
- allow for casting around;
- provide access to a wide range of internal data;
- tailoring and customising are important functions – again to meet individual preferences.

Expert systems

Expert systems have been described as another computer program that claims to draw on the knowledge of an expert, that is captured by the KBIS in order to solve problems, make decisions or address issues that normally require human expertise. Often known as knowledge-based expert systems they again attempt to represent knowledge as data or rules within the computer.

An example of the 'IF–THEN' approach might be as follows:

> 'Red sky at night shepherd's delight, red sky in the morning, shepherd's warning.'
>
> IF–THEN
> IF red in morning THEN watch out
> IF red at night THEN all's well
>
> Qualifiers, or the relevant questions, are:
>
> . . . what time of day is it?
> . . . what colour is the sky?

Based on these questions the expert system would give advice – also called *choices*. To the shepherd this might be to prepare for poor weather or not.

The *knowledge-base* comes from experts, extracted by interview for the system. They have been used in medicine, engineering, law etc. and have involved diagnosis, design and interpretation. For example:

> IF the infection is primary bacteremia AND the site of the culture is one of the sterile sites AND the suspected portal of entry is the gastrointestinal tract THEN there is suggestive evidence (0.7) that the infection is bacteroid.

In this specific example the knowledge being drawn on relates to the *content knowledge* of a medical professional. This is the knowledge that they have acquired through both study at medical school and through experience. As well as content knowledge, there is also *context knowledge* that is based more upon the knowledge that comes from being able to identify 'how things are done around here'. This can be how to 'work the system' in order to get something done more effectively and can relate to the social relationships that are significant or important at any particular time or in relation to a specific issue or problem.

Social networks play a significant part in the identification and application of context knowledge, perhaps based on the old saying, 'not what you know but who you know'. Organisations can be aligned with the relationships that make them up between departments, groups, stakeholders and individuals.

> Norms of cooperation can establish a strong foundation for the creation of knowledge. This is because such norms influence social processes by opening up access to individuals for the exchange of knowledge and ensuring the motivation to engage in such an exchange.
>
> (Chua 2002: 377)

Through a shared language and through such techniques as storytelling, individuals, groups and communities share their experiences and their knowledge. However, understanding these relationships, the structures they form and the cultural practices they embed in organisations can be viewed as a key element in relation to the KBIS, where we are asking where knowledge resides in our organisation.

Social network analysis

Social network analysis (SNA), as a mapping technique, has offered some insight into how we might practically go about identifying this knowledge resource. The aim here is to identify relationships and how these flow within any given organisation. Orgnet (2015) specialises in the application of SNA, via their SNA software *inFlow* (see Figure 10.1).

Figure 10.1 illustrates how this particular piece of software will present social networks and it will allow for different levels of analysis that will indicate the consequences of shifts or changes in the different relationships being represented.

The early work in this area focused on the recognition of social dynamics as discernible phenomena, in other words there are patterns to the ways in which we socially interact with one another and we can discover these patterns and work with these patterns. This led to the development and presentation of the 'sociometric star' which highlighted an

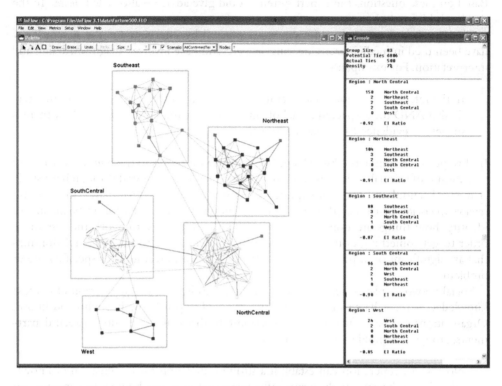

Figure 10.1 inFlow social network analysis diagram

individual's centrality within a social configuration. Literally the 'star' held a position of some authority, they were:

> ... the recipient of numerous and frequent choices from others, and who, therefore, held a position of great popularity and leadership.

> (Scott 2000: 10)

Social identity and social group formation, therefore, become significant elements in relation to organisational behaviour. The individual is not submerged by this focus on the social, it is not a question of the group over the individual, rather it is more accepting of the social 'field' within which the individual operates.

Through the generation of graphs organisational relationships can be presented and analysed. *Adjacency, neighbourhood* and *degree*, along with *path, length* and *distance* are the key criteria relating to the points that make up any *relationship graph*. Essentially, the actors or individuals are the points and lines used to connect two points to represent that they are adjacent. All the points represent a neighbourhood and the degree is the number of connections that one point will have within any neighbourhood (degree can be read therefore as degree of connection). The path forms the connection (the line on the graph between two points) and its length refers to the number of lines that make it up. Where a point passes through another point to a third point then there is more than one path present and the length is, therefore, valued as 2. The distance is the length of the shortest path that connects two points.

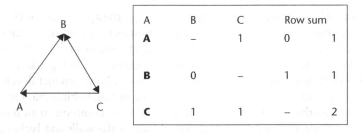

	A	B	C	Row sum
A	–	1	0	1
B	0	–	1	1
C	1	1	–	2

Figure 10.2 Directed graph and matrix
Source: Scott, 2000: 67.

The other basic element in the development of these relationship graphs is the notion of direction. Obviously if we are concerned with relationships then we do need to identify if it is going from A to B or B to A or both, and illustrate the number of lines that are directed towards it and the number of lines radiating from it. Figure 10.2 illustrates this.

What we are beginning to put together here is a graphic representation of relationships within the organisation (this is represented in Figure 10.2 as column and row sums):

Indegree – the number of lines that are directed to a particular point and
Outdegree – the number of lines that emanate from a particular point.

Another key measurement claim of SNA relates to the notion of *centrality*. The ability to assess the central position of individuals within social networks is clearly an important part of the knowledge mapping process.

> It is important to recognize that the measurement of local centrality does not involve the idea that there will be any unique 'central' point in the network.
>
> (Scott 2000: 84)

Any claim to centrality in relation to organisational relationships will be partial. No individual or group can claim or hope to be regarded as the real 'centre' of the organisation and these relationships are constantly changing and fluid. The purpose of SNA and the production of the type of detailed relationship graphs is simply to give a snapshot or an insight into how relationships are forming. They will highlight for us a richer view of the type of structures within the organisation that relate more closely to the knowledge and to learning readiness. Where, for example, we have well-established relationships or where we can clearly identify isolated individuals then we have identified areas where we need to focus some attention in order to discover why this might be happening.

Social network analysis might be criticised as too prescriptive and tends to present a two-dimensional view of relationships. Social network analysis might lack depth, but in attempting to include notions such as centrality or inclusiveness it is developing more depth and as a supporting tool it does offer a significant view of the organisation and in particular the content knowledge of that organisation.

Systems development life cycle (SDLC)

Both context and content knowledge can be supported through the application of IS. It is, therefore, important to ensure that the knowledge-based information system develops in a way that ensures that it is adequately assessed and evaluated. The use of a life-cycle model ensures that at each stage of development the appropriate questions are being asked.

The notion of a life cycle is not unique to information systems. New product development, for example, uses a similar pattern of development. The notion behind them is that in any construction process the stages within construction will be common to all buildings. This might be the preparation of the foundations, building the walls and lastly putting on the roof. The buildings themselves will look quite different but the stages will be the same. This is why there are different systems methodologies – they are more to do with building a particular type of system – while SDLC is an outline of the common process.

Feasibility: This is the stage at which the systems analyst, or the team of systems analysts, attempts to quantify the project and estimate what it will take to carry out the process as a whole. The systems analyst might be looking at existing hardware and software or at individual attitudes to a new system. A technique that is used at this stage is the rich picture, which is simply a diagrammatic representation of both attitudes and information stores, possible areas of conflict and so on. Software is now available to help individuals create these diagrams.

Systems investigation: This essentially asks, what is the current system? This will attempt to identify the way in which the organisation is exploiting its information resource. What relevant practices are in place, how are we using the information asset and what type of barriers are currently impacting upon the sharing of organisational knowledge?

Both feasibility and investigation stages are introspective, largely concerned with identifying the nature of current practice. They will be an opportunity for key individuals to reflect on what they do, without at this stage asking why.

Systems analysis – This begins the process of analysing how effective the current system is. It will look at data and how they are created, received, used and moved, and ultimately their relationship with other sources of data. It will consider the processes performed on data to make them useful (this might be the creation of management reports). Where is the information stored – in a filing cabinet, on a database or in someone's drawer? How is the information stored – in a file structure within a database or simply collected in a filing cabinet or drawer in no particular order? In carrying this out it will also be necessary to estimate the attitude to data and how individual users perceive their use of information. Finally, the relationships within the organisation to the use of information as a resource and how existing systems cooperate or not as the case may be.

Systems design – Having considered the current system with the first few stages of the life cycle, it is then necessary to begin the process of creating a more effective and efficient system. The system design stage will aim to provide the organisation with a logical model of the data and processes within the current system.

Implementation – The purpose here is to make recommendations on how to develop the existing systems in order to meet the specified objectives. It will be considering hardware and software, file and database specifications, programme specifications and procedure.

Review and maintenance – The system is now built; what remains is the need to test the system prior to implementation. This will include the training of staff and the installation of the equipment.

The life cycle will identify and consider key questions for the organisation. These questions are around learning and how we can understand learning as it takes place within the organisation. Training, within this context, does not simply become central, but is replaced by an engagement with a process of continuous learning, where management priorities are focused on understanding and encouraging learner motivation and where the manager's own responsibilities are more explicitly focused on these learning processes and the creation and integration of this into the policy statements of the organisation.

Increasingly, this requires the manager to consider the technological infrastructure. The network, for example, will enhance collaborative working and the creation of valuable social capital and ultimately will help to assess the preparedness of the organisation to move from the creation of shared databases to the implementation of communities of practice (CoP). The roles of IS and of information and communication technologies (ICT) are central to the management of knowledge and, therefore, to the embedding of learning as an organisational activity.

Not least ICT will help *to create the knowledge-base* and the various repositories of knowledge upon which this will be based. The principles of knowledge organisation will be used to ensure that these repositories are comprehensive and searchable. Individuals need to be able to find information when they need it and, importantly, they need to be willing for their information to form part of this knowledge-base. Information and communication technologies will provide the technical structure to support the embedding of discrete or explicit knowledge assets, but they cannot necessarily address the issue of willingness to share. Where an organisation places an emphasis upon the knowledge-base as a repository of explicit knowledge and that all knowledge can be made explicit then it will fail to appreciate the function of learning within the organisation.

This latter element emphasises the use of ICT in enhancing and supporting the communication and collaboration within an organisation.

> Research suggests that many ICT-enabled knowledge management initiatives have been unsuccessful, arguably because they focussed almost exclusively on technological issues and typically played down, if not completely ignored, social, cultural and political factors which have since been shown to be key in influencing the willingness of people to participate in knowledge management initiatives.
>
> (Hislop 2009: 226–7)

Rather than ICT being used to store, move and manipulate data and information, the challenge associated with the knowledge-based information system, or the application of ICT to OL is the extent to which these technologies can support collaboration. This is more than simply facilitating collaboration. Can ICT make collaboration more effective, do they help to build the relationship between the individual and the organisation and do they help to build the necessary trust that underpins this relationship?

Concluding remarks

In considering OL we must attempt to maintain a view of this discipline as a series of related but diverse questions. On the one hand we are interested in how we can use databases and networks to create an information infrastructure that is robust and adds real value to the organisation. Here we must concern ourselves with the functionality of technologies. On the other hand we also need to ask questions about how we create the knowledge that will feed this information system. This draws us towards individual engagement with the organisation itself and although this might present us with relatively straightforward questions about group working and team spirit, these in turn are underpinned by complex questions related to power dynamics that get to the heart of the organisation and its wider purpose within the socio-cultural and economic context within which it sits.

Our view, therefore, of OL is complex. Its origins, its goals and its purpose are increasingly seen as vital components for economic well-being, but the questions that have emerged go beyond this. We may well find ourselves dealing with the management of a technically based infrastructure with all of the practical organisational issues that this involves but unless we are able to at least recognise the wider implications of our potential actions then we cannot claim to be engaging with the questions inherent within OL. This is why we have spent some time, and will continue to do so, looking at the sociological implications of knowledge as an organisational asset.

Part 4

SPADES

Sustainable Pedagogy for Applying and Designing Experiential-learning cycleS

11 Introduction to the SPADES model

The SPADES model (see Table 11.1) seeks to present a coherent approach to the embedding of an OLP. It recognises the shift from a more traditional pedagogical model to one that is more fully based upon collaboration and the role of all who are engaged in learning having an equal contribution to make as both teacher and learner. Experience forms the basis of the content of these learning programmes, but it is also recognised that the process of collaboration itself makes a positive contribution to the application of this experience and ultimately the designing and sustaining of the experiential-learning cycles. As a continuous process there is an emphasis upon cycles, plural. As with the iterative and positive spiral associated with the SECI model, so SPADES too becomes a spiral learning from itself and able to sustain itself. A sustainable pedagogy for applying and designing experiential-learning cycles.

Planting

Planting requires the creation of the 'right' learning environments. This environment needs to meet the expectations of those engaged with learning. In an OL context where learning is a collaborative and social activity there is a primary need to ensure that the environment is able to reflect this. In more traditional pedagogical models there is an expectation that the delivery of content will be the responsibility of the tutor. In an OL context this will be a shared responsibility, with each member of the teaching and learning team being able to not only engage with material that is presented to them but also to be able to present material themselves. It cannot be assumed that all individuals being asked to participate in collaborative learning will necessarily have the required skills or capabilities. In creating an environment that is driven by the dialogues that allow us to share our learning, we are assuming that we have the capabilities to have meaningful discussion, that we can tell an engaging story of our experiences, but this is an assumption too far. To create an opportunity for there to be two-way discussion does not mean that there will be a discussion, let alone a meaningful one. The technical environment needs to reflect, not the strategic commitment to learning but the operational acceptance of its value. Without this, learning will not be sustainable and the virtuous cycle of learning from experience will not be achieved. This will be explored further in this model, but initially there is a need to be able to identify good practice in relation to the environment.

Nurturing

Nurturing requires the building of the relationships that will sustain the OLP. This will be the development of collaborative learning groups and consideration will be given to

Table 11.1 The SPADES model

Element	Content
Planting: Providing the right environment	**The technical perspective:** e-learning course design **The cultural perspective:** Critical discourse analysis
Nurturing: Ensuring early stage development	**Socialisation: onboarding storytelling** After action review (AAR)
Growing: Building on good practice	**Mentoring scenario planning**
Propagating: Spreading the message	**Communities of practice (CoP) Reflection**

the development of groups and group working within organisations with a particular emphasis on where and how this might ultimately relate to the creation of CoP. The key to this and other models of social learning is an understanding of the collaborative nature of learning. Questions to be considered here are:

- What will support the development of effective group working?
- How will the purpose of the group be established?
- How should these groups be led?

Through the processes associated with socialisation, for example, onboarding, the collaborative group will help identify the value of the learning processes they are being expected to engage with. In many respects they will drive and determine the values that will underpin the working of these groups. In identifying these values they will begin to embed the skills that will be necessary for successful organisational learning. This will include the ability to tell stories and the value of doing so. As part of the nurturing element of the SPADES model the capabilities associated with storytelling are explicitly identified. It can be taken for granted that we all have a story to tell but not that we can all tell a story.

Growing

Growing looks to develop from the creation of the right environment and the nurturing of the collaborative basis for group working. In all learning groups the size of the group, the environment within which it is being asked to operate and the perceptions of the members in terms of where the group has come from, where it is currently situated and ultimately where is likely to be heading, will all have a bearing on how members of a group will understand their position within the group. The size of the group will impact upon its effectiveness with smaller groups being able to develop more cohesion more quickly but larger groups being more capable when it comes to key tasks such as brainstorming.

At the outset there needs to be a clear identification of two key dimensions:

- social dimension
- task dimension.

Groups can vary in relation to the overall balance that may exist between these two dimensions with less formal groups tending to focus more on the social dimension of the group where it is the interaction itself that is the key goal or purpose and where there is a clear expectation that the engagement with the group will be enjoyable. The task, for these less formal groups, might be a less defined consequence of the social interaction. Where the task is the focus, the emphasis on the social dimension is lessened and the output or outcome is more defined and precise. Mentoring and scenario planning express these two dimensions of group working. Often, it is the relationship that is formed during mentoring that outweighs the value of any explicit knowledge that might be externalised and this can be carried on as mentees themselves become mentors. They sustain a close connect that can transcend the organisation and can become a longer term professional connection. With scenario planning it is the ability to accept plurality and the embedded fluidity of the organisational environment that will drive imaginative and ultimately valuable 'views' of the possible future. Growing this across a broad base of the organisation is significant at this stage of the SPADES model.

Propagating

Propagating is the final element within the model and also the start of the process. The practices that sustain collaborative group learning are themselves reflected upon and identified as the next seeds become ready for planting – thus starting the whole process off again. With the CoP model there is perhaps something to be said about exactly where the balance might lie between social and task dimensions. On the one hand the model is underpinned by a sense of participation that is driven by a genuine enthusiasm for and enjoyment of the practice around which the CoP is formed. In professionalised workforces there is a higher expectation of there being a more 'personal' level of engagement with the discipline, an embedded passion for the discipline and where there is less of a disconnect between an individual's perception of work and life then again the expectation might be that there is an underlying motivation in relation to any engagement with the discipline.

The CoP model is therefore a tool that can be applied to a mature OLP. It is not a model that can be introduced at an early stage as the expectation of the value to be gained from the relationships with a CoP have not been sufficiently developed.

Wood Group examples

With the key elements within this model there is included a brief example from Wood Group PSN, based in Aberdeen, Scotland.

Company introduction

Wood Group is a leading international energy services company composed of three businesses – Wood Group PSN, Wood Group Kenny and Wood Group Mustang (www. woodgroup.com).

Wood Group PSN is a global oil and gas market leader in production facilities support, offering high integrity services that optimise the performance of facilities, maintain production, reduce operating costs, ensure asset integrity and extend the operating life of fields. Annual revenues are around US$3 billion and the company has over 30,000 personnel operating in more than 40 countries. The company was formed in April 2011 following the merger of Wood Group's Production Facilities business and Production Services Network (PSN).

Wood Group PSN's ambition is to be the best production services company to work for, the best production services company to work with, with a relentless focus on continuous improvement. To achieve this, it puts seven core values at the centre of what it does; these define who they are and how they work.

Wood Group's core values are:

1   safety and assurance
2   relationships
3   social responsibility
4   people
5   innovation
6   financial responsibility
7   integrity.

For Wood Group CEO Bob Keiller,

> Core Values are the DNA of our business – they're a global gold standard that guides our thinking, determines our behaviour, and allows us to adapt to local needs.
>
> Our ambition, stated in the introduction, is our destination and our journey to get there is started and progressed by our people. They bring our Core Values to life and that is why our **People Core Value** is in the middle of the others, at the heart of our business.
>
> Sustainable learning within our organisation is impossible without our people and their behaviours in terms of willingness to collaborate, learn, generate ideas, and challenge established working practices to find more efficient optimal solutions. Every person in the organisation owns and engages with learning, with the CEO and his direct reports having specific responsibilities to ensure that collaborative activities are stimulated and delivered in their teams. This encompasses all teams in all locations.

12 Planting an experiential-learning community

Introduction

To plant an experiential-learning cycle the technical environment needs to sit within a cultural context that will use the functionality of the technical environment in accordance with the principles associated with the OLP. Here the need to identify and to 'work with' the dominant discourse within the organisation is crucial and the environment of the OLP will be a blending of these technical and cultural elements. An emphasis on the technical environment that undervalues the cultural dimension will result in the underutilisation of the functionality of the technologies being applied. This is not the same as the absence of the use of these technologies and indeed in many instances there may be statistics to illustrate a great deal of use. However, this might reflect an organisational imperative to 'produce results' or a misplaced appreciation of the indicators of value.

The 'right' environment is one that facilitates the genuine engagement of individuals associated with collaborative learning. It will reflect the ethical nature of this engagement and look to challenge those elements that impose themselves upon and actively impede this learning.

Providing the right environment

Learning management systems (LMS) or virtual learning environments (VLE) provide the technical environment within which collaborative learning can take place. Good practice in relation to course design and a thorough knowledge of the functionality of these systems is necessary to ensure the delivery of effective learning.

The technical environment

There are many technical products to choose from when looking to develop the OL environment. This might be a learning management system such as Moodle (www.moodle. org) or Blackboard (www.blackboard.com), two of the most popular learning environments that are used worldwide by numerous educational institutions to support the delivery of their courses. They aim to be complete environments that will control and manage all of the functions associated with learning. This will include the delivery of content, the registration of learners, the tracking of their performance and so on. There are many other systems that provide comprehensive learning environments, such as Litmos (www.litmos. com) which has proved popular with HR professionals. The core features of Litmos are:

- course builder
- assessment and quizzes

- survey and feedback
- checklists and tasks
- course library
- reports and dashboards
- instructional led training
- eCommerce
- gamification
- messaging
- certification
- corporate compliance
- learning paths.

As well as these complete environments there are other tools that can be used to support specific functions. The key issue here is to be aware of the range of tools and to be in a position to make an informed decision as to which tool will support which need. This level of *digital literacy* is increasingly significant for OL practitioners. Here the use of social media is important and individuals within organisations often bring to that organisation the 'connectedness' that will ultimately enhance their performance. Some reluctance by organisations to embrace or even allow the use of social media in the workplace can inhibit this. However, the uncritical acceptance of the use of social media can also be detrimental.

The embedding of digital literacy becomes a key component part of the OLP and can be recognised as a core capability. All of these capabilities need to be assessed in terms of the extent to which they are embedded within the individuals who make up the organisation. Here a form of auditing is required.

The *learning skills assessment* (see Figure 12.1) can be used to identify the levels of competence that individuals might have in relation to key aspects of learning. Similarly, an assessment of digital literacy skills will look to identify the level of competence in relation to:

- The use of personal computers and mobile devices.
- The use of key software packages and apps, such as the Microsoft suite, for word processing, spreadsheets or databases.
- Searching strategies on the Internet.
- Using social networks to support professional practice.

In order to enhance these skills there is a further need to keep up-to-speed with the development of different software packages and apps and increasingly individuals need to create strategies to ensure that they are able to maintain professional networks. This will include the use of key social media such as Facebook and Twitter.

- Who is being followed?
- What groups or individuals will inform a specific area of expertise?
- What software or apps will be useful to support the development of the learning environment?

In this rapidly changing and adapting environment it requires a conscious strategy on the part of both groups and individuals to maintain the currency of their knowledge.

LEARNING SKILLS ASSESSMENT

Rate your competence in the skill areas in this proforma using the following rating scale (tick as appropriate):

A   Expert with a high degree of skill and/or comprehensive knowledge (fully competent)
B   Proficient in the knowledge or skill and able to show others how to use it (high level of competency)
C   Familiar with and able to use the knowledge or skill (some competency)
D   Some awareness but not sufficiently competent to use it (awareness but limited competency)
E   No current knowledge or skill (no awareness or current competency)
F   No interest in acquiring the skill or competency

	A	B	C	D	E	F
ORGANISATION OF LEARNING						
I have strategies to help me to plan and manage my time						
I am able to effectively prioritise my tasks and activities						
I am able to work to deadlines						
I am aware of what makes my learning more effective (e.g. place to study, time to study etc)						
INFORMATION SEEKING SKILLS						
I am able to find a specific book or journal in the library using the on-line catalogue						
I am able to use a variety of different sources to find information (e.g. journals, books, electronic resources)						
I am able to access and search electronic resources (on-line databases, electronic journals, CD-ROMs)						
I am able to use search gateways on the Internet to find information						
I am able to evaluate the information I find						

Figure 12.1 Learning skills assessment

Note: This figure is derived from an internal RGU document.

 Pause for thought – keeping up-to-speed

Consider Jane Hart's website Directory of Learning and Performance Tools and Services (C4LPT, 2015)

This site compiles a list of tools under key headings:

Places to learn online
Social and collaboration platforms
Other collaboration and sharing tools

Communication tools
Web meeting and conferencing tools
Instructional tools
Document, presentation and spreadsheet tools
Blogging, web and wiki tools
Image tools
Audio tools
Video tools
Personal productivity tools
Browsers, players and readers

There is also a combined list of the Top 100 tools (http://c4lpt.co.uk/directory/top-100-tools/)

Digital literacy is a key element of any OLP and needs to be embedded in practice in order to ensure that the necessary level of engagement is maintained and informed. It will underpin the design of the learning environment and determine the level of functionality. The design of the environment needs to be regarded as a collaborative task, drawing on the expertise of web designers, but crucially supported by the users of this environment who are capable of informing the design process and linking design features to the pedagogical functions.

E-learning course design

A systemic approach should be adopted for the planning and design of an OLP. There needs to be a view of how the proposed development will relate to both its *environment* and in terms of the organisational *boundary* within which it sits. Here key questions need to be considered in relation to the nature and level of support that can be expected. This will range from the operational to the strategic level. For example, what resources already exist and what is the perception of the 'will' to see this development succeed? Is there a need to enhance both of these and acquire the necessary software, and will some preliminary dialogue be required to ensure that there is the necessary buy-in from the senior staff? Without a good understanding of what you have or need to acquire and a clear appreciation of the level of support across the organisation the attempt to develop the OLP will be undermined.

GOOD PRACTICE IN WEB DESIGN FOR OL

Creating a successful web page is not entirely divorced from the principles associated with the creation of a successful printed journal or text. There is a need to ensure that:

- The web page identifies the legitimacy of the 'speaker'. Who is speaking and is it clear that they have some authority or legitimacy to speak about the topic under consideration?
- It is clear from the title or heading, what the document is about.

- There is an explicit mechanism to ensure that the content being presented is timely and accurate.
- There is a route back to the origins or the 'home page' of the document that might have been located within a complex site.

For any website it is crucial for the user to be able to meaningfully navigate within the site. This highlights a crucial difference between websites and traditionally published documents, the enhanced ability to move through the site in a non-linear fashion. Essentially, this is the function of hyperlinks and the response to this needs to be a careful consideration of how to navigate within a site. The aids to navigation need to be made explicit.

Button bars are used to provide a consistent and simple mechanism for navigating within a website. This also highlights the need to ensure that any site maintains a high level of consistency, in relation to how information is presented. The use of *tabbed navigation* is a popular technique that mirrors tab pages in a paper ring binder. By clicking on a tab the content appears to be brought to the front. This aligns itself with the principle that good navigation of a site should appear to be invisible.

Although no real conventions have been set that will explicitly identify best practice in relation to navigation features, the principle of simplicity and a convention through practice has seen a particular style emerging. This is often a residual reflection of past practices where printed documents or libraries are used as the familiar model for information presentation. More practically the stability of a site, its accessibility under the World Wide Web Consortium (W3C) standards and the provision or the opportunity to engage with the users, are key design features.

> Don't get so lost in the novelty of Web pages that basic standards of editorial and graphic design are tossed aside.
>
> (Lynch and Horton 2001: 18)

To begin to organise information on the web there is an initial need to ensure that there is a good understanding of the needs of the potential user of the site. Based on this, information needs to be presented in the most useful and accessible way. This will require the creation of an explicit structure for the information that will be arranged in a hierarchical fashion designed to maximise use. In the first instance the presentation of small amounts of information has been recognised as the most effective way to ensure engagement. This is based on the belief that on average individuals will only hold five or six discrete parcels of information at any one time. Based on this, the information within a site needs to move logically from general to specific. This developing structure is often referred to as the architecture of the site and its success will depend upon how well this architecture has captured the way in which the users of the site will expect to find and locate information. Are the relationships between discrete parcels of information what would be expected and ultimately are users able to move through the site with ease and efficiency?

According to Lynch and Horton (2001) there are three structures that can be used to present information on the web:

- *Sequences*
  The chronological progression of a discrete body of information, arranged alphabetically (similar to an index in a text) or following a logical progress from general to

specific provides a clear path to the user and is often applied in relation to training and other educational content delivery.

- *Hierarchies*
  More complex bodies of information can be presented in hierarchical structures and these are a familiar structure for those operating within an organisational context. The organisation itself is often structured in this way.
- *Webs*
  The presentation of information in a web-like structure reflects the nature of the Web itself and allows individuals to engage with the material in a free and open fashion. However, in doing so it inevitably loses the structures associated with *sequences* and *hierarchies* and is therefore a more challenging structure to apply.

However the website is structured the individual sections and sub-sections that make it up need to be useful for the potential user. Creating a sitemap can help when developing a site to see how each of the sections relate to one another. The input of those using the site is important and this can be as simple as asking a small group of users to sort index cards in a way that they find to be logical and helpful.

Elements of good design for web pages include:

- Using *thirds* which suggest that dividing a page into thirds looks more harmonious.
- Limiting the use of centred text.
- 'Above the fold' – ensuring that what is seen first is the most significant detail.
- Consistent use of text size, the bigger the text the more significant the message.
- Use of black text on white background for core content as it provides the most contrast.

Basic design features should support the overall aims of the OLP and the elements within it need to be presented in a logical and engaging way. The technical environment will draw on a range of tools that will be used to support the aims. These tools need to be configured and presented in a way that will support key elements of the OLP. In the following box is a consideration of a key tool.

Focus on Moodle

Moodle is a virtual learning environment (VLE) that is popular with higher education institutions throughout the world. It is used to deliver content to students and to engage with these students in a positive learning experience. It is a technical learning environment employing a range of techniques which are embedded within its functionality to add value to the student experience of learning. Similar tools are used throughout the HE sector elsewhere to deliver training and other L&D related activities. Jane Hart's directory, shown previously, illustrates the range of tools that are available and they are constantly being assessed and evaluated through practice and subsequently redeveloped to meet the ever-changing perception of needs or priorities. At the time of writing Moodle was at number 12 in the top 100 tools for learning, 2014.

Moodle is a learning platform designed to provide educators, administrators and learners with a **single robust, secure and integrated system** to create

personalised learning environments. You can download the software onto your own web server or ask one of our knowledgeable Moodle Partners to assist you.
(Moodle, 2015)

Moodle looks to align itself with a social constructionist pedagogy which aims to build on social dynamics to drive learning within a collaborative environment. The functionality of Moodle, the use of the group working function, is illustrated next (see Figure 12.2).

Groups

Within modules, Moodle has the functionality to allow you to assign students into groups. Once this is done, the groups feature can then be applied to any of the Moodle activities. For example, if you set up a forum and choose to apply 'separate groups' to it, then the members of a particular group in the forum can communicate only with each other. As another example, if you set up a chat activity and apply 'separate groups' to it then members of a group will only be able to see other members of their own group in the chat room and will only be able to chat to them. The tutor or facilitator will be able to see all the contributions of all members of all groups in each activity.

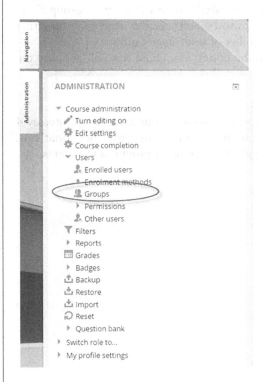

Figure 12.2 Moodle groups

Note: Drawn with permission from Robert Gordon University user guide.

Groupings is a feature new to Moodle 2. A grouping is a set of groups. Using groupings you can arrange to have different sets of groups collaborating and communicating for each different activity in your study area.

Setting up groups: To access the tool to set up your groups go to the study area and then click on:

- settings tab
- course administration
- users
- groups.

You will then see a page with two boxes, one titled *Groups* and the other *Members of* (see Figure 12.3). You now have two options to consider. If you do not mind which students are allocated into a group together, then you can let Moodle automatically allocate them into groups for you. If you have already decided the memberships of collaboration teams, then you can manually set up the groups.

Auto-create groups: If you wish Moodle to auto-create your groups, click on the *Auto-create* button (Figure 12.4).

General naming scheme: This uses the @ and # symbols. If you type 'Group@' in this field, then the groups generated will be called 'Group A', 'Group B', 'Group C' etc. If you type 'Group#' in this field, the groups will be called 'Group 1', 'Group 2', 'Group 3' etc.

Auto-create based on: Allows the groups to be auto-created depending on either number of groups you want, or the number of students per group.

Group/member count: Depending on the option you chose this will populate the groups.

For example:

- *Number of groups* – If you know you want to split your students up into, say 4 groups, then choose this option and put 4 in the 'Group/member count' box. If you have 24 students they will get allocated into 4 groups of 6 students.

Figure 12.3 Moodle group membership

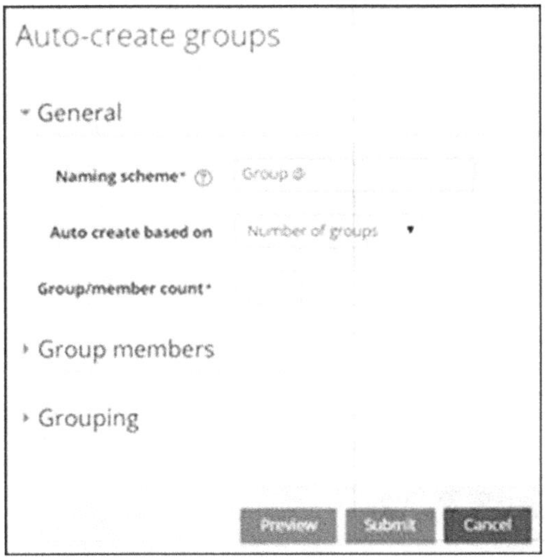

Figure 12.4 Moodle auto-create groups

- *Members per group* – If, instead, you are thinking in terms of the size of the groups and you would like to have 8 students per group then choose this option and put 8 in the 'Group/member count' box. If you have 24 students, this setting will result in 3 groups being set up, each containing 8 students.

Group members: Select members with role If you choose *All* here, then everyone who is in the module (including tutors and non-editing tutors etc.) will be allocated into a group. It is probably best to choose *Student* here, thereby sorting the students into groups. Once the groups are set up, you will be able to make amendments and add tutors and non-editing tutors (see Figure 12.5).

Allocate members You can have Moodle allocate the members, randomly or alphabetically by first or second name.

Present last small group When selected, Moodle will allocate additional members to an existing group rather than create a new group with few members.

Ignore users in group This should be ticked if you only want to select group members for users who are not already in a group.

Grouping: Grouping of auto-created groups You can use this tool to place your groups into groupings. A grouping is an aggregate of groups. You can apply different groupings to different activities in your study area. If you already have some groupings set up in your study area, you can choose the one you want from the drop-down list. Or you can create a new one by choosing *New grouping* in the drop-down list and give it a title in the *Grouping name* field. If you don't want your new groups to be in a Grouping, choose *No grouping* in the drop-down list (see Figure 12.6).

Applying groups to activities When you set up any activity on Moodle, whether it is a forum, chat, database or choice, you are asked to select a *Group mode* for the activity.

Figure 12.5 Moodle group members

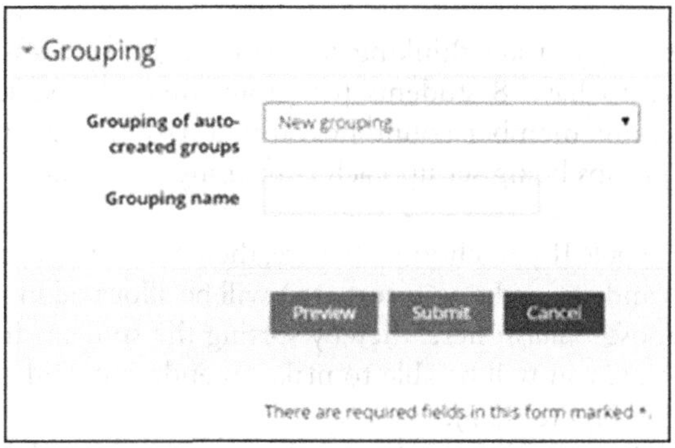

Figure 12.6 Auto-created groupings

The choices are:

- *No groups* – in this case you have decided that you want everybody in the module to be able to participate in this activity as part of one big community.
- *Separate groups* – in this case each group member can only see and respond to the contributions of the other members of their own group.
- *Visible groups* – in this case each group works in their own group, but can also see what the other groups are doing, though they cannot take part.

Example of applying groups to a forum activity

When you set up a discussion forum the *Common module settings* are the last thing you have to consider (see Figure 12.7). In the *Group mode* drop-down list you can opt whether or not to apply your groups to the forum.

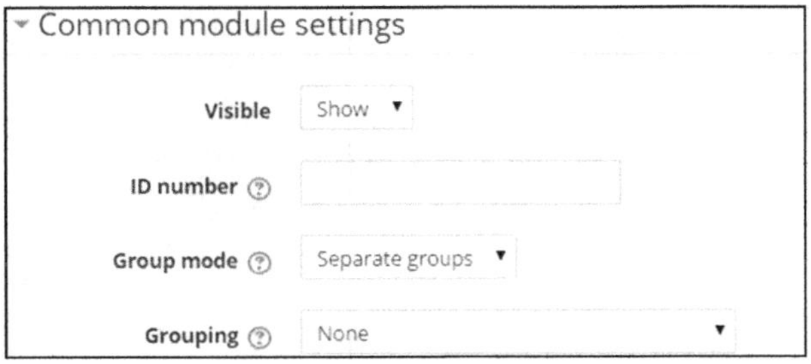

Figure 12.7 Forum activity for groups

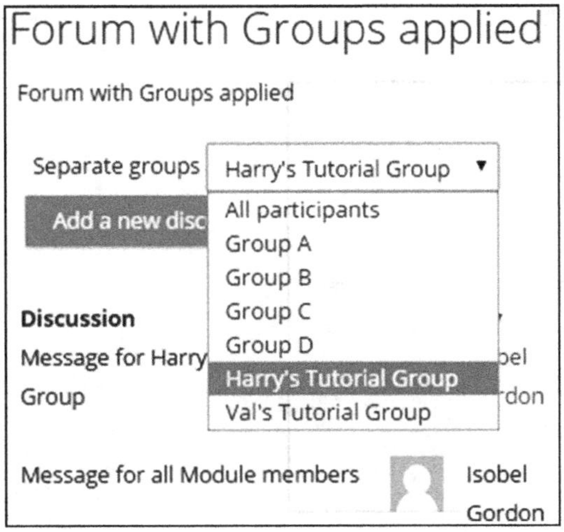

Figure 12.8 List of forum groups

If you choose *Separate groups* then you will be able to direct your postings to the students in separate groups and they will be able to communicate and collaborate with each other, within their group.

Now when you go into the discussion forum you'll see text in the top left-hand corner saying that *Separate groups* are applied. In the drop-down list beside this text, you'll see a list of all the groups in your study area (see Figure 12.8).

If you want to post a message to the students in one of the groups, e.g. *Harry's Tutorial Group*, then select that group from the drop-down list, then click *Add a new discussion topic*.

Once the posting is made you can see from the entry in the *Group* column that it was made to *Harry's Tutorial Group* (Figure 12.9).

Your new posting will only be seen by the students in *Harry's Tutorial Group*, and only *Harry's Tutorial Group* will receive the email (if subscriptions have been allowed).

If you select *All participants* from the drop-down list you can see all the postings in the forum regardless of the group.

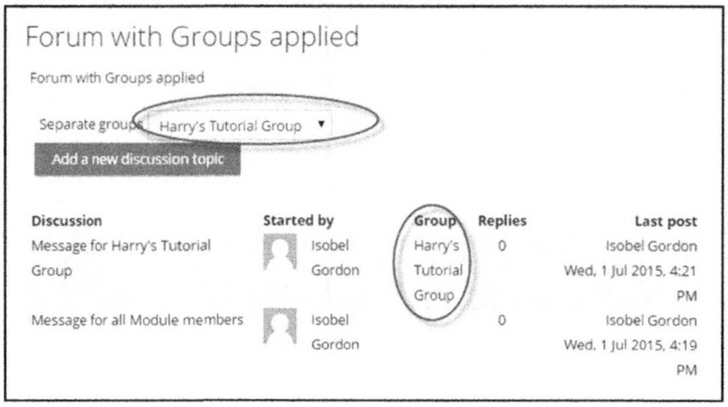

Figure 12.9 Posting a message to a group

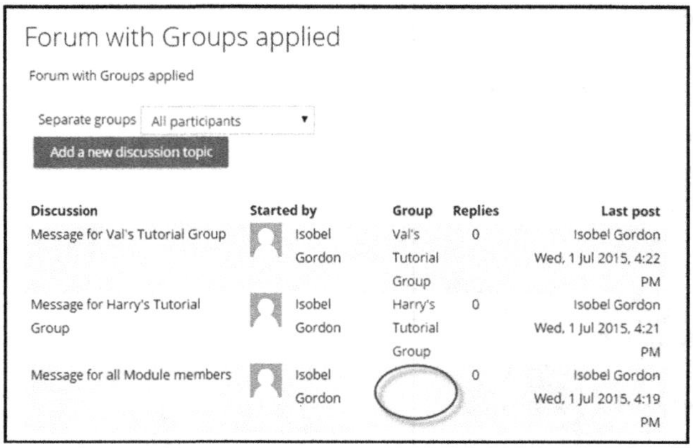

Figure 12.10 Group postings

In Figure 12.10 you can see from the entries in the *Group* column, that there is also a posting made to *Val's Tutorial Group*.

The reason both discussions are visible here is because *All participants* was selected from the drop-down list after each posting was made. If you select one of the groups from the drop-down list, you will only be able to see the postings for that group. You as a tutor are able to make this choice and are able to see and take part in each group. Students are unable to do this.

Please note that there is also a posting in Figure 12.10 which doesn't have a group in the *Group* column. This posting was made to *All participants*.

NOTE: Take care – if a posting is made to *All participants*, all the students can see the posting, but none of them can reply. They don't have the 'Reply' link to click in the posting. This is because the posting wasn't made to their group.

NOTE:

- If *Separate groups* has been applied to the forum, then the students will see only the postings that belong to their group and they can reply to them and start new discussions.

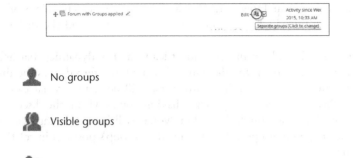

👤 No groups

👥 Visible groups

👥 Separate groups

Figure 12.11 Group forum

- If *Visible groups* has been applied, then the students also have a drop-down list and are able to choose whether or not to view the discussions of the other group(s). However, they are unable to respond in any way. They cannot reply to the other group's postings or start a new discussion for them.

In the module, when editing is switched on, the icons shown in Figure 12.11 are visible beside the forum (and every other activity that has been set up):
If you click on these icons, the activity toggles between each of the group types.

NOTE: You are able, at any time, to change how groups are applied to the forum. For example, you can start the activity off as separate group work and then after a couple of weeks or so update your forum either to make the groups visible to each other, or to open up the forum completely.

NOTE: If you have groups selected and you make a posting to *All participants*, please note that everyone will receive the posting, but none of your students will be able to reply to it because it was not posted to their own group. This is a common pitfall! If you want to send a message to all your groups, to which everyone can reply, you'll have to make a posting to each individual group.

This ability to configure and manipulate group working is just one of the many features of tools such as Moodle and other learning management systems. OLP are dependent upon the appropriate use of this functionality to support the development of learning within the organisation. The ability to configure Moodle or any other VLE to support group working does not necessarily mean that these groups will function as intended or hoped. The functionality of the technical environment is just one crucial element of this part of the experiential-learning cycle. The cultural environment will more directly relate to the engagement with this technical environment and together they will both determine the success or otherwise of the planting of the OLP.

The cultural environment

Communication and dialogue are at the heart of any OLP and where we might use the technical environment to facilitate this dialogue what it does not do is determine the content of the dialogue. From an OL perspective this dialogue should be meaningful and ultimately useful for the organisation. However, what we say and what can be said is often a product of the context within which it is said. Change the context and the dialogue changes.

Given this it is necessary to be able to understand, at least, the key dynamics that help to determine what is said or what forms the dialogue. This is often referred to as the discourse within an organisation and the dominant discourse will determine what can be said. Being dominant in this respect essentially means having power within the discourse and part of this is the 'voice' that one might have. This 'voice' will have differing degrees of legitimacy or authority depending upon the individual or group's position in relation to this dominant discourse.

Embedded within the cultural environment will be the elements of the dominant discourse and this, as much as the technical environment, needs to be aligned with the OLP. As well as digital literacy there is a need to be able to identify and analyse this discourse.

Critical discourse analysis

Discourse analysis (Fairclough, 2003; Gee, 2005; Van Dijk, 2011), as it relates to organisations (Fairhurst and Putnam, 2006) concerns itself with both the macro and micro level. At the macro level, discourse is presented with a capital 'D' – Discourse. This Discourse forms and presents the dominant characteristics that will drive the functioning of the organisation as a social entity. At the micro level, discourse is presented with a small 'd' – discourse. This discourse concerns itself with the way in which everyday interaction and communication forms itself into the process by which meaning is established and sustained. What drives Discourse/discourse is either the actions of the individual members or the embedded structures or a combination of both. It is through the various discursive forms that meaning is established and the legitimacy of individual or collective voices will be determined. Organisational learning is embedded in these discursive forms. Our ability to identify them, to understand them and to work with them, therefore, forms the basis of any OLP.

When we operate within organisations we make assumptions about individuals. This is often based on the key external features. For example, academic qualifications append letters after a name and externalise the level of education gained by that individual. Similarly, completing a doctorate or PhD will add letters before a name enhancing this position in relation to level of education gained and so on. Within the academic community and beyond these are recognised, largely, as valid indicators and will confer status and legitimacy, especially from within the academic community. All organisations can be regarded as communities formed around specific disciplines, be that engineering, nursing, legal practice and so on. A position within an explicit organisational structure will also confer status and legitimacy and this manifests itself in the authority an individual can command in relevant contexts.

Individual characteristics can be coupled with these more socially acquired characteristics to further enhance the legitimacy of an individual voice. Gender, race and age may also play a part here, if only in the negative acceptance of embedded prejudices. What we can 'say' emerges from this context, this rich communication, and forms itself around key cultural elements that emerge as the language that we use. Discourse is this rich communication and it appears as language, the specific language that we often regard as being freely formed but which is in reality being formed through this dominant discourse.

The significance of discourse needs to be recognised in the development of an OLP. In studying discourse we are studying the use of language and as OL is about dialogue, language is at the heart of any OLP. This language will be the words used, the body language and the context within which it is said. This later element will include the assumptions that are made about the individual who is communicating through this use of language. This can relate to the content but also to the manner in which it is delivered. Is it formal or informal, does it use technical language and so on. With this textbook the message you receive from me will be more than the words I use and it is as much to do with you as it is with me! So, your engagement with this textbook is not entirely down to me, but also down to you and the assumptions that you make and re-make as you read the text.

In semiotic analysis there is a focus on the relationship between 'myth' and ideology at the level of individual signs, such as advertisements. This is quite a narrow focus to take and 'structuralists' such as Michel Foucault, conduct a broader analysis of the historical relationship between discourse and power. This does not deny the power of individual signs but moves away from a specific focus on these signs and towards the context or environment which produced these signs.

What Foucault was intent on illustrating was that specific concepts were expressions of a power discourse that was inherently embedded within society. Discourse, to a large extent represents the means by which power is expressed, but not exerted. The subtle difference here is that the very expression of power inhibits individual action and any exertion of power is entirely voluntary, it is self-imposed. If it were otherwise we would be talking about coercion. The discourse of power is not an exercise of power but it allows for only a certain type of action to take place. It does this because it simply defines for us what this acceptable action is and where there is a consensus of opinion about the efficacy of this action then it becomes naturalised.

We are engaged with a discourse that goes beyond individual signs and extends towards more fundamental and larger social, political contexts. Essentially, we become incapable of acting contrary to the discourse of power because to do so would place one outside of the consensus – beyond accepted bounds of behaviour.

When we talk about specific concepts and when we look at Foucault, we are focusing specifically on his studies of criminality, madness and sexuality. Foucault (1991) presents the idea that each of these concepts is deeply embedded in the discourse of power. The discourse of power in relation to punishment has changed over the centuries and we can identify what might be called a discourse shift. In the eighteenth century the dominant discourse was to demonstrate power through fear. This meant that the treatment of prisoners was used to support this discourse, which in turn meant that it became a spectacle. *If you challenge the legitimacy of the state then this is what will happen to you.* By the nineteenth century this discourse had moved away from control through fear and towards control through individual discipline. Within this discourse there is no need for punishment as a spectacle, instead punishment is moved away from view and deviation is hidden and becomes part of a powerful discourse that marginalises and largely defines opposition to the state as deviance.

Our understanding of deviance is largely negative, as is of course our view of madness. Again, Foucault presents a shifting discourse of power in relation to madness. If we think of this broadly we can appreciate that whoever has the right to say that somebody is mad, is entitled to treat that individual in a way that would be unacceptable to a 'normal' person. We are entitled to exert control over those who deviate from accepted social norms of behaviour, but the establishment of these norms and the identification of who has the right to set them will largely reflect the power structures that are in place within society. This will be equally true of organisations.

 Pause for thought – Legitimacy

In my organisation I have a right to claim legitimacy because of my position and my qualifications. Legitimacy is what counts here and my legitimacy is as much based upon your own inherent understanding as it is upon that made explicit by my position.

If we look at a political statement, such as that made by George W. Bush about terrorism, we can see that what he is creating is an object – the *war* on terrorism – and investing it with a reality that is difficult to deny. However, think about this statement emanating from a source that does not have this sense of legitimacy, perhaps Greenpeace or the Scottish Football Association. Neither of the bodies would create the 'reality' that we get with the speech that was made by the US President.

Embedded within this discourse is a series of questions relating to the inherent implications of the statement. A war, as an object, has implications. It is an extreme position and one in which 'normal' codes of behaviour can legitimately be ignored. In wartime we can operate at an emergency level and this allows actions that would not be tolerated in other circumstances. It sidelines the need to think of the causes, because this is a luxury that we cannot allow in wartime. In positioning the US in this way it forces groups and individuals to either be for or against the American position, because this is how it is in wartime.

What we say positions us in relation to the dominant discourse. For example, if I as an academic were to say that students should be expected to guide their own learning and that I as a tutor or supervisor should largely have a passive role, then I would be positioning myself negatively in relation to a dominant discourse where the student is regarded as a customer but positively where it is accepted that responsibility for learning within higher education largely rests with the student and that this ties into adult learning theories associated with self-direction and autonomy in learning. A middle ground may be identifiable here also, but however many variations may exist in individual organisations the key point is that there will be a pressure placed on any individual and what they might feel 'able' to say depending upon the prevailing discourse.

What we are considering here is *what we are able to say* and identifying or considering the point that this is not random or entirely controlled by the individual, but part of a largely social mechanism and that we as individuals are capable of discerning and adjusting both our behaviour and our speech accordingly. It was Ferdinand de Saussure (1857–1913) who presented the distinction between *langue* and *parole*. The former is an abstract structural system, while the latter is actual speech. It is the distinction between the two that is being highlighted and emphasised. This distinction is focused upon the social characteristics of language and social semiology rests upon meaning as being a negotiated process deeply embedded within the constantly changing, fluid and dynamic struggle for power that is social legitimacy. It is the struggle to not only be able to claim legitimate knowledge of something, but of course to have this claim accepted.

This takes us back to Foucault and the power/knowledge discourse, where we now have discourse as the central element in what we can say to be true. Here, social embeddedness is at the root of this fluid and dynamic environment within which we are operating. Its significance lies in the recognition that any text is in the first instance dependent upon its own production and ultimately its meaning and reception will be dependent upon the interpretation of the receiver. How I read a text will be different from you – there is no explicit meaning, if we understand the same thing this is coincidence and also very, very unlikely.

Antonio Gramsci (1891–1937) an Italian communist, writing in the 1930s reinforced this crucial social nature of intellectual activity. He talked about what he called the 'organic' intellectual and presented the view that all social groups seeks to articulate a hegemonic project, in other words, present an overwhelmingly powerful agenda for their own legitimacy. This is ideology – the social acceptance of knowledge or an idea. Ideology is a consensus, it is what we agree to be the case. In Gramsci's terms ideology is what we seek to produce and all social groups seek to have their ideology placed within a dominant position. It is the role of the intellectual, according to Gramsci, who forms and presents the representation of social ideas or social knowledge. When it is accepted it can be said to be hegemonic.

So, we are talking about more than a text. We are talking about a context and an engagement for both the individual and the social. What we say is dependent upon who says it and who receives it. At any one time there exist identifiable structures that invest legitimacy upon groups in terms of what they may or may not claim to be a truth. Production and reception both relate to one another, both influence one another, with the text in the middle as an entirely vague, fluid, partial entity. It only becomes solid when it is received, but it will never be received in the same way twice, hence its inherent fluidity.

In models of critical discourse analysis (CDA) (Fairclough, 2003) the text is presented as an element nested within the context of its production. In the first instance we describe the text and then apply our interpretation of it, which itself sits within the wider context of socio-cultural behaviours or norms. We can view this as the text being a product of the 'layers' within which it sits. The socio-cultural norms inform the interpretation of what can then be presented within any text. By text we can mean a written text or verbal communication through the dialogues that form the basis of OL.

Carrying out discourse analysis is a lot more than simply considering the linguistic meaning embedded within a particular text. It is about seeking to understand why the text is presented in the way that it is – what elements of the complex social relationships produced it? Also it asks you to consider your own engagement with this text. What elements within your own view of the world will impact upon your understanding of this text? To understand a text we can no longer look at it in isolation. We must be able to identify the nature of the discourse. To do this Fairclough (2003: 25; Figure 12.12) suggests three key stages:

- *Description*: What grammatical techniques are used to present a particular perspective? Exclamations that seek to deny any consideration of a contrary position.
- *Interpretation*: Upon what elements does the text seek to play – sympathy, empathy and so on?

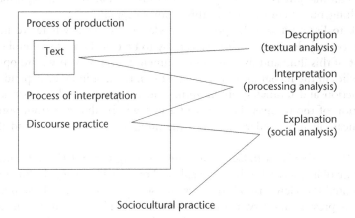

Figure 12.12 Fairclough's dimensions of discourse analysis

- *Explanation*: Where is the discourse placed within the understanding of the social processes that have produced it?

This reflective and critical evaluation and analysis of texts embodies the notion of discourse. It is accepting of the rich contextuality that is inherent within the production and reception of all types of communication.

There are many linguistic features that we can examine or consider that express the power that we are looking at in relation to the discourse. We can look at the emotive use of a specific word, carefully placed within the text to elicit a certain response. How we say something using passive or more declarative forms that also have a meaning embedded within them. The form of the text, who produced it, the relationships that can be identified within it and not least the reality that the producer perceives – what is there to identify the social position of the individual making these statements?

We could, for example, look at the power inherent in the use and application of a standardised language. A standard language is a form of representation, it presents a standard, normalising form of something. This is true of language. In relation to standard English its roots are said to go back to the merchant classes that began to emerge from late medieval England. This language was, therefore, linked directly to the mercantile class, to capital and to consumerism. Standard English had already by this time fought its battle in relation to other languages such as French and Latin which also had a claim to legitimacy and importantly had a status that was directly related to power structures as they existed in society at that time. The monasteries used Latin, and the Roman Catholic Church still does, to create a barrier to knowledge and understanding, simply because only they speak Latin. They place themselves, their institution, between the individual and what is known. This position of the mediator is a powerful one. The aristocracy in feudal England used French as their language for exactly the same reasons. We may now all speak the same language but there remains within it the same types of barriers in relation to the access that one might have to what is legitimate knowledge. Standardisation is at the root of this and is a form of codification which in turn is about attaining minimal variation. Texts on grammar, dictionaries and so on explicitly mapped and presented the language.

Pause for thought – Received pronunciation

Received pronunciation (RP) has embedded within it a legitimacy that has manifested itself in relation to the access that one might have to employment. We only need to think of the BBC in the 1930s to see how an institution valued RP as a means of identifying a certain 'standard' of individual.

Where now in the BBC do we see the deliberate use of non-standard English and why has there been an pronounced increase in the use of presenters with regional accents? What does this suggest to us about language and discourse?

Paul Ricoeur (1913–2005) recognised that a text, when distanced from the author deprives that author of control in terms of its *illocutionary* and *perlocutionary* effect, that is the mood of the statement in relation to the former and the reaction of the reader in relation to the latter. This distancing and lack of control highlights for us the need to appreciate the contextual elements that begin to define the discourse and which focus primarily on the reader as interpreter and, in turn, the context which will influence the interpretation of the reader.

Ways of interpreting the elements of a discourse might include analysing the different activities and how they are presented:

- Who is the ideal reader of the text?
- Are there any presuppositions about who will be reading it?

This might be where there is a deliberate attempt to tap into the prejudices or fears or hopes of a recipient. Often texts that deal with contentious issues such as asylum seekers can be seen to be written for an intended audience – perhaps those who fear the consequences of large-scale population movement.

Questions to be asked in seeking an explanation of the discourse should include some detailing of the way in which the discourse has been formed and why it will present a text and other forms of communication in the way that it does. Let's take an example of this and draw on Foucault (1991) to do so. He highlighted power structures as the contextual embodiment of the discourse. In other words what we say, why we say it and how we receive it (the message) is dependent upon our understanding and appreciation of the power structures at play. We can look at this at any number of levels, for example in the former Soviet Union an esoteric language was employed to deal with, to a large extent, the media. When a high ranking communist official was punished and sent off to Siberia, he was said to be having a *rest* from his taxing duties. Commentators, in understanding the application of this type of language within this specific context could then understand the meaning of it, in this case that the individual had been removed from power. The trick is to understand the discourse and be willing and able to engage with it.

Therefore, there is an inherent purpose to the production of language and it is one that is inherently linked to power or hegemony – as Gramsci refers to it. Language in this sense becomes a means of control and can be identified in the use of different linguistic terms and structures. Any analysis of discourse should be sensitive to the agenda from which it emerges and the purposes for which it is presented. These change and are reflected in the changing meaning of the same words and terms. This can be very easily seen when we look at the disparity between a historical context and contemporary writing, for example the changing attitude to the imperialist policies that defined Britain's foreign policy in the nineteenth century. This was at one time seen as a glorious attempt to spread civilisation to bring untold benefits to *backward* looking peoples. It is now often presented as an invasion and forced oppression of different cultural groups for the sole benefit of a mercantile class in Britain.

Foucault is equating what we can know with representations of existing power structures. The punishment that Foucault gruesomely describes at the start of *Discipline and Punish* (1991) reflects the accepted purpose of punishment as a means of control. This desire to control remains as an inherent element within the discourse of power but its instrument changes and we see a shift from spectacle to isolation and marginalisation. Control is exerted most effectively through self-regulation and this is exerted by the imposition of social pressures based upon the simple premise of observation.

The discourse shifts in relation to the power inherent within society and these shifts reflect themselves in the very way we are able to apply and to interpret the language that we use. Discourse analysis is about identifying present positions within the discourse as well as shifts that might have been taken or be taking place.

Language sits within a wider discourse and its purpose is to promote the legitimacy of an ideological position. This can be on the grand scale and be a political ideology that seeks national dominance or it might be an organisation eager to ensure its right to present it aims and objectives as valid and beneficial. To do so it must look to its own position within the discourse – what credibility does it have in relation to the knowledge claims it wants to make? It may present the venerable history of the institution or hold on to linguistic forms that support it. As OL practitioners we can also look to the way in which these legitimate knowledge claims are sustained. They are sustained through the use and application of language embedded as it is within the social.

When we talk or hold a conversation we are part of a two-way process that has its own conventions, not least of taking turns, listening and interacting. Below are two contrasting methods that can be used to work with dialogues in the organisation. The first is described as an ethno-methodological (Garfinkel, 1967) approach that focuses on the conversation and avoids any attempt to contextualise the conversation or draw on any external factors or influences as determinants of the content of the conversation. The second is very much concerned with the context and the dynamics which form and shape what can be said within any specific dialogue. In looking at both of these methods the intention is not to argue for one approach over another but to simply present the different ways in which dialogues can be regarded and used as the core data for any OLP. The issue is one of scale, the minutiae of the conversation is as significant as its relation to the dominant discourses within the organisation. Not least the orderly and efficient conduct of a conversation is as important to OL (a dialogue-rich approach) as any other factor or element that will ensure the creation of the necessary respect and trust that will underpin any OLP.

Conversation analysis

Conversation analysis (CA) is associated with Harvey Sacks (1935–1975) and focuses on the dynamic of turn-taking. The basic mechanics of a conversation are based on these two key elements:

- *Turn constructional units* – what an individual chooses to say when they have 'the floor'.
- *Turn transition relevance place* – the point at which the conversation moves from one participant to another.

The 'rules' of conversation are presented in relation to these two key elements and any divergence is seen as disruptive. For example, in speech we can either *overlap* or *interrupt* speech with the former being a mistaken identification of the ending of a turn and the latter a more hostile attempt to wrest control of the conversation from the current speaker.

In everyday or 'ordinary' speech there are patterns of behaviour that illustrate how any conversation will proceed. In an organisational setting there are further elements that act as determinants to the progress or otherwise of the conversation. Not least, the opportunity to ask questions is often more restricted in institutional conversations. One speaker can claim a right to ask questions while the other is, not necessarily denied, but conventionally restrained.

The position of the questioner is a powerful one and in OL there is, therefore, a need to not only be aware of this as a conversational convention but also to counter this and to ensure that there is the necessary balance and that each party is able to maximise their contribution. To an extent the OLP would look to counter some of the characteristics of institutional conversations and attempt to embed characteristics associated with an ordinary conversation.

> Whatever else we do with words, when we speak we are always telling our listeners something about ourselves.
>
> (Cameron 2001: 170)

In our ordinary conversations and the conversations we might have in organisations, what we say and the way we say it will present us in a very specific way. We make choices here about what 'identity' we might want to present and what this presentation might mean. How we make these choices will be drawn from the prevailing and dominant characteristics of our environment. Openly resisting this is common and certainly possible but in doing so the individual or group becomes non-compliant and risks marginalisation.

 Pause for thought – Transcription convention
(drawn from Cameron, 2001)

In order to be able to analyse and consider conversations there is a need to follow transcription conventions, as follows:

/ ...tone unit boundary
[...indicates start of simultaneous speech (overlap)
(.) ...indicates pause of less than 0.1 sec
(2.5) ...pause measured in seconds
= ...indicates turn transition with no gap or overlap
? ...indicates non-verbal or indecipherable comment

'   . . . indicates prominent stress
_   . . . indicates emphatic stress.

Tony Blair (ex-prime minister of UK) responds in a BBC interview to the news of the death of Princess Diana:

BLAIR: (2.5) I feel like / everyone 'else in this 'country today/ (0.3) / utterly / (0.7) / devastated / (3.3) / our 'thoughts and prayers are / with / (.) Princess Di'ana's family

Tony Blair uses both formal and informal styles, and emotive language. He was considered to be 'sincere' in this speech.
    The transcription aims to include all pauses and other non-verbal interactions or cues. Sarcasm, facial expressions (such as frowns, grimaces or smiles and grins) can all add to the 'meaning' of the word.

Working with discourse

Let's consider the following transcript:

INTERVIEWER: Please tell me something about your experience of team working in this department.
RESPONDENT A: I'm a team leader and I have been here for some time. I think we are a great team, a great group of lads, we all work together and support each other. If someone needs to know something then another lad will chip in and help.
INTERVIEWER: How has this come about, how has this team spirit been developed?
RESPONDENT A: Well, we've gone out of our way to be informal and to do things socially. We all regularly go out and have a good laugh together. We try to get to the pub at least once a month and it's usually a great laugh.
INTERVIEWER: Do all of the team go out to the pub?
RESPONDENT A: Usually. Some stay longer than others and there is a core of people who make a good night of it.
INTERVIEWER: Is it always the same individuals who drift away early?
RESPONDENT A: Usually, not everyone likes to stay.
INTERVIEWER: Who?
RESPONDENT A: 'T' usually needs to be encouraged to come along, and he's more of a wine drinker than a beer drinker. He takes some stick for that, but in a good natured way.
INTERVIEWER: How is he encouraged to come along?
RESPONDENT A: We don't force him, it's up to him, but I think it is important that we all go together, as a team. Work together, play together.

Here we are considering the important discipline of team working and although the above transcript is fictitious, it is based on a real conversation. It highlights some issues for us relating to micro discourse analysis. Not least, it is open to many different interpretations. Here is mine:

This team is displaying some common characteristics of a gender (male) dominated working culture. The members are put under pressure to conform and will be marginalised if they do not. It is sustained by a belief that good teams are solely based on a level of commonality and conformity that, as a consequence, finds it difficult to accommodate any differences.

What needs to be done?

Little can be done on a single short transcript such as this but it would merit some more research into the characteristics of teams in this department. In particular, a conversation with 'T' might be illuminating. If this conversation confirms the pressure that is being identified from the first conversation then a case is being built for some direct intervention. The nature of this intervention might focus on the leadership of this team and might explore with this team the need to consider issues around difference and diversity in a team as a positive feature.

Let's consider another scenario:

At a meeting of a university strategic management team, which is represented by members from all departments, it is observed that the university library makes little if any contribution. After the meeting a conversation with the library representative is as follows:

INTERVIEWER: You didn't say much, did you not feel you had something to contribute?
REPRESENTATIVE: Oh, these meetings! We have far too many of them. We go to more and more meetings, leaving less time to get on with what needs to be done.
INTERVIEWER: So, you think these meetings have little value?
REPRESENTATIVE: Everybody knows what we do and I think we do a good job, when we're allowed to get on with it. We don't need to be constantly dragged into the management of the organisation. As long as we're doing what we're supposed to do then I'm happy with that.

My interpretation:

This is a part of the organisation that is becoming marginalised and allowing its value to be determined by operational criteria that if fulfilled will justify their position and continued existence. To an extent this part of the organisation is choosing to marginalise itself from the discourse.

Some questions form themselves from this:

- Why do they feel that it is easier to operate on the 'margins'?
- What has created the 'disconnect' between this department and the wider organisation?

With both of these examples the interpretation is mine and there might be alternative interpretations from others on the OL team.

Discourse at the macro level can be like getting involved in a fight and you need stamina for that. There is a dominant discourse but this will constantly be contested. Being able to consistently identify it and to not align yourself with it can be punishing. It can be better to simply 'go with the flow' to accept that things will be done in a particular way, that may not be to your liking but it can appear to be too difficult to change things.

If this type of characteristic is embedded too fully within an organisation then the ability of the organisation to change and to learn is impeded. It is important to be able to identify the extent of this type of issue and to work with it. In this case there is a need to look at issues concerning strategic management, key channels of communication, identify the significant individuals and how they are operating. Has the leadership of the organisation become too competitive and are there some 'hard hitters' dominating the field and looking to exert their control or enhance their power within the organisation?

Critical discourse analysis (CDA) concerns itself with identifying the key characteristics of an organisation and why it operates as it does. This will range from the micro-level relationship between colleagues and departments to the macro level and the strategic management of the organisation, its structure and its behaviour. The role of the OL practitioner is to carry out the necessary research into these relationships. This will be through a range of research methods (see Table 12.1).

The methodologies shown in Table 12.1 can be used to gather relevant data and information. Each requires specific skills to use them effectively. These might be in the construction of suitable questions for a semi-structured interview or conducting a focus group and so on. Once it has been gathered various tools can be used to analyse and 'make sense' of this data.

As well as CDA other analytical support tools are shown in Table 12.2.

Qualitative data analysis is a systematic search for meaning. It will require researchers or investigators (who can be OL professionals) to interpret and develop explanations

Table 12.1 Research methodologies

Methodology	Brief description	Quantitative/Qualitative
Ethnography	The attempt through embedded observation to identify the key cultural characteristics of a group of individuals.	Qualitative
Phenomenology	A reflective process that seeks to identify the essential properties of experience.	Qualitative
Semi-structured interviews	An interview process that allows new ideas to be introduced.	Qualitative
Focus groups	A facilitated group discussion that explores perceptions and attitudes.	Qualitative
Surveys	A technique, often questionnaires, that looks to sample a given population in relation to a specified topic.	Quantitative
Case study	An in-depth consideration of a subject of study – the case.	Quantitative/Qualitative

Table 12.2 Analytical support tools

Tool	Description
Coding (constant comparison analysis)	A dataset is analysed and either deductively matched to codes or, inductively, these codes are allowed to emerge from the data itself. Key themes are developed through this coding.
Content analysis	Similar to coding it is often used when it is worth counting the occurrence of codes themselves, often in larger datasets.

that will form the basis of the dialogues that are at the heart of any OLP. It is used to obtain insights into the experiences of both individuals and groups, but it remains less popular because of the issues around its practical application. Not least, it is open to, indeed founded upon, interpretation and this is always contested. An organisation needs to be fully reconciled to living and working with this level of contestation before it can successfully employ these techniques. Creating the right environment for OL will go some way to preparing the organisation for this. It will be technically able and culturally aware, at least, of the need to foster and embed dialogues as the key driver of learning.

Concluding remarks

To plant an experiential-learning community there needs to be a blend between the technical and cultural environment. It is not enough to create a technical environment with elaborate or sophisticated functionality if there is no attempt to understand the key cultural dynamics that drive the organisation. In this first instance, *planting*, looks to use technology to support CDA and its in-depth analysis of the organisation at both the macro and micro levels. To a large extent the necessary 'capabilities' at this stage are sound researching skills on the part of the OL practitioner. First, being able to identify key aims and objectives – what is it I want to find out and what do I need to do to address this? Next, identifying the appropriate methodological approach and tools and being able to effectively apply these. After application there is a need to analyse the results. The technical infrastructure will be dominated by tools that will facilitate the necessary investigation of the cultural dynamics. These investigations will form the origins and the basis of the dialogues that will form the OLP. From the questions raised by CDA at the macro and micro level the technical infrastructure needs to be able to facilitate further discussion and dialogue. The emphasis is very much on dialogue rather than discussion. *Discussion* is focused on talking, with a specific direction and focus, it will look to consider opinions, identify and analyse options and ultimately select the most favoured option. *Dialogue*, by contrast, is focused on listening, allowing a focus to emerge and generating ideas and options. The selection or adoption of any option is not required. The creation and development of key organisational dialogues is led by the OL practitioner and is diagnostic in nature. It seeks to produce a picture of the organisation, to identify key issues and create initial strategies for the exploration and understanding of these issues.

13 Nurturing an experiential-learning community

Introduction

Once an organisation has planted the experiential-learning community, it will then go on to nurture the emerging shoots of good practice. We will consider here some of the techniques that can be associated with this part of the process. Central to this is the social nature of the experiential-learning environment and this in turn focuses on group dynamics and how individuals relate to one another, build teams and learn collaboratively. The experiential-learning cycle looks to build the relationship between the individual and the organisation and the establishment of this relationship begins with processes of socialisation and onboarding.

Socialisation

Socialisation is the process through which individuals begin to lay the foundations of their relationship with the organisation. If planting looked to provide the right environment, with the technical and the cultural dimensions appropriately aligned, nurturing looks to ensure that at this early stage of development the right support and encouragement is provided to help foster collaborative learning. If they are embedded within the right environment their inclination or willingness to learn will be enhanced.

As with any relationship there are two sides. On the one hand there is an opportunity for the individual to exert some influence on the organisation and on the other, the organisation to exert some influence on the individual. This former element is often referred to as *individualisation* and can be more than simply personalising a work space. It can be an attempt to realign working schedules or renegotiate elements of the job description. Similarly, the process of socialisation can be both formal and informal, where informally individuals or groups within the organisation seek to influence a new member of staff and align them with their working practices.

Assimilation is the goal of the socialisation process, but this is not the blind acceptance by the individual of organisational rules and procedure. Rather, it is the first steps in an ongoing process that will allow the individual to build the necessary trust that in turn will drive their engagement with collaborative programmes of learning, the OLP.

The way in which an individual will engage with the organisation remains on the level of the individual. Generalisations, based on the theories in Table 13.1, will only provide some indications of the way in which an individual may go about the process of assimilation. They will look for information, they will draw on their own experience and so

Table 13.1 Theories of socialisation (drawn from Kramer, 2010)

Socialisation theory	Definition	Action	Key theorist
Uncertainty reduction theory (URT)	Cognitive uncertainty – not being able to predict motives. Predictive uncertainty – inability to predict behaviour. Explanatory uncertainty – inability to explain reasons for actions.	Information seeking behaviour to reduce uncertainty. Drawing on individual past experience or embedded assumptions.	Berger and Calabrese (1975)
Sense-making	Assigning meaning to experience.	Determining meaning through negotiation/ communication. Plausibility over accuracy.	Weick (1995)
Social exchange theory (SET)	Identifying the value and viability of social relationships and their maintenance.	Comparison level – cost-benefit analysis of single variable. Comparison level of alternatives – cost-benefit analysis of multiple variables.	Thibaut and Kelley (1959)
Social identity theory (SIT)	Identity formation as a factor in determining engagement with socialisation processes.	Personal identities – physical and cognitive characteristics. Social identities – perception and extent of a sense of belonging.	Ashforth and Mael (1989)

on, but what information they find and how they determine the value of that information remains rooted in their own personal experiences.

Any organisation has a choice about how it might approach socialisation. It can look to carry out either individual or group socialisation, it can adopt formal or less formal techniques and they can look to determine the extent of the pressure that might be placed on the individual. Military organisations might look to apply a high degree of pressure with a view to ensuring that individual characteristics are subordinated to the collective. Similar pressure is applied by or through the application of certain rules. This might be a dress code or, as is prevalent in the oil and gas industry, the focus on health and safety, requiring individuals to use hand rails while going down stairs, or even the strict imposition of reverse parking.

The ability to apply CDA will determine the extent to which the elements within the socialisation process can be viewed as care or an attempt to ensure higher levels of conformity. Individual perceptions of this will have a direct impact upon the creation of trust and the building of a positive learning culture. Again, this is not clear-cut in that individuals will vary in their analysis of these processes, but where there is prevalent a sense of imposed control then there will be negative implications for the development of the OLP.

The relationships within an organisation will determine and drive the dominant discourse. Within organisations the key relationships are between the manager and those being managed, and between peers. *Social penetration theory* (SPT) identifies the way in which individuals develop these relationships (Altman and Taylor, 1973). They add both depth and breadth by enhancing the level of intimacy and the amount of content that is shared. They do this as the relationship progresses, through the pace of self-disclosure as individuals open up and share their views, opinions and knowledge. The level of intimacy will mirror the trust that becomes embedded in the relationship and, of course, this can be lost as well as gained. Where this level is high then there will be more information disclosed and therefore shared.

As a model for understanding the development of relationships SPT tends to lack any of the more subtle elements of relationship building and relies on a generalised view of a linear process that is either advancing or retreating. This is presented, not surprisingly, in the form of an onion, with different layers leading towards the centre, or core, that represents the private self.

Socialisation supports the development of key organisational relationships and an understanding of how these relationships are forming. SPT is based on progressive stages of intimacy:

- *Orientation* – largely based on phatic communication that serves a basic social function.
- *Exploration* – beginning to reveal aspects of the self, exploring the possibility of further intimacy.
- *Affection* – a more trusting stage, where opinions are proffered.
- *Stabilisation* – deeper personal thoughts and ideas are shared.
- *Depenentration* – breakdown of the relationship, levels of intimacy decrease.

The key dyadic relationship between the manager and those being managed is inevitably based on a difference, namely the difference of level within the hierarchical structure of the organisation. Here the forming of a stable relationship within the organisational context is both crucial and problematic. The leader or manager will form relationships with a range of individuals which might fall into two broad categories, according to leader–member exchange (LMX) theory (Graen and Uhl-Bien, 1995):

- *High LMX* – a partnership, based on mutual trust where the communication is open and the relationship is stable. Consultation is preferred over direction and both commitment and performance are enhanced. Those forming part of this group are often referred to as the *in*-group. As the in-group this group is well resourced.
- *Low LMX* – a more antagonistic relationship that is perceived to require direction rather than collaboration. Communication is often one-way and the manager looks to direct. Levels of trust are low and as the *out*-group this group tends not to be well resourced. Both commitment and performance are limited.

Between high and low LMX will exist the fluid and changing relationships that characterises organisational 'reality'. These relationship are fluid, they will change over time and they are subject to the environment, which itself is increasingly fluid. The opportunity to develop stable relationships is to an extent compromised by the shifting workforce that looks to change positions more frequently than in the past. Nevertheless, the goal would be to create relationships associated with high LMX, where there is an opportunity for individuals to participate in decision making, where they are able to have a voice and be constructively critical of the organisation.

However, the in-group is by definition limited. Those in the out-group cannot be regarded as having no relevant knowledge or experience and this is largely lost when they remain outside. The need to draw all individuals into the in-group is a key goal of OL.

The goal of socialisation is to support this, in order to maximise the use of the embedded knowledge asset. Peer relationships are as significant here, not least for individuals first joining the organisation. The 'first contact' determines a great deal of the perception that individuals will have of the organisation – the crucial first impression.

As individuals tend to work as part of teams or groups within organisations it is the interaction within and between these groups that will determine the way in which organisational relationships will develop. Often teams or groups develop norms that will represent their values and it is expected that individuals becoming part of the group will conform to these norms. This becomes a negative element where it becomes a coercive force, an imposition that often characterises self-managed teams:

> Self-managed teams can create norms that serve as concertive control over their members. Concertive control can be more powerful than hierarchical or bureaucratic control because it involves self-enforcement by team members.
>
> (Kramer 2010: 133)

Embedded norms will form an important part of the relationship that will exist between individuals within an organisation and these need to be identified and aligned with the strategy of both the organisation and the OLP. Where they exclude individuals this needs to be recognised as a barrier to OL. Gender, age, class, sexual orientation, are all factors which can marginalise individuals. Those who form a minority are disadvantaged and as the disadvantaged they will not be in a position, or will be less inclined, to share their accumulated experience. The need to identify the changes to be made in organisational practice cannot exclude individuals and OL looks to identify and address this exclusion and aims to become more inclusive.

 Pause for thought – Legitimate peripheral participation (LPP)

In the development of communities of practice new members are asked to participate by performing minor but relevant tasks. In doing so, they are afforded an opportunity to observe experts and the practices of the community. Progressively, the tasks draw the individual towards the centre. During the process opportunity exists to reflect on the nature of these tasks and on the individual's role within the community. As the individual becomes a more central member of the community the ability to be constructively critical is embedded through these opportunities to reflect but importantly what comments they might want to make are fully informed by an understanding of the norms that exist within the community.

Think of the periods when you have been new to an organisation. Identify the way in which you were able to make some meaningful contribution to existing practice, highlighting any instances of opposition. To what extent was this opposition based on your 'lowly' social position within the group rather than upon the quality of the suggestion.

Where you are able to identify an instance of this, what might the organisation have done to address this type of situation?

Building organisational relationships is the primary function of the socialisation process and rather than this being a one-off induction session it is an on going nurturing process within the OLP. As well as addressing the theoretical and practical elements associated with induction, the process of socialisation needs to consider the interaction of individuals as part of prospective teams and groups. New members of staff need to know where they will sit, what they are being asked to do and how they will relate to the others in the organisation. This is the start of the onboarding process.

Onboarding

As organisations increasingly operate within an environment where recruitment forms a significant and ongoing part of their activity, where the recruitment of 'talent' is of crucial significance to the ability of the organisation to compete effectively and where there can be a reasonable expectation that attrition rates may rise as economic and other factors impact upon operations, then the ability to tap into the knowledge and skills of the individuals who are coming into the organisation becomes more critical.

The role of onboarding is to address this need to ensure that knowledge can be utilised efficiently and quickly. However, the purpose of onboarding as part of a nurturing process is not solely concerned with induction, with ensuring that individuals know what their role and tasks might be. It certainly goes beyond a tour of the office and the issuing of a password to the network. Onboarding can be seen as a vital element in the ongoing process of socialisation that will allow individuals to both embed quickly, to perceive their value to the organisation and through this further enhance the likelihood of retention – keeping the talent.

As part of a formal process that looks to build the relationship between the individual and the organisation, onboarding will or should explicitly benefit both the employer and the employee. There can be many reasons why individuals might feel marginalised and this is not necessarily exclusive to new employees. However, new employees can need assistance and support in building their relationship with the organisation and this can start with their professional network.

> To better nurture relationship building, firms should go beyond the scattered half-measures currently in place and embrace structured social programs that start very early and unfold progressively over the first year of the new hire's tenure. These programs should embrace both professional and personal networking, help new hires build networks both inside and outside the firm, mobilise stakeholders throughout the firm, including senior leadership, and also include provisions to ensure that new hires' families are comfortable.
>
> (Stein and Christiansen 2010: loc 1919 of 4551)

Without social relationships individuals become anxious and this will impact upon their motivation and commitment levels. As new generations join the workforce there is perhaps an enhanced need to recognise this as part of a more formal organisational process. There is perhaps an enhanced expectation amongst emerging generations that there will be a supportive professional network outside the organisation, as well as supportive teams or groups inside the organisation.

Inside the organisation many crucial networks need to be formed:

- *Task network*: aligned to the role and position within the organisation.
- *Social network*: providing less formal support and can be with individuals across the organisation, perhaps sharing an interest outside the organisation.
- *Authority network*: relations with those who control or have power over tasks.
- *Innovation network*: relations with those identified as having ideas relevant to tasks.

These networks will enhance an individual's effectiveness and efficiency, enhance motivation and commitment levels and lead to a greater willingness to engage with the collaborative learning necessary to drive the OLP. Where individuals experience openness and a willingness to share they are more likely to follow this behaviour and themselves share their knowledge. This in turn will help to build trust across the organisation.

 Pause for thought – The OL network

The OL external professional network includes a range of organisations, including:

The Tavistock Institute (www.tavinstitute.org)

> The Tavistock Institute of Human Relations (TIHR) applies social science to contemporary issues and problems. It was established as a not for profit organisation with charitable purpose in 1947.

> The Institute is engaged with evaluation and action research, organisational development and change consultancy, executive coaching and professional development, all in service of supporting sustainable change and ongoing learning.
>
> (The Tavistock Institute, 2015)

ODN Europe (www.odneurope.org/)

> ODN Europe is the European chapter of the Organization Development Network, an international professional association of organisation development practitioners.

> Our Mission
> Organisation Development is a field central to creating effective and healthy human systems in an inclusive world community.

> Our Vision
> ODN Europe is dedicated to being a leader in the advancement of the theory and practice of organisation development by:

> - Helping to define and communicate the values, purposes and benefits of organisation development.
> - Promoting the effective and ethical use of organisation development principles, tools and best practices.

- Supporting practitioners through enhanced learning and professional development opportunities.
- Providing a venue for OD practitioners, researchers and educators to discuss and exchange ideas about critical issues.
- Sharing leadership and partnering with other educational providers to achieve our vision.

(ODN Europe, 2015)

Society for Organizational Learning (www.solonline.org/)

Guiding Principles of SoL

The Drive to Learn – All human beings are born with an innate, lifelong desire and ability to learn, which should be enhanced by all organizations.

Learning is Social – People learn best from and with one another, and participation in learning communities is vital to their effectiveness, well-being and happiness in any work setting.

Learning Communities – The capacities and accomplishments of organisations are inseparable from, and dependent on, the capacities of the learning communities which they foster.

Aligning with Nature – It is essential that organisations evolve to be in greater harmony with human nature and with the natural world.

Core Learning Capabilities – Organisations must develop individual and collective capabilities to understand complex, interdependent issues; engage in reflective, generative conversation; and nurture personal and shared aspirations.

Cross-Organizational Collaboration – Learning communities that connect multiple organisations can significantly enhance their capacity for profound individual and organisational change.

(Society for Organizational Learning 2015)

Within the UK there are professional bodies, such as:

CIPD (www.cipd.co.uk/)

We're the CIPD – the professional body for HR and people development. We are the voice of a worldwide community of more than 140,000 members committed to championing better work and working lives.

We've been setting the benchmark for excellence in people and organisation development for more than 100 years. Through our expertise and research we provide a valuable point of view on the rapidly changing world of work. And for our members we're the career partner of choice, setting professional standards and providing the know-how to drive the HR and L&D professions forward.

We're independent and not-for-profit and hold a highly respected Royal Charter. We exist to make work and working lives better. And at a time of unprecedented change we have the vision, agility and strength to make a real difference to our members, to businesses, to the economy and to all working people.

(CIPD 2015)

ITOL (www.itol.org/)

> The Institute of Training and Occupational Learning (ITOL) is the UK's elite professional body for trainers and L&D Professionals. In the year 2000 the UK government granted 'Institute' status and since that time we have become recognised as the premier organisation for everyone involved in the world of learning and education.
>
> (ITOL, 2015)

Learning and Performance Institute (www.learningandperformanceinstitute.com/)

> The Learning and Performance Institute is a global Institute for Learning & Development professionals. Established in 1995 the Institute has grown on an annual basis to become the leading authority on Learning & Development.
>
> Through an unrivalled range of membership, certification, accreditation, events and bespoke consultancy services, the Institute focuses on enhancing and recognising the skills and professional status of individuals and organisations engaged in learning activities, and assessing the quality of learning services.
>
> (Learning and Performance Institute, 2015)

These organisations represent just a fraction of the relevant OL network that can be built. Other significant organisations (largely UK based) include Charities Learning Consortium and Towards Maturity. Equally, a range of individuals might be followed through social media (Facebook, Twitter and LinkedIn).

The accompanying website to this text expands on this list, but each individual is capable of contributing to this list and through that contribution not only sharing valuable information but also forming part of a broadly based process of socialisation, where the contribution of individuals is relevant and welcomed. Where this is made explicit individuals can feel more valued and this can enhance their commitment and motivation. This in turn begins to build organisational trust.

Many organisations need to embed this engagement more fully with social media as a powerful way to enhance the effectiveness of individual staff and to recognise that this will also play a part in the socialisation process. One reason why organisations do not fully engage with these social networks and often actively discourage it, is largely based on the lack of control that they can exercise over these social sites and that they are not entirely associated with working practices. Since when has Facebook been work? It becomes work when it supports the early assimilation of staff and contributes to the agility of the organisation in meeting the challenges of change and the many transitions it will face as it engages with the contemporary environment.

A key principle associated with onboarding is to initially focus on depth rather than breadth. A smaller group of individuals to act as a 'go-to' resource can be reassuring for a new member of staff. It can help them to build from this base quickly and effectively.

A strong, nurturing social life is both a basic human need and essential for career success. Yet most companies do not help nurture relationship building among new hires as fully as they might, and the organisation pays a price.

(Stein and Christiansen 2010: loc. 2220 of 4551)

Social media is transforming the way in which professional networks are being built and to be successful in building a network through social media there are key points to consider:

- Familiarity with the social media tools: how familiar are individuals with the type of tools available and how do they maintain this familiarity?
- Nurture each relationship: keep the request for information focused and show a clear awareness of the individual or group being asked. Are you asking an overly complex question which will take up too much of their time and effort and in doing so strain the relationship?
- Where possible look to stabilise the relationship by meeting face-to-face or at least using Skype or FaceTime to interact more informally with individuals.
- Ensure that you explicitly express the value you place on the connection. This can simply be thanking individuals for contributions.

This awareness of the position of others in relation to the building of organisational networks aligns itself with the ethical and professional standards that need to be embedded and associated with OL practice. Within a context of diversity and fluidity, where ethical behaviour cannot rest on prescribed or predetermined criteria and where the subjectivity of ethical or moral action is heightened, then the willingness to develop the capability to look at any instance from the others' point of view becomes more critical. Professional networks, built through social media, do not have their foundation within any formal structures. Behaviour, therefore, is determined by those who form part of this network. As a fluid network it cannot operate successfully without mutual respect and an awareness of the needs of others.

 Pause for thought – Twitter (www.twitter.com)

Twitter can be used to maintain professional knowledge and to keep up to date with relevant developments. In setting up a Twitter account it is important to decide:

- What it is you want to get from it. Is it entirely professional, a blend of social and professional or entirely social?
- What level of involvement are you wanting, are you prepared to make contributions and how often?

Present yourself appropriately and tweet before you follow. Build up a body of information about your interests and expect to build your following slowly. Previous colleagues and friends can be found by searching on Twitter but there are sites that will help you to identify professional leaders to follow, for example, Twellow (www.twellow.com). Regular and focused contributions are preferred to constant tweets, which can clog a twitter feed. Consider taking the extra step and arranging a face-to-face meeting with key individuals at professional events.

Tweetdeck (http://tweetdeck.twitter.com) can help to organise your engagement with Twitter, creating timelines, alerts and filtered searches.

Onboarding, as with any other process within an organisation, needs to be continuously developed. It will require the development of specific content to support specific functions. This might be presentation material around the building of professional networks, activities associated with creating a Twitter account or customising a Tweetdeck. This will be specific content that itself needs to be maintained and made available. Where is it to be stored, who will maintain it and who will be able to access it? This is the management of explicit knowledge and the knowledge-based information systems will be used to store material of this kind and provide access to it.

Building up materials and resources that relate to onboarding is just one part of the nurturing process. Creating other resources and making knowledge that is based on personal experience explicit requires individuals with the capability to externalise their knowledge. The willingness to do so is founded within the growing relationship between the individual and the organisation. Onboarding plays its part here. It presents an extended process of engagement for the individual within the organisation and the wider professional community.

> Successful on-boarding is far more than traditional orientation in new clothes; it is an innovative strategic program that can boost a company's bottom line and improve its future prospects. By establishing a program covering culture, social networks, early career support, and strategic insight, and integrating on-boarding into the infrastructure and processes of the company, you can reduce time to productivity, increase level of productivity and lower attrition.
>
> (Stein and Christiansen 2010: loc. 4069 of 4551)

As individuals engage with social networks and as they build their relationships within the organisation they enhance the value of their experience. The relationship itself becomes a positive contributor to the knowledge base. Making this knowledge explicit can happen in many number of ways, but the nurturing process needs to embed practice that will support this. Being able to tell a story has proved an effective means of doing this, but it cannot be taken for granted that we are all good storytellers. Organisationally there is a need to appreciate the value of storytelling and individually there is a need to at least identify the need to enhance storytelling skills.

Storytelling

Where learning situations and environments are complex, the use of narratives is often regarded as an effective way of capturing and communicating these situations and environments. Denning (2001) has identified five key characteristics of organisational stories:

- *Endurance* – stories will have longevity.
- *Salience* – stories will impact the emotions.

- *Sense-making* – stories will offer an explanation of something.
- *Comfort* – these stories will have a level of familiarity with the experience of the people engaging with these stories.
- *Authenticity* – the storyteller will be trusted.

A story is a particular type of narrative. We engage with a story in a particular way. Not least we give the teller of the story licence to embellish it, to embed their own sense of it, their perspective and ultimately their own prejudices. We expect to hear a story and we expect it to be imbued with the personality of the teller and we happily assume that this will most likely be different from our own perspective. To an extent we want to be entertained, amused, shocked or surprised. Our emotions should be engaged and positively anticipate the experience. We have anticipation because storytelling involves the embedding of an interpretation of an event. Why did something happen? Does it represent something more than its own actual occurrence, is it directed at me as an individual or does it have consequences and is there a meaning behind this story that will have future significance?

These questions lie at the heart of stories and they tell us many different things about life within an organisation. From the perspective of the developing experiential-learning programme, the use of this technique is largely for organisations that have embedded and appreciate the value of dialogue, and have experienced what can be achieved through dialogues that are open and built upon trust.

Storytelling as a technique has existed in a human social sense for as long as there has been social contact between peoples and our largely text-based contemporary culture was preceded by an oral culture where stories were passed down through the generations. Only some of these stories will have passed through this oral tradition into the written form that we are familiar with today. The most powerful of these are still very prominent today, be this religious texts, or ancient tales such as Homer's Odyssey and so on. Similarly, Viking sagas and other folktales were passed down orally before being written down.

The storyteller is a skilled individual and within the oral tradition they were often prominent individuals, revered and respected, but what is their place within the organisation? Organisations concern themselves with facts, with achieving explicit goals driven by the roles and functions embedded within their clearly identified and explicit structures. Stories engage emotions and these are less logical than most organisational operations. Nevertheless:

> A story, with its more or less continuous narrative, actively engages the sense-making faculties of listeners, making the story memorable and, when necessary, making it more economical than other ways of transmitting information.
>
> (Allan, Fairtlough and Heinzen 2001: 7)

Economy and efficiency are at the heart of stories within organisations. They engage emotions but in doing so they enhance and embellish facts with meaning. Meaning has a particular significance in that a series of facts can have multiple meanings depending on the perspective from which they are viewed. So, what facts an organisation might have will be brought to life when meaning is given to these facts. Stories create this meaning and they create it in many different ways and in ways that will change and alter these facts. To an extent facts are a step along the way of sense-making, the analytical and critical engagement with these facts is crucial and the mechanisms to carry this out are equally crucial.

Storytelling is one of the mechanisms and an *After Action Review* (AAR) is a practical opportunity to encourage and embed storytelling. A story:

> ...can be used to study an organisation's culture and politics, the psychological wishes and needs of its members, the nature of its surface and deep symbolism, the effectiveness of its structure, and the pervasiveness of its value.
>
> (Gabriel 2000: 136)

In 1993 the US Army published a training circular defining and outlining After Action Reviews. In this circular AAR are defined as:

> ...a professional discussion of an event, focused on performance standards, that enable soldiers to discover for themselves what happened, why it happened, and to sustain strengths and improve on weakness.
>
> (US Army 1993: 1)

Clearly there is an opportunity here to reflect on specific and potentially dramatic events. The story of these events will have the ingredients of drama and the purpose of the AAR is to capture these stories.

> It is important that the atmosphere of the AAR be one of open discussion, not one stifled by rank consciousness.
>
> (US Army 1993: 25)

Stories can be elicited directly from individuals by simply asking them to relate their experiences in relation to specific areas of interest. Here it is important that the OL practitioner is seen not as an objective observer standing at the periphery but as an active participant, a 'fellow-traveller'. In this role they may question the storyteller, but in a way that reflects their engagement with the story rather than as means of interrogation. The relationship within storytelling as an organisational mechanism is inherently collaborative and positive. There needs to be a clear statement of what the purpose of the exercise is, why are they being asked to tell stories? There needs to be an equally clear understanding of just how vulnerable individuals are when asked to tell stories and that they need reassurance about how the stories will be used. Trust, therefore, is an essential part of this process. Having a clear appreciation of the other, the position of the individual beyond yourself, is vital and this should inform the ethical approach to the nurturing of the OLP.

In setting up their AAR the US Army recommends that the actual site of the action is chosen to help recollection, that seating be arranged in a horseshoe shape, and the discussion leaders face the horseshoe and if necessary be elevated, if dealing with a large group.

> ...for a platoon AAR, the platoon leader and platoon sergeant should be seated in front and centre of the horseshoe, with their soldiers spread out to the left and right. The company commander and battalion commander would be located behind the back row of soldiers. This allows soldiers taking part in the AAR to feel that their comments are valued as much as those of senior leaders.
>
> (US Army 1993: 25)

The sentiment here is to provide a non-threatening and open environment where candid and detailed recollections of events will be forthcoming. The stories that emerge from AAR or from other opportunities form the basis of the data that will need to be properly transcribed and processed for future use. This information can be stored and should follow a prescribed method of recording (drawn from Gabriel, 2000: 144–5):

- serial number
- author
- organisation
- type of story
- theme (one line description)
- full text
- emotions described and generated
- moral (if any)
- main characters
- keywords
- subjective assessment of quality.

Although almost anybody can tell a story this does not mean that everyone is a good storyteller. Within organisational storytelling the quality of the story will vary, some will engage the listener while others will not. The value of the story cannot be based solely on how engaging it might be, nor can its value be based on the extent to which it might be said to reinforce any preconceived ideas of those gathering these stories. The value of these stories lies in the richness of their own subjectivity. They can be used to support multiple ideas, often contradictory ideas.

Storytelling skills, like all other skills, can be improved and developed. Similar to the training that might be provided to colleagues to enhance presentation skills, perhaps a report following a project. A clear structure, with the content presented at the beginning, shifting from the general to the specific. Stories similarly, follow certain patterns that can help in their construction. A good story will use language to engage the listener. For example, rhythm, alliteration and metaphor are all used to help the listener remember the content of the story. A successful story needs (drawn from Allan, Fairtlough and Heinzen, 2002):

- Movement – progress with resolution.
- Suspense – an ending that is not clear throughout.
- Characters – identifiable characteristics that can easily be identified with.
- Emotion – characters or situations that will touch the listener.
- Relevance – has some 'connect' with the listener.
- Pace – too long will bore, too short will confuse.
- Simplicity – too much detail can be a burden for a story.

It will have characters, a purpose or direction, an obstacle to be overcome and an outcome. To develop storytelling skills a key approach is simply to write for a set period of time, say 20 minutes without any intention to read what is being written. The story can be disjointed and conform to none of the elements above that apply to good storytelling. The intention here is to simply allow an individual to focus on the process of writing itself. Following on from this exercise, another story can be written, again without any intention of following good storytelling guidelines. However, on this occasion there should be a specific focus in mind – an incident, happening or event. With this focus different elements can be added to the outline, characters, perspectives, emotion and so on.

Storytelling is a qualitative research technique being applied to organisational practices. It is dialogue based, will be embedded within the dominant discourse and will require interpretation. It aligns itself with the view of knowledge as ever-changing and fluid. Knowledge in this sense is not a thing, it is embedded within our experiences and understanding of the world around us. Storytelling engages our emotions rather than our rationality. As Boje (2008) highlights, the purpose of narratives within organisations has often been to reflect the current order, to draw us towards the centre, to be a mechanism that looks to embed conformity, while stories have sought to push away from the centre and embed the more subjective elements that seek to challenge and question.

> ... narrative, over the course of modernity, has become a (centripetal) centring force of control and order. The counter-force is that story (when not totally subservient to narrative order) can constitute a (centrifugal) decentring force of diversity and disorder. Narrative has been influenced by modernity to aspire to abstraction and generality, while story, here and there, has retained more grounded interplay with the life world.
>
> (Boje 2008: 1)

For many organisations it is this shift from centring to decentring, from order to disorder, that is the most challenging. Stories can, therefore, be unsettling and they require the organisation to recognise this and to actively and positively embrace this. They need to become good at existing with the fluidity associated with constant dialogue and to see this as not idle chatter that fails *to get things done*, but as the life of the organisation.

Case study: Storytelling

Organisational learning within Wood Group PSN is incorporated into our Core Values. Looking in particular at our Relationships Core Value this promotes a deep understanding of needs and a desire to exceed expectations (see Figure 13.1).

Relationships core value

Our business depends on healthy relationships with customers, business partners and suppliers. We build and nurture strong relationships that are mutually beneficial, making sure that we deeply understand the people we deal with, so that we can anticipate their needs and always aim to exceed their expectations. Everyone in our organisation contributes to the quality of the relationships we build and we actively seek feedback.

Looking at the elements of this Core Value through the lens of the RGU SPADES model this fits with the NURTURING principle. Storytelling within WGPSN takes on many forms and is not always explicitly known as storytelling.

Figure 13.1 Wood Group: Relationships

A list of some activities that involve storytelling is listed below. This is not an exhaustive list:

- HSE incident investigation reports;
- lesson capture;
- success story capture;
- lunch and learns;
- contract performance reviews;
- new contract tenders;
- contract extension proposals.

For HSE Incident reports, lesson capture, success stories and lunch and learns, storytelling is pivotal to the success of these processes. By ensuring the story behind an incident is properly told and documented enables the proper use of root cause analysis to identify key causes of the incident. If we were unable to tell the story properly these root causes would not be identified and we would be unable to learn and prevent a repeat of the incident.

The same is true of lessons and success stories. If we are unable to give the clear articulation of the background/context to the event, a clear description of what actually happened and the impact of this it becomes difficult for people to first, understand when they are in similar situations or contexts to the story and what potential risk or opportunity they are exposed to. Both lessons and success stories in WGPSN have a structure design to clearly articulate the required elements of a story.

Lessons Structure: Title, Background, Event & Impact, Recommendation
Success Story: Title, Overview, Response, Results

To socialise the learning properly we utilise *lunch and learns, safety moments* and *tool box talks.* These more cognitive learning events enable a richer learning experience. Recognising that as humans we only retain around 10 per cent through reading, 20 per cent from a classroom-style event and 70 per cent from experience we also ensure any changes to competency or training are captured through the lesson action process.

Looking at the activities designed to grow existing business or win new business storytelling is hugely important. The majority of responses to invitation to tenders (ITT) are formulated around success stories, lessons and experience. Where we are looking to grow existing relationships it is important to articulate to existing customers where we have exceeded their expectations but also where we are doing that with other customers. Success stories are a perfect mechanism for this. We have a success story library that is available globally and contains over 150 stories that articulate where we have exceeded expectations, lived our core values in our delivery and delighted our customers. We have documented nearly £50 million in direct savings to our customers through our success story process.

WGPSN success story examples

One success story in our library articulates how a contract was looking to improve safety performance through improving the safety cultures on the sites and offices. Their response was to implement a behavioural based safety programme that involved a top down and bottom up approach to safety. The response they got was positive and demonstrated a commitment to safety and assurance. Safety stats improved to over 1000 days incident free. Over 76 volunteers were trained and there was a drastic increase in participation in risk identification and intervention processes. On the back of this success story this programme has now been implemented across the operator's other contracts.

Another story in our library tells the story of how we wanted to take a different approach to inspection on one of the platforms we provided services to. To carry out some inspection activities on a drilling derrick would have required drilling facilities to be taken out of commission for 3 weeks. In response to this challenge the contract utilised a remote operated aerial vehicle (ROAV). This is a metre-long, feather-light helicopter unit, complete with mounted camera and GP. This ROAV carried out a detailed structural and coating inspection of the drilling derrick. Operated from the platform's helideck by skilled technicians, the miniature helicopter took high-resolution photographs of the derrick as part of a technical survey to assess the integrity of the facilities, prior to topsides removals. This was a first for offshore UKCS deployment. The ROAV was able to carry out the derrick inspection concurrent with drilling activities removing the need for these to be shut down for around 3 weeks at a cost of £1,680,000. More importantly, it eliminated the need for four inspectors to carry out the work, which would have required significant use of rope access, thereby virtually eliminating any risk to safety.

Concluding remarks

Nurturing is an emotive term and its use here is deliberate. OL is about engaging with emotions, as it is through this that individuals will be able to build the necessary and appropriate relationship with the organisation.

The emotional/rational dichotomy approximates the folk distinction between 'heart' and 'head'; knowing something is right in 'in your heart' is a different order of conviction – somehow a deeper kind of certainty – than thinking so with your rational mind.

(Goleman 1996: 8)

If trust can be placed at the heart of the OLP then there will be a necessary emotional connect between the individuals who are being asked to share their experiences.

... if more and more people take care to learn the art of the story, then there could be a big shift in organisational culture. Command-and-control organisational models inevitably suppress emotions.

(Allan, Fairtlough and Heinzen 2002: 277)

As the OLP begins to develop it will be able to use the technical environment in a very specific way that will reflect the cultural dynamics associated with the OLP. The VLE will become less of a mechanism to facilitate dialogue and more of an opportunity to support centripetal forces. The priority here is less around the need to create a structure, from the top, than to allow that structure to be created, from the peripheries. In the 'traditional' model within HE the tutor takes responsibility for the structure and content of a taught module. Each topic within the module may conform to principles of good practice, but to a large extent it is this that is being challenged. The pedagogy associated with OL, if there is one, would require the content and structure to be determined by those engaged with it. This takes a crucial element of control away from the tutor and spreads responsibility across all individuals.

Similarly, in an organisational context the technical environment will or should be fashioned by the cultural dynamic inherent within this less traditional pedagogical model. Essentially, it is a collaborative model that embeds this collaboration within the structure of the environment within which it operates. This can be seen as a challenge for those required to relinquish control and for those required to accept greater responsibility. The role of the OL practitioner at the nurturing stage is to support the embedding of these more dispersed responsibilities. By initiating an onboarding process the focus is fully on the creation of a relationship. To externalise an individual's engagement with the organisation they need to develop the ability to create stories around this engagement. This means that storytelling needs to importantly engage with both content and context knowledge.

Stories around the projects, the incidents and the happenings of an organisation must also be blended with stories around the way in which individuals perceive the organisation and their position within it. After action review can be a mechanism for both. It can encourage recollection which focuses on the meaning of past events but also projects ahead to not only their consequences but also to how this might impact upon the individual's perception of themselves. Perhaps the story will highlight surprise, and that this surprise disappoints or fails to meet expectations. This begins to drive a more negative perception of the organisation or of individual roles within it. Creating a story around this, however, acts as a cathartic exercise and opens it up to individual reflection and group interpretation. This can help to challenge the build-up of negative perceptions and more positively build trust.

Stories are an externalisation of the relationship that is established during the processes associated with onboarding. The relationship between the individual and the organisation is central to OL and the OL practitioner's role is to help create and sustain this relationship through processes that will externalise it. Individuals as storytellers require key capabilities to construct and present these stories but also require the organisation to recognise the significance of storytelling as a centrifugal force and that it represents the type of organisational culture that can be appropriately associated with OL. This is, essentially, a statement on the power dynamics within the organisation.

What is being nurtured here is not solely the capabilities associated with the process of onboarding or the techniques associated with storytelling, but the appropriate perception and understanding of power and control. Storytelling will embed a practical process of knowledge capture but will also embed a specific understanding of roles and responsibilities. The voice of the storyteller will present specific content and help establish the legitimacy of this voice within the wider organisational discourse. Storytelling commits the organisation to the creation and development of a technical or technologically based knowledge base and to a cultural shift.

Nurturing, therefore, has the most significant role within the SPADES model, in that it sets the appropriate direction for the development of both the technical and cultural environment. If the duality of this approach is not fully engaged with then there is a danger that the OLP will become too technologically focused and that ultimately the KBIS will simply be a repository of data that fails to stimulate learning and at best offers a database of eclectic information that is in danger of becoming an expensive white elephant.

14 Growing an experiential-learning community

Introduction

Once an organisation has planted and nurtured the experiential-learning community, it will then go on to grow those parts that have proved to be most beneficial. It will continue to develop the relationship between the individual and the organisation. The mentoring process enhances the relationship between key individuals and needs to be a cyclical process with mentees taking on the role of mentor. Within this relationship the ability to share knowledge through the storytelling function is also maintained and developed. This is developed further in the creation of possible futures that is at the heart of scenario planning, where individuals are allowed to use their imagination to create possible futures, to anticipate possible challenges and to create a meaningful dialogue around the implications of these possible futures.

Mentoring

Mentoring is by no means a new concept. For centuries wise men and women have provided help, advice and guidance for young people with aspirations of success. Mentors are usually much more senior and experienced managers, whose knowledge and judgement is respected by the mentee. Experience is more significant than seniority and it is not inconceivable that a mentor may be less senior than the mentee. Within the emerging digital context there are many skills and capabilities associated with this context that make this a more likely possibility, but it requires a great deal of trust and respect for this to operate successfully.

The role of the mentor is somewhat different to that of a coach in that although assistance with work issues can be given, other, and much wider issues, are covered. The mentor's role is very much about giving the individual the benefit of their experience, in effect 'short circuiting' the learning process by giving the individual information today which in other circumstances may take him or her years to discover. This will help to improve performance and individual career development, and embed the practice of knowledge sharing.

Mentoring is a mechanism that can support the transfer of tacit knowledge and can form part of an organisational learning programme that supports both the mentor and the mentee. For the mentor there is created an opportunity for them to reflect on what they themselves have learnt through their experience and for the mentee they can acquire knowledge not only drawn from the mentor but also from the process itself.

For both the mentor and the mentee there is a need to establish a relationship that is founded upon a mutual appreciation of the value to be gained from the relationship.

This two-way process highlights the value that initially is to be gained by the mentor. By engaging with this process the mentor can clarify their own experience and in doing so engage with the key tacit to explicit model. The incentive to do so, can come from an altruistic desire to pass on what has been learnt, based on a recognition of the value of what has been learnt. It is an opportunity to have experience challenged, opened up to scrutiny and to be changed. In doing so, the mentor will also gain further experience of forming knowledge in such a way as to make it accessible to others. For the mentee the incentive to enter into a mentoring relationship will emerge from recognising that valuable and necessary knowledge is missing and that in order to develop the necessary skills the acquisition of new knowledge is needed.

A mentee will look for key characteristics in a mentor.

- An individual who is respected in the field.
- An individual who will willingly engage with a process of knowledge transfer.
- An individual who is capable of effectively sharing their knowledge.

On this basis the mentor and the mentee can expect to establish a relationship that is based on mutual trust and respect. Given this as a basis for a relationship the mentor/mentee relationship is one of shared responsibility. The mentor is not responsible for the success of the exercise any more or any less than the mentee. Accountability rests between the two or between the groups. This makes mentoring somewhat different from coaching or training where there is less evenly distributed accountability and responsibility.

Any shift in this basic relationship needs to be made explicit, whether this is an aim to achieve a specific goal or develop individuals in a specific way. Not doing so will jeopardise the relationship between the mentor and the mentee. The building of this relationship is a key part of this mechanism and it needs to address crucial questions around how the relationship will be managed.

What level of support is necessary and how will this take place?

An appropriate style needs to be mutually approved. This might be the 'wise counsel' or the 'facilitator' with a light touch, looking to encourage the mentee to take decisions for themselves. Whatever approach might be adopted mentoring is characterised by generosity, care and a benevolence that should transcend any of the embedded issues within an organisation.

Mutual respect is, therefore, necessary and needs to be both established and maintained. This can be an issue at the early stages of mentoring and can be undermined when it is not clear what the 'value' of the mentor is. Perhaps the mentor is unknown to the mentee and their specific area of expertise is not recognised or known. This may form itself into a lack of respect. It is necessary to ensure that this absence of respect does not embed itself and lead on to an active contempt. Equally, at these early stages a mentee needs to be engaged meaningfully with the purpose or aim of the mentoring, and treated with respect. Here the mentor needs to avoid presenting themselves as the fount of all knowledge, to show that they are 'human', approachable and fallible. To an extent this is looking to empower the mentee in relation to the process. This looks to create a more equitable relationship where the mentee is not managed or led but accepts at an early stage that they are required to take responsibility for their own learning.

It cannot be expected that there will automatically be the necessary respect between mentor and mentee. Indeed, some degree of friction should be considered as the 'norm'. After all this is a challenging context for both individuals, one where they feel uncertainty and it is likely that they will be anxious about this process. If there is no clear identification of the value of this process then these initial anxieties are likely to express themselves as various excuses to disengage. 'Taking too much time', 'can't make it for the next meeting' and so on. This raises a key issue for the mentor concerning their own position within the relationship. Rather than being about encouraging the mentee to do things as you do, there is a need to recognise that they may choose to do things differently. If the mentor feels that this undermines their power or control then this is likely to be indicating the imposition of the mentor's ego.

Given the need for organisations to constantly acquire and continue to acquire new knowledge the mentoring process has attracted a great deal of interest over the last few years. Whether the need is to ensure that knowledge is not being lost or, as in some instances, that the organisation can be said to be haemorrhaging tacit knowledge, or that there is a need to stop reinventing the wheel and to use the accumulating knowledge more efficiently, the development of an effective scheme of mentoring can be an effective tool.

The mentoring scheme can be applied at various points within any organisation. This might be to directly develop individuals for specific purposes, either to enhance the organisational knowledge base or to encourage/support the individual at a particular point. Exactly how this might be measured as a 'return on intervention' may be difficult to identify. Just as trust exists within the mentoring relationship, so its outcome will require a degree of organisational trust in order for it to be effective.

 Pause for thought – Trust

At this point there is something that we are being asked to accept, namely that there is an embedded degree of trust within the organisation, and this may simply not be the case. Trust crops up at various points, it is embedded in the basic tacit to explicit model, in that, we trust that a whole series of processes will take place and create a substantial knowledge base for the organisation. We trust the altruism of those around us and yet accept that what is around us, is in fact a highly competitive environment. It would appear to be more prudent for us to assume a lack of trust.

So, trust has consistently presented itself as a key component of the developing OLP. It certainly merits not being taken for granted. Where opportunities exist to build trust then this itself is positive for the OLP, but how might this be measured? Here some qualitative techniques might be applied, trust might be ethnographically observed and it might even be quantified.

Take some time to think about how and where we might look for evidence of trust being embedded in organisational practices.

The goal or aim of mentoring is to produce individuals who are more capable and can apply their developing knowledge base more effectively. Here the individual is often being asked to challenge themselves or meet a specific fear. This is a fruitful ground for knowledge creation. Doubt and uncertainty sharpens senses and to an extent the mentoring relationship offers an opportunity to embark on a learning process where the mentee is moving into an area that is uncertain to them. The mentor is there to ensure that this uncertainty does not overwhelm the individual.

Here, the process of mentoring might be aligned with Senge's discipline of mental models. A mental model is an embedded pattern of behaviour that imposes itself negatively on practice. By presenting alternative patterns of behaviour this can initially help to externalise the embedded mental model and allow the mentee to acknowledge it. Having acknowledged it, its iterative and detrimental effects can be challenged through further dialogue.

 Pause for thought – Mental models and Senge

Senge was concerned with the individual's ability to identify their own 'position' in relation to the organisation and he talks about turning the mirror inwards. Try to think about this introspective approach and identify one thing that you think characterises your approach to work. This need not be negative but might look to identify where your own practice has become routine or taken for granted. In doing this, reflect also on just how uncomfortable a question this is. Would you expect everyone to be capable of this introspection, would some be more capable than others?

This is a clear opportunity to create a specific dialogue. It encourages introspection and there needs to be a clear and accepted purpose behind it. It cannot be idle chatter, in a phrase try to define the purpose of this activity.

Through a redistribution of responsibility fostered by mechanisms such as mentoring, there is or should be fostered a greater openness within the organisation. This may or may not impact directly on the overall coordination and control of the organisation. Building relationships and regarding this process of building as a key component element of the mentoring process characterises or represents the capabilities of the good mentor. Skills, knowledge or other types of ability are secondary to this, simply because without the perspective of a good mentor it becomes more difficult to turn those skills into an asset for the organisation.

Mentoring, therefore, helps to build the trust that is so necessary in the development of the key disciplines associated with the learning organisation. It does this through the development of effective dialogues that can start with:

Listening: through being an effective listener the mentor will build a more collaborative or sharing context for themselves and the mentee. This will be achieved only where the individual mentor fully invests in the relationship. Similarly, the mentee needs to identify the goal or purpose of the context. Where there is this clarity and level of investment then the relationship should succeed.

Trust: a mentor must ensure that the relationship is allowed to develop and that they positively maintain a position and an attitude that will not undermine the developing trust between mentor and mentee. This can happen naturally as individuals become more familiar with one another and where the genuineness of the connection is made. Being genuine can relate to a free and open acceptance of limitations, the mentor can be seen to have limitations.

Limitations: these will emerge in relation to the task set and the role of the mentor is to ensure that challenges and obstacles are overcome along the way. By drawing on experience the mentor will be in a position to offer a more informed view or option to the mentee.

Assisting an individual to gain knowledge from the mentoring process is the principal goal. It is focused on the creation of a sound and ongoing dialogue that is at the heart of any OLP. In establishing a relationship there needs to be an initial meeting that focuses not on what might or might not be learnt but the *extent of the commitment* to the process. The potential relationship or the extent to which individuals might feel some affinity for one another is secondary at this early stage. Rather, it is important to get to know the personal and professional background of both the mentor and the mentee, and on exploring the expectation of the process itself:

*   How long they think meetings should last?
*   How frequent these meeting should be?

Creating this practical structure is the goal at this stage and if successful there is a basis for the necessary commitment to the process. After this has been established successfully it can be developed. This can start by restating the perceptions of the first meeting and in these early stages it is important to allow the structure to help embed practice and to establish a routine for the dialogue. This can then be followed by a more *detailed consideration of just what the content might be*. What expertise is being sought? What does the mentee want to know or more likely what does the mentee think they need to know? Guidance at this stage can be given to help form what will be the trajectory for the relationship. Again, using an explicit or even formal structure can help to establish the necessary pattern of practice.

Once this pattern of practice becomes embedded then the real 'work' of mentoring begins. To sustain it the mentor needs to ensure that they fulfil or *meet the expectations* that have been agreed. They need to be present, they need to gauge the required level of support and to avoid being overbearing or too *laissez-faire*. The pace and tone of the relationship will emerge and it is to be expected that there will be some issues or concerns along the way. Again, drawing on structure and recognising the soundness of the foundations helps to sustain the relationship as it develops and both parties need to recognise that they will be developing – the mentor in terms of being a mentor and the mentee, hopefully in terms of what they have identified as their learning goals. Being self-reflective assists this process and mentors need to consider how they are performing and how they might develop the skills they are acquiring and needing to support the mentee.

As part of this review there is inevitably an *assessment of the outcomes* that will ultimately form an end for the process as a whole. It has been established at the outset that this relationship and the dialogues embedded within it are finite. This might be agreed at the first meeting, it might be a set number of meetings, or a specific time period. At this stage the OLP can grow further by either an agreement to sustain the process for an extended period or to use it to form the basis of further mentoring schemes involving other colleagues. Acknowledging that useful conversations and the close relationship that is developed during any mentoring scheme have an explicit value for the organisation is crucial as it argues for their retention and development.

The mentoring process can be a challenging one for those individuals asked to be either a mentor or a mentee. As has been seen, as part of the nurturing process, socialisation has a role to play in ensuring that the individuals and groups understand and appreciate the aims and objectives of the OLP. Primarily, the need to establish the appropriate relationships is emphasised and this applies to the mentoring process. In doing so, it needs to consider some of the key challenges.

- The mentor needs to balance their responsibilities, attempting to do too much will reduce an individual's ability to sustain the momentum necessary for this process. More importantly, the mentor needs to maintain the collaborative nature of the OLP and avoid placing the mentor in a position of power or authority over the mentee, tempting as this might be.
- There needs to be a clear identification of what is to be achieved and how it is to be achieved. This will be explicitly outlined in the opening exchanges and will be drawn from the process of socialisation. Where there is this established and embedded trust then the mentoring process can progress positively, it can avoid any negative behaviours that might express themselves in less constructive dialogues.

 Pause for thought – Truth test

How equal are you?

Identify a relationship where you might assume some authority or greater status and ask yourself:

I can easily acknowledge a sense of sameness with this person.
True
False

I can be comfortable disclosing information about myself to this person.
True
False

Domestically, I would be happy to make this person a cup of coffee.
True
False

This person has something to offer me.
True
False

Would I reconsider my own view if this person's view differed from it?
True
False

The purpose of these questions is to encourage self-reflection. If the answers are predominantly 'true' then there is likely to be a perceived level of equality. If false then a perceived difference of status exists and this may impact upon the development of a successful mentoring process/relationship.

The challenge of the mentoring process is to sustain this balanced relationship and encourage a reflective approach to its establishment and development. Particularly on the part of the mentor there is a need to ensure that they do not place themselves in a 'superior' position to the mentee and recognise that the purpose of the relationship is to create gains for both parties on equal terms. The principal challenge here is to ensure mutual dependency and this again requires an explicit opportunity to reflect on the process and perhaps to recognise the role of a third party as a neutral observer of the mentoring process.

The OL practitioner can undertake this role of neutral observer in relation to mentoring relationships. Importantly, the function here is not to be critical of either the mentor or the mentee but to encourage both parties to take some time themselves to consider how the process has been working, how it has changed and is changing. Are these changes disturbing the balance of the relationship or enhancing it? Is there evidence that one party has become too dependent on the other?

Observation of both the mentor and the mentee can identify where a mentee might be requiring validation from the mentor too often and inhibiting their ability to act or make decisions. This may be an issue with the mentor who has imposed too much control within the relationship or with the mentee who is placing too much emphasis on the status of the mentor as an expert or guru. It may indeed be a combination of these issues. The role of the OL practitioner is to identify this as an issue and to make it explicit. Through the embedded dialogue between the mentoring partners and the OL practitioner this type of issue can be addressed.

As a part of the OLP, mentoring will help to grow learning as an organisational activity. It should become an iterative process where mentees look to become mentors. Equally, as specific skills develop there can be an open presentation of these as potential opportunities for mentoring as a mechanism to share these skills. It is not inconceivable that a former mentee might mentor a former mentor.

Case study: Wood Group, Aberdeen

People core value

People are the heart of our business.

We are professional, high performing team players focused on delivering and drawing on our global expertise.

We aim to attract, develop and retain the best people, treating each other with honesty, compassion and respect.

We create a stimulating, fun and open work culture that promotes personal development and work/life balance, rewards competitively and celebrates success.

Looking at this Core Value through the lens of the SPADES model this fits with the GROWING element, particularly mentoring and storytelling (see Figure 14.1).

As the core value says 'People are the heart of our business' and we pride ourselves on having some of the best people in the industry. With recent studies suggesting that 50 per cent of the technical community in the oil and gas industry will retire in the next 5 years and that it can take 8.2 years for new engineers to reach the same knowledge level of those about to retire it is hugely important to the business that we leverage our collective experience as much as possible in developing and retaining our emerging talent.

Figure 14.1 Wood Group: People

Our goal is to create a development organisation and environment that encourages continued development at all levels. Our developing talent population is key to the future success of the organisation and as such the partnership between our developing talent population and the leadership of the business is critical. This is a reciprocal relationship, where the organisation commits to providing an environment where our employees can develop and progress and in return we have committed and loyal employees.

Feedback is a feature of our organisation – we encourage honest and open feedback between all our employees. It is one of our most effective means of development and we have tools available to help ensure it happens. The developing talent programme is a two-way partnership between the business and the developing talent population.

Our people core value is explicit in outlining that WGPSN encourages personal development. We believe that employees and the company have a shared responsibility for career and competence development. We recognise the need for employees to acquire additional skills, knowledge and experience to meet the short-term needs of the job, as well as the longer-term needs of themselves and the company. Our approach to developing talent focuses on developing well rounded employees who are technically competent and have a drive to develop within the organisation. All our development interventions are aligned to our core values and our leadership framework. We achieve this through:

- High energy onboarding programme designed to immerse new employees in the Wood Group culture.
- Opportunity to access a substantial development package including on-the-job training and support.

- A structured training plan, developed to help you achieve increased competence in your chosen discipline.
- Top quality training courses related to your training plan as well as access to a range of general business and personal development skills development.
- Opportunity to attend conferences and events.
- Structured mentoring programmes with senior leadership.
- Professional guidance, support and feedback from within your discipline/function.
- Regular performance discussion through my success plan, our tool to record what you plan to do to be successful and how.
- Guidance and support from the talent development team regarding opportunities available to you to help you drive your career forward.
- Access to a peer network through the Developing Talent Committee.

The structured mentoring programme is of particular value to our developing talent community as it allows one to one interaction with an assigned senior leader. This relationship is based on trust and on mutual benefit. First, for the mentee to learn and grow from the experience of the senior leaders and second, for the mentor to play a vital role in sharing experience and learning to further the development of a Wood Group employee.

The mentor and mentee enter into a Monitoring contract which they both develop and sign. This contract provides some boundaries to the relationship and guidance on particular areas of interest or development for the mentee.

Scenario planning

Planning represents a key function of management. The purpose of any plan is to achieve specific aims and objectives, but to do this within an organisation there is a need to identify where it is at present and to be clear about where it might want to go, or is likely to be going, in the future. To an extent all planning is linked to forecasting. The value of information and knowledge plays an important part here, as they largely form the raw materials of planning and decision making. Without good data and information, without the statistics or the numbers identifying the possible trends, planning ahead would be impossible.

However, planning is extended beyond a rather simplistic projection based on statistics that might represent growth in specific areas/markets or in relation to specific products/services. Raw data of this sort forms just one part of a more complex consideration of a range of information sources. As planning extends itself into the future this becomes more pertinent. Scenario planning, therefore, that might look 10 or 20 years ahead, needs to be based on a range of information sources that will look to identify how an organisation will or may look to operate within its wider environment. In doing so, this challenges the embedded assumptions based on the 'way things are done' and promotes a willingness to more readily accept that there may be a need to do things differently.

Incremental and evolutionary change is unlikely to be the experience of most organisations over the next 20 years. For many it is certain that there will be unexpected developments that will require at times a radical change of direction. The unexpected nature of these developments shifts the planning process from one that focuses on what view we might create of the past, based on available data and information, to the creation of potential views of the future. Planning for the future is not about extending the view of the past beyond the present but accepting that the future can potentially be varied, but that these variations need to be identified and their implications considered.

Accuracy is not a necessity here. A range of possible futures that are fully articulated will allow organisations to consider their potential responses to the implications embedded in each (*if we are likely to face . . ., then we will need to be better at . . .*). Questions are raised about just how flexible and responsive the organisation may need to be or what capability it will require if such a future were to emerge.

> Instead of relying on projections that basically paint a picture of your future business landscape as a variation on the way it currently looks, scenario planning challenges the very idea that there is **a** future that is 'most likely' to emerge.
>
> (Wade 2012: loc. 275 of 3385)

Failing to plan for the future or to be able to see the likely direction that a market may take can be catastrophic for an organisation. For example, in 2011 the Polaroid Corporation filed for bankruptcy and this was partly put down to its inability to fully appreciate the impact that digital technologies would have on their core photography business. To plan for the future is, therefore, a necessity, but one that has obvious difficulties. Not least, it is almost impossible to predict the future with any certainty which leaves scenario planning as an imprecise activity that will fail in some respects and to some degree. Nevertheless, even if it cannot claim to be entirely accurate, there may still be value in both the process itself and in the identification of general trends that can inform decision making.

The oil company Shell has been associated with the use of scenarios:

> Shell has been using scenarios since the early 1970s to allow generations of leaders make better business decisions. Over time, the Shell Scenarios have gained a global following among governments, academia and other businesses. They have helped deepen understanding of how the world might appear decades ahead.
>
> (Royal Dutch Shell 2015)

The systemic or holistic view is essential for successful scenario planning and this, therefore, links this process with Senge's key discipline of *systemic thinking*. Here, it is necessary to view the environment within which any organisation will be placed, as well as the inter-connected nature of the activities that make up the organisation within its own boundary. From a range of complex variables a future will emerge, but just exactly what future this will be is uncertain. Rather than focusing on attempting to identify this single future, scenario planning is about accepting that there will be a range of possible futures and the organisation needs to be prepared to meet all of the challenges inherent in these futures.

This is fundamentally what scenario planning is aiming to do and shifting the mindset of the organisation away from certainties and into the less defined context of multiple or variable certainties is very much the embracing of a postmodern concept of the organisation. The emphasis here is on flexibility, agility, responsiveness and the willingness to explore and extrapolate with a view to identifying just how able the organisation is to meet the challenge of this fluid environment.

To embed scenario planning as a valid organisational practice there needs to be, as has been seen above, a certain mentality or way of thinking. Within the SPADES model the *planting* and *nurturing* elements will look to ensure that this mentality is well established and that scenario planning will be supported by both the appropriate technological infrastructure and the key cultural characteristics that are rooted in a trusting, open and sharing environment.

The process:

1   Identify key drivers and explore embedded assumptions.
2   Identify the commonality between the key drivers.
3   Create around eight initial scenarios based on the key drivers.
4   Refine these initial scenarios to two or three.
5   Produce draft scenarios and create stories.
6   Consider key issues and implications.
7   Monitor and update.

The success of scenario planning will ultimately be based on the nature of the participants' engagement with the process. Success will be down to the willingness of individuals to collectively learn from each other, to challenge their own assumptions and accept that the other participants have valid and constructive contributions to make. This is very much the environment that the OLP is seeking to create, making scenario planning a more mature element within the development of the OLP.

A key capability will also be the ability of individuals to communicate and to create strong narratives. In producing scenarios they are essentially producing stories around the organisation's future and these need to have legitimacy, in other words the teller needs to have the authority to tell this story based on respect for them within the organisation, as well as being able to create entertaining and engaging stories. Storytelling is, therefore, a key part of scenario planning.

The stories themselves will be dependent upon the information used to help create them. These stories need to be informed and to be based on sound data, information and knowledge about the organisation and its environment. To help identify key drivers the PEST model can be useful:

Political – what political issues impact upon the organisation, significance of government intervention or the introduction of relevant legislation?
Economic – which economic developments will be likely to have an impact, a fall in prices or significant new players in the market?
Social – what social trends will be significant, an increasing concern for personal health and fitness, a concern for the environment?
Technological – where are the emerging technological developments and is the organisation capable of keeping up to speed with these developments?

Being able to access and effectively and critically consider what might be a large amount of information cannot be assumed. The ability to interrogate a database, the availability of the relevant databases and so on are capabilities necessary to drive this exercise. Again there may be a requirement here to collect primary data and this may be done through *semi-structured interviews* of key individuals.

The purpose of a semi-structured interview is to create a series of questions that allow for new ideas to emerge during the interview process. However, there needs to be a clear understanding of the overall aim or purpose of the interview, in order to ensure that it does not stray into related or even unrelated areas. The skill of the interviewer here is to identify where this divergence may be occurring and then to be able to draw the conversation back to the key area or areas.

Similarly, key abilities at the early stage of this process will include:

Brainstorming

In order to identify the key drivers the group tasked with creating the scenarios will be required to share ideas and produce stories. Brainstorming is an established technique used to facilitate this type of communication. It is a technique associated with Alex F. Osborn (1888–1966) who developed it as a method for creative problem solving.

As with any group-working technique it is the dynamic of the group itself that will determine either its success or failure. Individuals need to feel confident that their contribution will have value and that they have had sufficient opportunity to form their own ideas. Therefore, preparatory work ahead of a brainstorming exercise is to allow individuals an opportunity to consider the question, in this case building scenarios. The validity of each individual member's contribution needs to be firmly established and as part of a more mature OLP this should be already established. However, this can be emphasised in order to avoid any blocking or free riding where individuals feel reluctant to present their ideas.

> Choosing the actual participants is an important task needing some real consideration. If the scenario planning is to have the greatest potential value, then the people who help create the scenarios should be open, intelligent, motivated, imaginative and strategic thinkers.
>
> (Wade 2012: loc. 543 of 3385)

According to the Osborn method there are two key principles:

- defer judgement
- reach for quality.

In the first instance the aim is to generate the ideas that will help to identify the stories that will be used to create the scenarios. All participants will present their ideas and form a comprehensive list. This will then be considered and commonality between these ideas will be used to refine this initial list into a first collective list of ideas. At this point the purpose of the brainstorming exercise has been achieved.

In beginning to analyse the results of the brainstorming exercise the two key characteristics that are being sought are:

- potential impact – high or low;
- uncertainty – high or low.

There may not be complete agreement about how each driver might relate to its potential impact or its level of uncertainty but through constructive discussion some consensus can and should be reached. The aim of scenario planning is to focus on those drivers that are high impact with a high degree of uncertainty – the *critical uncertainties*. It is the critical uncertainties that will form the final scenarios. Each scenario can be named in order to provide it with a suitable identity, just as any good story will have a title. Each element or driver within each scenario should be discussed further to develop ideas and thoughts around their significance in terms of their overall impact and the nature or implications of this impact. For example, the need to embed technologies identifies a range of issues around the skills base and the ability of the workforce to assimilate an increasing pace of technological innovation. Perhaps key individuals or groups will need specific support, which will have a significant financial impact or even a social impact. Perhaps it will negatively impact upon group dynamics if it creates a greater turnover in staff and disrupts an innovative and highly motivated group or team.

Compiling these stories is in itself a challenge. The assumption being that they will have the capabilities of the creative writer. This is enhanced by the fact that this is a team-working exercise. Having clarity in relation to the scenario and being willing to alter the parameters of that scenario where it is proving too difficult to construct a meaningful or coherent story is necessary. Mixing individuals around between the scenarios being considered can provide a valuable insight into how the narrative is forming. As with most narratives it is helpful to identify a structure or an outline of the story. Where will it start, what are its key elements and where is it heading?

In judging the quality of the final scenario, its plausibility, clarity, relevance and comprehensiveness are the key factors. Is the story recognisable from the current position, does it progress logically from its starting point, does it maintain a sound focus of what is being considered and does it contain all that it would be expected to contain?

The purpose of the scenario is to present a possible view of the future with a reasonable expectation that this is realistic. Given this, the organisation then needs to develop some strategic option for meeting the challenges inherent in these possible and realistic scenarios. It is helpful at this stage to identify where there might be some indications of which scenario is potentially emerging. What key signs might indicate that a particular scenario is emerging? Working with the scenario, these indicators can be used to adapt and update the scenario, to reflect where specific impacts might have been under- or overestimated.

Case study: VisitScotland

Executives of VisitScotland used scenario planning to identify the key challenges for Scottish tourism, an industry that is normally expected to contribute around £1 billion to the Scottish economy. Scotland was looking to boost both its international and domestic tourist trade, by attracting more visitors from abroad and from the rest of the UK. A high-level team from across the sector, including representatives from the Scottish Arts Council, Scottish Natural Heritage and the Scottish Government discussed, analysed and identified the key drivers. From the discussions four scenarios emerged.

Exclusive Scotland – attracting high spending international tourists in the face of a collapse of the domestic market. High unemployment and high costs undermine the domestic market but a favourable exchange rate will attract wealthy visitors. Exclusive resorts are prioritised, offering key activities around gambling, hunting, fishing or relaxation.

Weekend getaway – placing the emphasis on entertainment and consumption based on key recreational activities. This will be dependent upon falling air fares, cheaper train travel and moderate hotel fees, attracting casual visitors to Scotland for short breaks. The focus here would be on attracting visitors from Europe rather than further afield.

Yesterday's destination – a moribund industry, lacking any real drivers for change. The direction of travel is from rather than to Scotland. The industry becomes complacent and cheaper more attractive destinations can be found elsewhere. Exchange rates do not favour Scotland.

Dynamic Scotland – creating an industry that will generate around £10 billion for the Scottish economy. This will be dependent upon a favourable exchange rate, growing disposable incomes, lower rates of income tax, lower oil prices and an enhanced infrastructure.

In 2003 the executives at VisitScotland worked with these scenarios and had to contend with major occurrences and events including the terror attacks on the US and the outbreaks of both foot and mouth disease and avian flu. From the terror attacks and the subsequent war in Iraq there could either be major economic disruption or just a short-term hiatus. The four scenarios become:

Global Northern Ireland – major disruption to tourism due to terror attack.
Into the Valley of Death – major military disaster in Iraq leading to a financial crisis.
New Dawn – major assault on Iraq which causes instability in the market, but a new order emerges.
How the West was Won – conflict is localised and has no major impact upon Scotland.

The *How the West was Won* scenario proved to be the closest to what actually transpired and although this has impacted negatively on tourism the fact that VisitScotland could consider plans for this eventuality made its occurrence less traumatic. It was not an unexpected event that might cause panic or high levels of insecurity. It was an externalised possibility and as such some consideration had already been given to what actions might need to be taken. VisitScotland was able to prepare for a downturn in the US market, for an unfavourable exchange rate and to shift their efforts to the European market, preferably through direct flights to Scottish airports avoiding the London hubs. (Based on details in Wade, 2012)

Scenario planning aims to highlight the benefits to be gained from foresight and to potentially avoid the many pitfalls that might be easily identified with hindsight. It requires an organisation to value the experience of individuals and to allow those individuals to reflect on this experience. This is not solely to look at operational or even tactical issues, but also at the strategic level. Scenario planning is at this strategic level, it does ask questions about the direction of the organisation as it sits within its environment. It is not going to ensure that any organisation is 'future-proof' but it can lessen the impact of future events. Not least it can help to build a mentality that favours imaginative and critical thought, that embeds a deeper approach to learning rather than a more practically focused and limited strategic approach to learning. It is a shift away from linear thinking and a more liberating approach to the crucial attempt to understand change.

Concluding remarks

Growing the OLP allows the organisation to deploy more effectively the groundwork that has been carried out at both the *planting* and *nurturing* stages of the SPADES model. Both mentoring and scenario planning are underpinned by the technical and cultural context that has been, and is being, created. The development of the mutually beneficial relationship that underpins mentoring is founded on trust, similarly the group dynamics at work within scenario planning requires mutual respect to be well embedded in the culture of the organisation.

Similarly, the conversations that both of these techniques will produce will also form part of a wider data resource that the OL practitioner can use as part of a systematic and thorough analysis of the underlying discourse within the organisation. How are individuals relating to one another, what characteristics can be identified that might impede OL?

The key element of trust has been highlighted here and it is important to recognise that trust can either mean that individuals will have some freedom to explore their own thoughts and ideas, and to challenge existing practices, or it can mean that they feel they will be protected when challenged. Where organisations are tasked with dealing with the consequences of a fluid and dynamic environment, where their familiar patterns of behaviour are challenged, then there is a strong tendency to regard this as a threat and to act defensively.

> Attempts to introduce doubts and uncertainty mobilise powerful social defences that push away disturbing information, distort reality, and erode the atmosphere of genuine trust. The way to deal with this threat is to help organisational members understand that the realities they experience are, at least in part, objects of their own construction.
>
> (Lipshitz, Friedman and Popper 2006: 248)

Without an appropriate understanding of what is expected of individuals in relation to key techniques, such as mentoring and scenario planning, their effectiveness will be limited or at least stalled by the need to either establish the correct approach or attitude amongst the participants, or to identify and counter behaviours that emerge during the application of these techniques. This is both time consuming and costly. A well-established technical environment, offering the appropriate opportunities for motivated individuals, within a cultural context characterised by an equally appropriate understanding of trust, to identify and externalise their experience will drive the development of the OLP.

15 Propagating practices in an experiential-learning community

Spreading the message

Introduction

Once an organisation has planted, nurtured and grown the practices associated with experiential learning, it will then go on to propagate and spread the practice more effectively and comprehensively across the organisation. This is the mature stage of the experiential-learning cycle where the technical and cultural environment has been well embedded and individuals and groups have a clear appreciation of the value of knowledge sharing.

Through processes such as mentoring, the individual has learnt the value of collaboration over competition and has actively sought to develop the skills that will be needed to externalise their own knowledge, for example, storytelling. The OL practitioner is developing a rich understanding of the conversations that make up the dialogue of the organisation in order to further enhance this cycle of experiential learning.

To complete the experiential-learning cycle and to stimulate the necessary momentum to ensure that it becomes the iterative process of learning that is at the heart of the OLP, we will focus on the *communities of practice* (CoP) model and the process of *reflection*. As a model that focuses on the notion of 'community' there is a clear sense of this being a model that aligns itself with a very specific view of the relationships that should be existing within organisations that aim to fully embed the OLP.

Communities of practice

The sense of *community* is one of respect, trust and mutual assistance. In a community individuals are both apolitical and altruistic. A community is independent of agency and therefore requires no external management. It is self-organising and self-sustaining. More than this, communities or the sense of community is where we want to be. It has positive connotations of security and of a comfortable, familiar companionship.

> In a community, we all understand each other well, we may trust what we hear, we are safe most of the time and hardly ever puzzled or taken aback. We are never strangers to each other.
>
> (Bauman 2001: loc. 43 of 2338)

We actively seek to be a part of a community, and to an extent within the contemporary environment we have been deprived of this within the wider social context of the digital age. Our fragmented lives have often broken down along with the sense of commonality that once existed. We source our information in many different ways, there are multiple means to access the world around us and we are less dependent upon the news media to provide us with their mediated view. This view is no longer shared and through social media we are forming a range of disparate networks that seek out commonality and a sense of shared experience. Similarly, in an organisation plurality is the norm, from patterns of work to behavioural norms and the need to embrace difference.

The strength of the community is now recognised as being embedded within its ability to embrace this difference. A community will embrace diverse views and be able to appropriately assimilate the views of all. Through this the organisation will be capable of sustaining efficiency and effectiveness.

The focus on *practice* links this to the activities and actions associated with professionals within organisations. Because all individuals have a familiarity with the other members of the community, there is less time spent searching for information. They are familiar with who knows what and can justify expecting this knowledge to be made available when required. This lowers the costs associated with information seeking and transfer. Where this becomes mutually supporting, as it should in a community, the need for enforcement is also reduced.

> Communities of practice embody the ability to learn and collaborate. In other words, communities of practice provide an essential platform that fosters learning and collaborating across the organisation. Communities function as tangible vessels that enable organisations to meet important challenges presented by the knowledge era.
>
> (Saint-Onge and Wallace 2003: loc. 1184 of 6840)

This 'knowledge era' has thrown up the need for organisations to respond to more complex demands from customers, users and other stakeholders. Both internally and externally the demands made of the traditional hierarchical model of organisations cannot easily be met. Instead, the demands are requiring a more collaborative and cross-functional structure. The organisation needs to draw on its collective know-how to a greater extent and this creates many challenges for organisations that are embedded in traditional hierarchical structures and relying on accountability to drive action.

To shift the organisation towards a more cross-functional structure requires the concept of collaboration to be embedded in the strategy of the organisation. This strategy needs to adopt a comprehensive view of knowledge as an organisational asset and should seek to provide universal access to information and avoid any segmentation of knowledge exchange. All individuals and groups need to be given access to the knowledge base, through the appropriate technological mechanisms. In supporting the principle of universal access it is also beginning to embed and develop trust. As individuals take up their personal responsibility for sharing their tacit knowledge they are opening themselves up, making themselves more visible and at this point there needs to be explicit reassurance of the way in which this enhanced visibility will be respected by the organisation.

Corporate intranets are, therefore, more than functional repositories: they are also testing grounds for intentions and attitudes. To an extent they challenge the organisation to 'come clean' on the impetus behind any knowledge-based strategy for its OLP. It will soon become apparent when an organisation might be looking at this to enhance visibility as a mechanism for control and for imposing greater restraint on individuals rather than allowing them to openly develop key relationships and networks that will support and enhance OL.

The CoP model

The CoP model requires an appropriate environment and it requires individuals to behave in a particular way that reflects this inherent respect for the Other, the ethical foundation stone of OL. It also reflects the strengthening view of knowledge as a collective resource, rather than an individual one. The CoP model, therefore, can be aligned both with the humanistic elements associated with OD and the postmodern ethics that we have aligned with all of the OL practices considered throughout this text. It will negate the panoptic effects of technology by reducing the need for agency and monitoring. Removing this need will in turn build trust, which sustains the experiential-learning cycle.

The consideration of communities of practice as mechanisms for learning in organisations is aligned to the practice-based approach that acknowledges the importance of day-to-day experience as the catalyst for the generation of tacit knowledge (Brown and Duguid, 1991; Lave and Wenger, 1991, Wenger, 1998). To a large extent the question that is being considered here, is – how ready are we to learn for the organisation? What will motivate us to share our tacit knowledge and where are our opportunities to do so? These are what von Krogh (2011) refers to as *opportunity structures*.

> Opportunity structures refer to the benefits of sharing knowledge in the community and occasions for doing so. Since interest and knowledge are intimately connected, and since it takes more effort to identify sharing possibilities if affiliates have diverse interests (irrespective of community size), the opportunity structure of a community is a particularly important factor in the problem of knowledge sharing.
>
> (von Krogh 2011: 416)

The role of the OL practitioner is to understand or appreciate the nature of the opportunities that might exist within an organisation. Are these *narrow*, affording few opportunities or more *broad* with greater opportunities available to community members? Primarily, this will require us to overcome the issue embedded in the tacit to explicit model where there is a recognition that knowledge creation is initially on an individual level but for it to be of real value to the organisation it must be externalised in some form, usually through dialogue or other communicative mechanisms.

> Knowledge is localised in individual heads and is largely tacit, being expressed in professional skills. For knowledge to exist at the organisational level it must be shared by individuals and it is usual to assume that individuals are reluctant to share their personal knowledge with each other.
>
> (Stacey 2001: 40)

We cannot accept that sharing is a natural or 'normal' process that will inevitably follow from the application of increasingly sophisticated communication technologies. As we have established elsewhere, the social dimension of OL is seeking to present us with a view of how we might stimulate and encourage an organisational culture where we can address the barriers to knowledge sharing and ultimately create an environment that is conducive to learning at the organisational level. To an extent, it is this sense of community that bridges the gap between the individual and the organisation. In a genuine community there is a positive answer to whether or not individuals are willing to share their own tacit knowledge for the benefit of the organisation. However, this has been hard won and will not emerge independently of actions to build the necessary relationships. The planting, nurturing and growing elements within the SPADES model are the actions that can be associated with this crucial process that will ultimately provide the cycle with the momentum it needs to be an ongoing and iterative process or spiral.

Communities will develop their own mechanisms for knowledge sharing that will reflect their own behavioural preferences and these will over time form routines and to an extent become expected. These can become ritualised and can provide positive certainty to proceedings, but can also ossify into rules that can stifle the spontaneity that is often the hallmark of knowledge sharing. CoP have emerged as a key approach to the deployment of OL within organisations. They are essentially group or team-working environments that are sympathetic to the global networked environment experienced by many contemporary organisations.

Consider the following:

- A CoP is a network of people who share a common interest in a specific area of knowledge or competence and are willing to work and learn together over a period of time to develop and share that knowledge.
- Etienne Wenger is credited with coining the term CoP. He defines them as groups of people who share a concern, a set of problems, or a passion about a topic, and who deepen their knowledge and expertise by interacting on an ongoing basis.
- Wenger also believes that learning is a social activity and that people learn best in groups.

Etienne Wenger (1998) states that CoP differ from teams or work groups in a number of fundamental ways:

Voluntary membership
> Whereas teams and work groups are formed by management, membership of a community of practice is voluntary.

Specific focus
> Teams and work groups are formed to focus on a specific objective or activity, while communities of practice are not necessarily; they may have some stated goals, but they are more general and fluid.

No expectation of tangible results
> Teams and work groups are required to deliver tangible results, whereas communities of practice are not necessarily required to do so.

Existence defined by group members
> Teams and work groups are disbanded or reorganised once they have achieved their goals, while communities of practice last as long as their members want them to last. The CoP can be said to follow a distinct life cycle (Saint-Onge and Wallace, 2003). It will begin with the identification of potential and why the community might need to be formed. Once formed the community will come together and form a specific identity; it will then grow and this identity will manifest itself in specific types of practices, behaviours and routines; this maturity will begin to plateau and the community may fragment or look to transform itself by changing focus or simply come to an end.

Melissie Rumizen (2001) calls CoP 'the killer knowledge management application' which:

- provides a valuable vehicle for developing, sharing and managing specialist knowledge;
- avoids 'reinventing the wheel';

- cuts across departmental boundaries and formal reporting lines;
- can be more flexible than traditional organisational units;
- generates new knowledge in response to problems and opportunities;
- provides early warning of potential opportunities and threats;
- can be a vehicle for cultural change (creating a knowledge sharing culture);
- are largely self-organising.

As well as the organisational benefits, CoP also provides benefits for individual community members, including:

- having access to expert help to expand horizons, gain knowledge and seek help in addressing work challenges;
- enabling members to feel more conscious of, and confident in, their own personal knowledge;
- providing a non-threatening forum to explore and test ideas or validate courses of action;
- fostering a greater sense of professional commitment and enhancing members' professional reputation.

CoP, therefore, are a key component element in relation to OL. They are more than an electronic forum. Three elements make up the model, according to Wenger:

Domain – the knowledge base that defines the discipline or area of interest.
Community – the individuals who make up the community.
Practice – the activity of the community that drives its collaborative learning.

Many different types of CoP have been presented, such as *communities of interest* or *communities of learning*, and these have manifested themselves in organisations in a number of different forms. Some have been highly formalised with a defined purpose and structure, while others have been highly limited and informal, with little structure. Each will reflect the nature of the commitment of the organisation to the model. It can be argued that the more formalised and structured CoP begins to move away from the crucial elements that define and distinguish the CoP from other work related teams and groups. It is the informality of the model that is its defining characteristic and any compromise on this will simply create a working group that will not function as a CoP and cannot be presented as one.

CoP are fundamentally collaborative and cooperative. They are based on a recognition by individuals that they have a need to know and that the knowledge they require will be acquired more effectively through this collaboration and cooperation. In turn, this recognition ensures that the community will be self-regulating or self-managing. On this basis it will generate knowledge that supports and is relevant to the domain of practice, and it will use a range of opportunities to support this activity. The organisation must support this, must appreciate the benefits to be gained but must 'trust' the CoP to be doing what it is has been created to do. This can be the greatest challenge for organisations but it forms an important part of the trust that underpins the model and the OLP more generally.

Fundamentally, the CoP is a social space and the learning that takes place within it is a form of social learning. As with any social context different dynamics will determine the way in which the community functions. Different roles will be played by specific individuals. Saint-Onge and Wallace (2003) have proposed:

Connectors – these are the good networks, able to make connections and form relationships with a broad range of individuals. They have high levels of energy and sociability.
Mavens – these are the good communicators of information, who know a lot and are looking to share it.
Salespeople – these are the persuaders, the individuals who are enthusiastic and want to promote action.

Within these broad types there are individuals who will naturally question and seek debate, others who will add their own 'tuppence' worth, or be good at drawing disparate ideas together. This rich dialogue is the basis for the CoP and a successful CoP will be exchanging knowledge and creating knowledge, using a range of different tools and techniques that are made available to the community, often through the embedded social networking technologies, which in turn make up the knowledge-based information system.

There is, clearly, a social dimension in relation to the knowledge creation that defines the purpose of the CoP. Rather than making explicit discrete knowledge artefacts that can be embedded within specific knowledge-based technologies, the *process* through which sense-making takes place is given precedence. Here the communicative environment is central and the skills that are prized over all others are those which allow us as individual professionals to effectively externalise the skills and expertise that represent our developing personal knowledge base.

> . . . they take a sense-making approach to think about organisational knowledge in the context of communities of practice in which individuals convey what they know about practice to each other through storytelling.
>
> (Stacey 2001: 41)

CoP, therefore, pull together a number of key elements that we have been considering. They are, in very simple terms, a networked environment, very similar in functionality to many other such social networking environments. These are contexts that facilitate and support a level of connectivity that previously could not be considered. Groups or teams as well as individuals can all communicate in increasingly diverse and convenient ways, where geography, in terms of both time and space, is virtually no longer seen as a barrier – geography is history!

However, CoP should not be seen primarily in terms of the functionality that they represent. Rather they help to create a series of dialogues and these dialogues are the drivers behind the value that is to be gained from the application of CoP. These dialogues, according to Wenger, address four key areas:

Meaning – learning as experience
    Here we are encouraged to engage in a dialogue around our changing abilities and how our experience helps us to form our understanding of the world. In a purely organisational context we are talking about how we understand that organisation and how we experience it. Why do I have the view of the organisation that I have? How has this changed? Most of us can recognise the type of issue here, where, perhaps, we have thought we understood the organisation and 'how it works' but how this has

been altered when the organisation 'acts' in a way that we find unusual. In these cases we alter our view or understanding of the organisation. Dialogue around meaning is this type of experience.

Practice – learning as doing

Here we have a dialogue around how it is we do things within the organisation, because of specific configurations, such as social formations or other resources. This might be structural, the way the organisation is set up, perhaps, hierarchical. In talking about practice we are looking for a way of talking about the shared historical and social resources, frameworks and perspectives that can sustain mutual engagement in action.

Community – learning as belonging

Here we have a dialogue around our social configurations, talking about our understanding of the community that we are part of, our own position within it and our understanding of the position of others. Do these social configurations meet our expectations and are they adequate for the intended purpose? Our view of this community will tell us a lot about the social relationships that will underpin the crucial elements of the organisation's culture.

Identity – learning as becoming

Here we have a dialogue around how our learning changes who we are and creates personal histories of becoming in the context of our communities. We are going through a reflective process, looking at our own personal development as part of a specific community, what we do, why we do it in the way that we do it and how this contributes to the wider community.

CoP are, therefore, a series of dialogues. These dialogues then form the basis of the meaning that defines and describes practice. This description is the 'product' of the CoP, it is the externalised tacit knowledge that will be shared and that will ultimately drive the learning within the organisation. As a dialogue, there is a need to consider language as a crucial element in the dynamic actions of the CoP as it is language that will describe the meaning that defines the practice.

> ... understandings of the processes by means of which communities of practice are constituted and maintained require attention to the role of language within these processes.
>
> (Barton and Tusting 2005: 41)

As a dialogue-based discipline OL will inevitably focus on language and indeed we have considered communication, conversation and discourse analysis as techniques or elements that support this focus on the use of language. Inherently there is a focus on the use of qualitative research tools or techniques to explore the rich dialogues that define an organisation and will represent its ability to embed OL. Language is the bedrock of the CoP model and to have any meaningful understanding of the value it can offer to an organisation will inevitably require an active engagement with the language we use to communicate.

Building the community

The first task here, in establishing the CoP model, is to understand the definition of the model. What is it, what is its purpose and what is it looking to achieve? Clearly, the term community and its key definition as a group of individuals who share a common passion can cover a range of different collectives – an informal club or a high-level scientific research group. The engagement with these groups will be quite distinct from an organisational point of view and this can undermine the common understanding that we might have about their purpose or how they might relate to the structures of authority and control within the organisation.

We can distinguish between organisational communities, project teams, informal or formal learning communities or communities of practice. Learning communities might informally share knowledge but this would not necessarily be the key professional focus for the group. The CoP does have this professional focus and looks to drive innovation.

According to Plaskoff (2011) there are three key elements that help to create the basis for the relationship that will underpin a CoP, the three Bs:

Believing
> This looks to establish the common identity of the potential community. This will be based on the shared practice of the group and their understanding of the parameters that make up this practice. It will identify and recognise the value of this practice to the achievement of key organisational goals and what might be the nature of the challenges for this practice.

Behaving
> A maturing CoP establishes ways in which it will operate. It will establish mechanisms for communication and indeed styles of communication, perhaps more informal, among members. More practically this will also manifest itself in terms of the production of knowledge artefacts, how documents or records might be produced and presented.

Belonging
> A fully mature CoP will have embedded trust and respect. This in turn will generate the type of engagement that will encourage and foster innovation and risk. It will be able to make mistakes and to learn from them, rather than attribute blame for any failure. All of this is based on the depth of the relationship that has been allowed to develop between the community members.

The emphasis here is on the relationships that exist within the community. It is important when establishing a CoP that the core members are identified carefully and that they represent a range of 'abilities' in relation to the practice around which the community will be formed. There should be a blend of experienced and the less experienced, in order to ensure that the founding principles of the community will be broadly based. Given that the early members of any group will determine the cultural norms for that group, this broad base is essential. It is important to recognise the need to embed diversity at this early stage and to emphasise that communities should be inclusive and egalitarian in nature.

Saint-Onge and Wallace (2003) outline four key elements in establishing a framework for the CoP:

Productive inquiry: this is the spark that brings real value to the knowledge base by stimulating discussion around the content. It is this discussion that adds value, more than the actual content itself.

Community conventions: it is possible to ask inappropriate questions and it is the role of conventions to ensure that there is an appreciation of the purpose of the community and that inquiry needs to be aligned with this.

Generative capabilities: the discussions of the CoP form the 'data' that will be archived and made available for further consideration. As with all knowledge assets its true value is in its availability for reuse.

Tools and technology infrastructure: rather than simply being a repository for data, information and knowledge, they also need to be able to support and facilitate the social aspects of the community, providing areas and opportunities for discussion and exchange, both formally and informally.

The first task of this initial group is to establish the agenda for the community. Like pioneers, the early members need to identify the elements that will help this fledgling community to survive and then thrive. Survival comes down to the right environment and other essentials. What are the dangers and challenges that the community might face?

Brainstorming is used to create this initial sense of purpose for the community. Some consideration will also be given to how the community will assess its own success. This activity will forge the initial relationships within the community, and the actual launching of the community should only be attempted when there is a strong sense amongst these early members that the purpose of the community is clear, and that they themselves have a strong commitment to it and each other.

After the establishment of the community it is important to ensure that the initial members do not dominate and that all subsequent members have clear opportunities to change or adapt the agenda of the community. This should be an iterative process and the community should be allowed to change and evolve for as long as there are members to sustain it.

Given many of the expectations associated with the launching and sustaining of the CoP it is necessary to be working with individuals who have an appreciation of the implications associated with OL. This makes the CoP model a late tool in the SPADES model and in the development of an OLP. To a large extent the planting, nurturing and growing stages are addressing the expectation associated with the CoP, they are embedding trust and identifying the value of knowledge sharing as an organisational activity. This makes CoP members responsible rather than accountable:

> Unlike the accountability model, individuals driven by responsibility feel an emotional tie and commitment to other individuals or entities in their joint enterprise who, in turn, have the same emotional tie.
>
> (Plaskoff 2011: 219)

Individuals who have had an opportunity to form close relationships through mentoring processes and who have been allowed an opportunity to express their relationship with the organisation in the form of constructed narratives will be more inclined or able to identify the value of the CoP model and to participate in an appropriate way. Indeed mentoring can be extended into the functioning of the CoP itself.

The centrality of teams

The CoP model represents what effort we might put in place to understand and appreciate the social context of the organisation, both from the individual point of view and from the collective point of view. Hislop (2009) emphasises the two basic premises upon which CoP are based:

> The community of practice is based on two central premises: the practice-based perspective on knowledge, and the group-based character of organisational activity.
>
> (Hislop 2009: 59)

Group-based activity recognises that initially there will be more naturally forming teams that will gravitate together based on their shared actions – they will share a primary focus. Rather than bringing together individuals to form the CoP it is more likely to be the bringing together of groups that will be the initial challenge. Communication, in the form of stories, needs to be able to flow between these teams.

> Teams are the building blocks of community structure: they are the Lego bricks that build an army of volunteers united by a mission. But as building blocks, they fit together in many different ways, with countless variations and possibilities in how they are constructed.
>
> (Bacon 2009: loc. 31 of 3570)

Roloff, Woolley and Edmondson (2011) identify three concepts relating to team learning:

Outcome improvement: Concerned with measuring performance and factors that can impede or support team working.
Task mastery: Considers how knowledge sharing and collaboration can drive the mastery of the specific tasks.
Group process: Identifies the type of behaviour that will be conducive to team learning.

Teams are significant not just as productive units but also as contributors to the necessary cultural dynamic that will support both the development of CoP and drive the OLP. Specifically, they drive the important sense of belonging, which in turn will create a more open learning environment and enhance trust. Importantly, they can break down larger communities into more manageable, coherent or less intimidating smaller groups. This will allow new members to feel able to contribute when they might only have to deal with a relatively small number of individuals rather than an entire community that might consist of hundreds.

In establishing teams it is important to allow them to freely form rather than be formally created for the members. Individuals will naturally gravitate towards those sharing common interests. Based on a clear appreciation of the overall goal, teams can make explicit their own specific goals and how this relates to and supports the wider community goal.

Different approaches to communication need to be applied to the different functions of these teams and the wider community. A more formal communication style might support technical knowledge sharing sessions, while building the crucial sense of belongingness will likely require a less formal style.

The emphasis here is on knowledge emerging from what we do, in other words, from our work-based learning or experiential learning. Also, this learning takes place within an explicitly social context and there is therefore a bridge created between the personal knowledge gained through experience and the need to share this knowledge across the organisation. A CoP, therefore, embodies the principles of OL and offers the necessary rationale for there being a perception of a need to share, rather than hoard knowledge for personal gain.

As a form of social learning it will not be surprising to find that there is an equal concern, within the CoP literature, for both identity and collective practice. Wenger, in his consideration of the former focuses on participation, or non-participation, and how individuals can attain a sense of belonging.

> Learning is the engine of practice, and practice is the history of that learning.
>
> (Wenger 1998: 96)

The CoP, it is said, is capable of sustaining high levels of organisational innovation through the knowledge creation process. It is the embodiment, to a large extent, of the knowledge sharing spirals that are at the heart of our understanding of the KM processes. These virtuous and iterative spirals can sustain learning through the generation of organisational trust and cooperation rather than conflict and competition.

From an OL perspective, therefore, CoP are directly related to the creation of knowledge and the establishment of a cultural context that will create and stimulate knowledge sharing practices.

> In terms of knowledge processes, communities of practice have the potential to provide benefits in two broad areas. Firstly, communities of practice can underpin levels of organisational innovativeness through supporting and encouraging the creation, development and use of knowledge ... Secondly, the common knowledge possessed by members of a community of practice, combined with their sense of collective identity, and system of shared values means they have the potential to facilitate individual and group learning, and the sharing of knowledge within the community.
>
> (Hislop 2009: 64)

Identity and values shared throughout the organisation address the organisational dilemma that has been highlighted by Chris Argyris (1993), but although there is little to argue with in terms of the sentiment being expressed here, there is equally little outlined as to how best to develop the appropriate identification with the values of the organisation. To a large extent this is dependent upon individual circumstances, but working with LO models (such as Senge's five disciplines) we do have an outline of the areas within which we need to work. We need to look at and explore how individuals create mental models of the organisation and what impact these have; we need to identify the aims and priorities of individuals and how to blend these into the work of teams or groups within the organisation.

To do this we need to engage in a dialogue and it is the function of the CoP to facilitate this process. To an extent this removes the CoP from the direct objective of sharing knowledge, rather it is an opportunity to reflect and explore, and to manage the larger task of potentially large organisations being able to know employees at a level most often associated with smaller organisations. The CoP, through the application of ICT, offers the opportunity to enhance or recapture the dynamic of familiarity associated with the smaller organisation and it is this function that characterises the CoP and distinguishes it from other network applications.

Define, establish and launch

To succeed, a CoP will need to be aligned with the strategic aims of the organisation and it must support the identified development needs of the individuals forming the community. In other words there needs to be a clear sense of the purpose of the CoP. This, in turn, will help to form the roles and responsibilities within the early CoP. To an extent the early elements within the SPADES model have already embedded these crucial elements and individuals will clearly see the value for enhanced knowledge sharing through a supported community approach.

The individuals should be able to drive this self-governing mode that, to an extent, is an extension of the mentoring practices that helped to nurture the OLP. Similarly, the conventions and norms that will govern the behaviour of individuals will also draw on nurtured cultural characteristics. Individuals will not feel inhibited in bringing their knowledge or experience to the community, they will actively engage with knowledge that is brought by others and will look to develop both the existing community and the spread of the practice. The community itself will act as the catalyst for the propagation of the practice, in an iterative cycle of experiential learning.

The CoP will be self-sustaining but it must be recognised that it operates within a fluid context, where its value needs to be made explicit, where its purpose needs to be championed and that internally it needs to ensure that it does not become dominated by individuals or groups for their own purposes. These are delicate balances to maintain.

Saint-Onge and Wallace (2003) identify the following factors:

- Shared sense of purpose and ownership.
- Self-initiated view of learning and readiness to learn from each other.
- Overall climate of trust and involvement.
- Partnering mindset and corresponding skills.
- Strong technology platform.
- Supportive context and leadership endorsement.
- Realistic expectation of return on investment.

Many of these characteristics have been embedded by earlier elements within the SPADES model. In launching a CoP this preparation is necessary, the members have been identified, the purpose established and there is a high expectation that the members will engage collaboratively to support the development of the OLP. The technical infrastructure is in place and initial conventions around communication style and method have been established. At this point the CoP is ready to launch.

The first view of the CoP can include:

Welcomes: this might be from the facilitator or recognised champion of the CoP or the key sponsor (a high-level manager) or from the technical team, outlining the functionality and offering any additional support.

Member profiles: self-created statements that identify the individual and will outline areas of expertise and interest along with some expectations about the CoP. Contact information will also be included.

Starter discussion topics: based on the agreed aims and goals of the CoP some content around these key areas will provide some stimulus to discussion.

Gather initial data: who has viewed the resource, how many discussions have been initiated or profiles updated? Identifying trends of use can be important for the sustaining of the CoP but this should not be allowed to be seen as a controlling element. There should not be predetermined figures for the number of expected contributions, individuals should not be 'followed' and encouraged to make more or less of a contribution. If this element is poorly managed and the CoP is seen as another context or opportunity for control of individual action then it will quickly become counterproductive. The perceived level of participation will be fulfilled as an exercise in itself, but this will likely be of limited value at best.

As the CoP develops there should be a perceptible shift in responsibility away from those organising or championing the CoP and towards the members themselves. In terms of both *content* and *context* the members should take the lead. The content should be driven by the members, what is it that they want to talk about, what are their key concerns? There may be a need here to keep these developing discussions on track and focused, but this needs to be done carefully and considerately. If not, the heavy hand of control can again be perceived to be present. The context will be evaluated by the members through practice and any functionality that might enhance the dialogue can be suggested by members or by CoP facilitators. Where a technique is proving useful in a more limited number of cases then there may be a training issue and this can be offered along with some examples of how it has already been applied successfully within the CoP.

Needs and a style will develop through use, as will the mechanisms to adapt and alter functionality to meet this. The facilitator's role remains significant and it is necessary to have an individual identified as responsible for the CoP. This helps to maintain them as a discrete function and support their development within the organisation, perhaps arguing for more resources to support specific functions. Along with emerging champions, this facilitator will initiate reflective conversations around the value of the CoP, identify development needs and encourage participation.

Feedback will be received and should be encouraged, constituting one of the ongoing dialogues within the CoP itself. Both formal and informal mechanisms for feedback can be established, gathering quantitative data around use and more qualitative data around value, relating to participation and engagement. Users need to be fully aware and supportive of all of these mechanisms. A formal reflective process should be put in place to allow participants to think about or consider their experience of the CoP and to highlight any content or context related issues.

As the community grows, where its value to the members becomes clear and this is also perceived by the organisation as a whole, there are often emerging issues. Not least the very value of the CoP can create friction. It can be seen as a power base in its own right and this can create conflict rather than reconcile it. The CoP itself can become a focus for individuals who might wish to use it for less collaborative and more competitive purposes. Careful consideration needs to be given to the dialogue around the CoP itself and discourse analysis techniques can be used to identify these shifting power dynamics.

Open consideration of how the CoP is developing needs to be ensured and this will also drive the development and expansion of the CoP. Full participation by community members needs to be maintained and it will be the qualitative reflections of the membership that will form the basis of the measurement of value. The CoP is there to support and enhance organisational learning which in turn will:

- *Enhance agility* – lessen the time required to meet to effect change.
- *Improve performance* – through collaboration individual development and training requirements can be met.
- *Retain talent* – by improving the job satisfaction of key or significant individuals.

Surveys and semi-structured interviews can all be carried out to determine the extent to which each of these elements has been perceived to be more effectively embedded within practice. This can then be used as evidence of value being created by the CoP – or not.

Various reasons might emerge for the non-use of the CoP. These commonly might be the perceived lack of time (related to the priority given to the CoP), lack of required skills to participate effectively and feeling that it was already duplicating effort. These issues can then be used to identify the questions that can be used to develop the CoP.

Lack of time/not a priority: this may relate to the sense of value or perceived sense of value of the CoP. Demonstrating the value can provide an explicit view of its worth, and when presented by a trusted colleague this becomes a persuasive tool. The ability to construct a narrative and tell a good story will be of considerable value at this stage.

Lack of required skills: on the face of it this can appear to be simply a training issue – identify the skill that was perceived to be lacking and then provide training. However, underlying this might be a more significant issue. Why would an individual feel disinclined to externalise this need? Did they feel they would be ridiculed? Does this indicate power dynamics at work that are detrimental to the development of a trusting and blame-free environment where individuals are comfortable to admit shortcomings or a need for further development? If so more needs to be done than providing training.

Duplicating effort: again, this relates to the issue of prioritising and perhaps a need to shift working practices. Underlying issues may relate to the reluctance to shift practices. Are individuals becoming over-reliant on embedded practices, to the point where they might be reluctant to change or adapt when required? How might they best be supported to address this issue?

Analysis and value measurement becomes a mechanism for development through the identification of issues that relate to behaviour and the wider nature of the engagement with the CoP. This qualitative approach can and should be supported by quantitative analyses that might identify:

- the number of members;
- frequency of use

  - by specific groups or even individuals;
  - by time – when is the most popular time?
  - by function, chat, uploading;

- number of discussion topics;
- average number of contributions;
- most popular discussions;
- most highly rated items.

Surveys can also be used to expand on the data that can be collected, fleshing out the figures and providing some indication of why certain patterns may be emerging or issues arising. To an extent once the CoP has become established and reached maturity, it will largely be self-sustaining. Communities will have moved beyond the need to explicitly present the value that they create for the organisation, there will be an inherent and embedded trust in their ultimate value and in the value of individual participation. This is the point at which CoP become an inherent part of the organisation, trust is an embedded feature and the speed and agility of the organisation to operate in its environment has been enhanced. This is the same as saying that trusting that the CoP creates value for the organisation is the only measurement of value that is required.

Reflecting on CoP

The CoP model pulls together the elements that make up the SPADES model. To an extent it represents a mature approach to knowledge sharing or social learning. They have been given a range of different names, including learning networks or thematic groups. They come in a similarly diverse range of sizes and using a variety of different technologies to facilitate and support their goal. Some are small and rely almost entirely on face-to-face meetings, while others deploy a range of technical tools to support a large community. They will cross organisational boundaries and will operate across organisations. They are not new, but there is value in drawing the practice associated with them into sharper focus.

CoP can, therefore, be closely aligned with OL and in many instances are regarded as the key tool: Rumizen's 'killer application'. A critique of the CoP model will alight on the perception of knowledge as an organisational resource, as a discrete entity rather than a social entity and on the extent to which it is seen to be creating a more visible environment based on this instrumental view of knowledge where practice determines the type of knowledge that informs organisational learning processes. Power and conflict are at the heart of the critique of CoP and this was recognised by Lave and Wenger (1991: 42) when they talk of 'unequal distribution of power'.

> There seems to be a void in the literature concerning the form of government suitable for a learning organisation and the role of political activity which, within the framework provided by that form, might facilitate the essential spontaneity of activity and relationship while safe-guarding the interests of the organisation's members.
>
> (Coopey 1995: 195)

The political and ideological environment within which organisations operate draws upon the notion of knowledge that is associated with power. Where knowledge becomes more embedded within social practice, as has been argued here, the power within the social, within the organisation, has an opportunity to adopt legitimacy within the wider discourse.

> While power is moderated by the facilities used by actors to draw upon or to frustrate the imbalance of resources within the structure, communication depends upon the meanings which can be articulated and shared within the constraints of structure and ideology, and sanctions rely on the application of norms which are institutionally legitimated. In totality, those involved in social interactions can attempt to exercise control of the dialectic through their discursive facility linked to any combination of resources and any negative and positive sanctions of coercion and inducements on which they can draw.
>
> (Coopey 1995: 198)

Communication within a context of organisational culture and behaviour forms a crucial power dynamic that in relation to OL highlights not a context of social cooperation, mutual support and trust, but of control.

This tradition represents a line of thought that directs attention to the structure of dominant and subordinate interest groups, to social conflict, and to power systems. Its principal thesis is that society is based on conflict and that, in the absence of open conflict, a process of domination prevails. In this tradition the social order is perceived as the outcome of a struggle between groups and individuals seeking to ensure that their own interests predominate over those of other.

(Gheradi and Nicolini 2001: 36)

Rather than expanding boundaries of self-directed and empowered individual action within a movement of democratic egalitarianism, social learning sustains, through visibility, transparency and the maintenance of a form of knowledge dependent upon the need to meet the challenges of change, a coercive, controlling and potentially oppressive management approach. It does this by emphasising the need to meet constant change and the subsequent reliance upon individual learning being embedded within the social context of the organisation.

Given that learning organisations are, by design, less structured than more traditional forms, and that structures themselves provide socially accepted rationalizations for specific types of activities, we should probably expect to find a high volume of informal communication as people seek to resolve the uncertainty created by ambiguous situations and the relative dearth of structural cues to behaviour.

(Coopey 1995: 202)

Where knowledge begins to emerge within the context of local narratives, where legitimacy is determined by the dynamics within the negotiated context of social environments it is inevitable that rhetorical and discursive capabilities become key elements in the defining of organisational knowledge. These new capabilities rest upon a dynamic that recognises the need for transparency and concealment.

Power and conflict render the circulation of knowledge non-transparent and conceal the social conditions of its production.

(Gheradi and Nicolini 2001: 37)

In developing the OLP and CoP as the principal tools, two largely opposing views can be identified. On the one hand it is seen as being idealistic and ultimately unrealistic. On the other it is a nightmare for those operating within it. It is about the continued exertion of political power over individuals within the organisation.

The CoP in this instance is a mechanism that seeks to challenge the concealment of knowledge by the exertion of control over the production of knowledge. It partly does this by emphasising the social nature of knowledge production and drawing the focus towards the value of the process of knowledge production rather than knowledge as an explicit or discrete outcome or product. This, to an extent, explains why the CoP model is often presented as having no leader, being informal and being self-organising.

However, the CoP can often be self-organising but many are cultivated and as the SPADES model has made clear, they are the end product of a great deal of effort that has gone into the creation or planting of the right environment and identification of key cultural characteristics. It is the nurturing of these characteristics through discrete practices and the growing of these practices into mature tools that add value in themselves but also lay down practices and dynamics that support social learning that ultimately forms the basis of measuring this value.

CoP can be formal as well as informal and they do need to be led. Leading a CoP is not about possessing more knowledge or acquiring a senior position in relation to community members. It is more about identifying an individual who has a heightened sense of the value of the CoP and is prepared to take a lead in its planting, nurturing and growth. They will spread the message and they will champion the model by talking to those who can support the development of the model. This might be financially, technically or culturally.

This is essentially asking for a re-addressing of the fundamental issue of what knowledge is as an organisational resource. If it is seen as a resource that can be codified, stored in a database, manipulated and moved through the organisation in its explicit forms, then there is an acceptance that knowledge is complex information. Complex information can be equated with scientific forms of knowledge that are distinguished only by the uncontested nature of this knowledge. The process of producing scientific knowledge is a method that ultimately seeks to rid knowledge of its contested nature.

However, the partiality of knowledge, the tacit and personal nature of knowledge, has always presented an opportunity to deny the claim that all knowledge can be defined as scientific (practice-based) knowledge and that in fact there are forms of knowledge that cannot be identified and codified in the ways outlined above. Rather it is a partial resource and, that given this, there is a need to seek to understand the process of knowledge and of being knowledgeable.

Reflection

Throughout this text there has been a recurring element, the element of reflection. The core of OL is a process of reflection, where individuals have the ability to consider who they are in relation to themselves as professionals, as members of different groups, teams and communities, as part of organisations and ultimately the wider social environment. The disciplines associated with OL are themselves encouraging a series of reflective activities. Mental models, for example, are asking us to consider why we act and think in the way that we do. OL is concerned with the ability of individuals to reflect. It cannot be taken for granted that we are able to reflect or even willing to reflect. Within this question of reflection is the crucial distinguishing characteristic of OL – the preparedness of individuals to use their reflective capacities and to channel these into the necessary dialogues that will define the OLP and drive each of the elements within the SPADES model.

Pedagogically it is sound to encourage you to reflect on the material that has been presented to you in this textbook and to value the need to do this.

The 'reflective practitioner'

OL is as much about valuing the development of individuals as it might be about data management or web page design. The relationship between the individual and the organisation is central and it is this that makes the consideration of reflection and programmes of learning of importance to OL practitioners.

The concept of the 'reflective practitioner' as developed by Donald Schön (1991) has generated a great deal of interest and helped to establish the broader concepts associated with OL, as espoused so forcefully by Peter Senge and others. This text has included the development of the 'reflective inquiry' method that seeks to identify, through reflection, key aspects of organisational learning.

We have mentioned and considered aspects of organisational learning and largely accepted that it is a positive and beneficial development. It represents an opportunity to reflect upon the knowledge that one has acquired and in doing so, offers both a means to disseminate that knowledge and to create new knowledge.

Schön has identified four characteristics of the knowledge that is represented by the professional, they are (1991: 23):

- specialised
- firmly bounded
- scientific
- standardised.

Importantly this makes the connection between knowledge and action or application. There is a need to ensure that the theoretical developments that are being made will be directly relevant to practice. As we considered briefly earlier, the positivist curriculum set in place a hierarchy where those who generated new thought and new theory were seen as being of more significance than those who applied that theory in practice. To a large extent this epitomises the separation that still exists between the activities of universities and of other organisations. Research – the building of theory – is seen as being the preserve of the university, of the 'higher thinkers', and the practitioners are those who await the results of these deliberations in order to improve their practice. For Schön this situation is represented by what is called 'technical rationality':

> From the perspective of Technical Rationality, professional practice is a process of problem solving. Problems of choice or decision are solved through the selection, from available means, of the best suited to establish ends. But with this emphasis on problem solving, we ignore problem setting, the process by which we define the decision to be made, the ends to be achieved, the means which may be chosen.
>
> (Schön 1991: 27)

Where there exist categories of applied theory then standardised techniques can be used to address them. However, where these categories do not exist then we are in a context where knowledge is only partial. We can recognise this in many professional contexts, such as within the different diagnoses that might be presented within psychiatry or in the presentation of proposals in relation to town planning. Essentially, this is the subjective context where there is not a clear and unequivocally correct answer or solution to the problem.

This is a central issue for OL:

> When we go about the spontaneous, intuitive performance of the actions of everyday life, we show ourselves to be knowledgeable in a special way.
>
> (Schön 1991: 49)

This ability to act knowledgeably can be distinguished from having knowledge. In particular it is more dynamic in nature and represents a process that can be reapplied and reused. It is not the knowledge that represents the end of a process, the answer to a question or the solution of a problem. It is the ability to identify the nature of the question, to address that question and to pose a solution to a problem. With the knowledge economy characterised as it is by the need to meet constant change, this *knowledgeability* would appear to be more appropriate than identifying specific items of knowledge, embodied in answers that are expected to solve problems. Schön refers to this, essentially as 'reflection-in-action'.

> . . . the practitioner allows himself to experience surprise, puzzlement, or confusion in a situation which he finds uncertain or unique. He reflects on the phenomenon before him, and on the prior understandings which have been implicit in his behaviour.
>
> (Schön 1991: 68)

Reflection, therefore, can be said to represent a form of learning, and indeed it is regarded as being an essential element that will distinguish the surface or strategic learner from the deep learner. The ability to reassess and re-present their material is the goal of education. It is not to reproduce from predefined contexts or from within predefined parameters. It is the ability to operate effectively within different contexts and with different and changing parameters. It is these characteristics that largely represent the organisational context within which we have been considering OL. Therefore, we need to consider more fully the nature of reflection.

The nature of reflection

Reflection is related to thinking and to learning, and within the context of OL we are clearly identifying reflection and the reflective process as one that will have a positive bearing upon the generation of knowledge. If we do accept this then there must be some opportunity to reflect; there must be ways in which reflection can be supported both physically through the environment and in terms of it being recognised as a worthwhile process. This might manifest itself in 'quiet rooms' or designated times, either at specific times or an acceptance that so many hours within the week will be put aside for it. Reflection, in other words, must form part of the knowledge strategy of an organisation.

In doing this we are supporting the view expressed by John Dewey (1997) where he considered not the outcome of reflection to be the real value but the process underpinning it. He goes beyond considering the physical environment and concerns himself more with being able to identify how able or otherwise we as individuals might be in being reflective. In considering this he describes a journey through what he referred to as 'perplexity'.

There is a growing realisation that the body of knowledge that might represent a profession is constantly changing. Knowledge itself is in a state of flux and as such it is a partial resource. As Schön himself has said:

> As the tasks change, so will the demands for usable knowledge, and the patterns of task and knowledge are inherently unstable.
>
> (Schön 1991: 15)

Where there is no belief that specific behaviours or actions can be understood and interpreted by examining them in themselves, we are left with the need to examine the processes upon which they might be said to have been based. This essentially, is a reflective process, it is learning from our everyday experiences and from one moment to the next.

It is the manifestation of the responsibilities inherent in the self-direction and autonomy associated with the adult learner. Where learning becomes the responsibility of the individual, the need to engage with and embed self-inquiry becomes significant. *What am I doing, why am I doing it in this way?* The iterative engagement with these questions builds the basis of the trust that is central to OL – this is the ability or the capacity to trust oneself.

The position of the individual is central to reflection as a process. Rather than viewing reflection as something that can be carried out for a specific purpose, it should be viewed more ontologically as a more embedded part of identity. Reflection looks to identify aspects of the individual rather than looking at a discrete activity that the individual might have done or engaged with. Reflection is self-exploration and the ability and willingness to see the value in this self-exploration.

The value itself will be based on the extent to which the individual can maintain the capabilities necessary for the changing dynamics of their environment. This is at the heart of what Schön refers to as 'reflection-in action':

> Reflection-in-action accounts for the artistry of professional performance in the short term and high levels of performance in the long term.
>
> (Lipshitz, Friedman and Popper 2006: 34)

To work with reflection there needs to be this recognition of its inherent value. However, this will be difficult to quantify; it will be difficult to add to any balance sheet. It will be subjective, based on intuition, it will be personal. Johns (2013) supports this view of learning as understanding, as being first based on an understanding of each element, which in turn is understood within the context of the whole. Both the parts and the whole are engaged with through, first, the construction of a narrative or story and second through the performance or presentation of that narrative. Through a series of dialogues known as the hermeneutic circle (Johns, 2013) the narrative is constructed:

Self: creating a story as a text. The spontaneous application of the imagination can drive the development of this story. It should not be planned but should allow the experience itself to drive it. In this way the imposition of previous opinions and previous experience is kept to a minimum. To do this effectively there needs to be provided the right environment. For example, the use of 'quiet rooms' has grown over the last few years and these provide a space to reflect to avoid any disturbances and should form part of a programme of reflective 'opportunities', made available at specific and defined times, as well as being available for more spontaneous use.
Story: reflecting on the story.
Insights: considering the outcome of the reflection on the story.
Community: shared consideration of the story.
Insights: considering the outcome of the communal reflection, producing a narrative text.
Narrative text: wider communal reflection on this narrative and its social implications.

Similarly Hay (2007) outlines a model for reflection in practice and the construction of the narratives upon which this is based:

1   Capture events as they occur.
2   Reviewing specific events.

3 Reviewing to look for patterns.
4 Planning ahead to incorporate learning generally.
5 Planning for a specific event.
6 Implementing your learning.

The purpose here is to record as accurately as possible the events being considered. This need not be a direct process of constant note taking but a willingness to allow for some time and space for reflection and a more considered description of the event. It is useful to simply write down what was observed rather than attempt at this stage to consider it in any depth, this can come later. Technology can play a part here and recording obviously provides an opportunity to revisit and reflect upon an event or session. For example, teachers might have a teaching session recorded in order to conduct peer assessment at a later stage. This requires to be carried out with the explicit agreement of all parties and this must be based on the trust that has become embedded within the OLP. Confidentiality and the 'proper' use of recorded material must be assured to the satisfaction of all taking part. The consideration of narratives can be done individually or collectively, but always openly and constructively. What patterns emerge from these narratives and how will these translate into action? Once an action is identified then further work can be done to ensure that it is embedded effectively and in accordance with the understanding of all those involved in the process.

With these models reflection becomes a discrete part of the learning process, ideally something that will happen automatically and form a part of the everyday actions of all those who have something to contribute to the learning of the organisation – namely everyone. This is not an inconsiderable commitment by either the individual or the organisation. OL, through its roots in both the HR and KM elements of the organisation, offers an opportunity to draw the complexity of this commitment into the realms of the possible. However, without the 'groundwork' of the SPADES model, setting the appropriate environment in the first instance, this will remain something of an unrealisable ideal.

Concluding remarks

The CoP is a very specific network application that can be aligned with the aims and objectives associated with OL. As a communicative environment it can facilitate the externalisation of key issues related to understanding the relationship between the individual and the organisation. Rather than specifically being regarded as a direct opportunity to share knowledge, it should be regarded as a more introspective tool that can support the development of the OLP.

As a tool for externalisation we can critically consider the underlying purpose of CoP, as we can most of the tools associated with KM and OL. CoP will enhance visibility; they require individuals to be open with and to trust the organisation – a goal that is very difficult to assess, if very easy to value. The CoP, essentially, is an OL focused tool that uses network functionality to support the cultural imperatives embedded within OL. CoP are therefore very different from portals or other network applications. This difference is very much related to the way in which they are applied rather than any distinct functional characteristics.

More broadly, reflection is the process that underpins the OLP. As an embedded part of organisational practice it makes the SPADES model a sustainable pedagogical approach.

By starting from the self and creating narratives around the self this can then be extended to the organisation. The willingness to do so is established by the earlier elements within the SPADES model that have the primary function of building the necessary trust to shift individual narratives to organisational narratives. Essentially, therefore, OL is an organisation's ability to successfully shift these individual narratives to organisational narratives and this is done through an embedded process of reflection.

Part 5

Reflection on the discipline of organisational learning

This part reflects on the content of this textbook to present a view of OL as a discipline. OL can mean a great many things to a great many people and to an extent this is its key weakness. It lacks clarity and can only be defined in very broad terms. This textbook has attempted to do two things, first, to present a view of OL from a particular perspective and second, to identify how related tools and techniques might be applied from this perspective. Rather ironically, the postmodern perspective (itself difficult to define with any confidence) has been drawn on here. This perspective rests on plurality, multiplicity and stands somewhat opposed to the rational and logical position of positivism and more modernist perspectives. The postmodern perspective most applied to OL identifies its potentially controlling nature and the creation of a context that through visibility will entrap individuals and subject them to a scrutiny that will ultimately lead to a form of self-imposed control. This is the panoptic effect of the true surveillance society.

16 Reflection on the discipline of organisational learning

Introduction

Given the origins of the LO within the wider concept of OD, what type of organisational structures best support the principles embedded in this model? Is there an inevitable move away from more hierarchical structures towards a more collaborative model? Or, does the application of information and communication technologies sustain a more positivist view of what the purpose of the reflective practitioner might be? In considering the concept of the reflective practitioner as an outcome of the application of the principles of organisational learning there remains a need to critically consider the nature of the reflective practitioner that is being produced. Is it one capable of engaging with an increasingly diverse technical environment that is able to manage large data sets, or one capable of positively challenging and questioning the structures that make up the organisation? Are these mutually exclusive?

Also, organisations cannot learn as they are not conscious entities and if learning can be ascribed to them then this is a form of unjustifiable anthropomorphism. It is only individuals who can learn and the organisation can at best contain within it individuals who are capable of engaging with learning, or not. OL in seeking to be a discipline that claims to be able to make this key shift from individual to OL is doing so on a very questionable basis. On the one hand it appears to be a very appealing analogy, to consider the organisation as a human being, but this only masks the complexity of trying to embed practices that are essentially designed for the individual and expecting these to be adopted across the collective that is an organisation.

The extent to which the value of education and learning remains a potent element within a wider social context, to an extent, has driven the development of OL and the concept of the LO. Learning is largely regarded as a positive process. The more we learn, the more knowledge we seek, the better, the more informed, we become. To be educated, to have a degree, are the trappings of success and within the wider discourse many organisations are seeking to draw on the legitimate symbols of education to hopefully acquire some of this legitimacy for themselves. Ironically, this has often blurred the role and position of traditional educational institutions such as universities. Questions around what or who drives the content and development of the curriculum within higher education and particularly at masters level and beyond are being formed. To what extent do external professional bodies, such as CIPD, determine the content of taught undergraduate and postgraduate qualifications within HE institutions? Is there any real issue with them doing so? One issue may relate to the shift that will inevitably occur in relation to the existing discourse, which in turn is effectively a contest for legitimacy or a legitimate voice.

The position of the university in relation to statements about professional practice is different from that of other organisations. Different perspectives have different priorities and these can often be seen as competing. The question now becomes one of just how aware we might be of these differing priorities and whether or not this enhanced contestation within the discourse will shift the legitimate voice in a particular direction.

Part of this shift is OL itself, the formalising of learning and education as a part of organisational practices. Apprenticeships and training have been replaced by learning programmes which become, within the knowledge-economy, more central to organisational well-being. The LO will capture the 'hidden gold' that is the intellectual capital that is embedded within the organisation. It will do so as the only genuinely sustainable resource and allow organisations to sustain their competitive edge. Given these claims for the LO it is not surprising that the potential benefits are attractive and that subsequently the notion of the LO has already attained mythical status.

However, how an organisation is to attain the exalted position of an LO remains unclear. Few examples can be found that are convincing in their claims to be organisations that can learn. Rather there are modest claims to progress towards this utopian ideal. There are claims made for different tools and techniques, this might be the application of learning technologies or learning management systems. There can equally be claims to cultural breakthroughs that empower individuals and transform the way in which organisational structures are being flattened. This range and depth of claims can itself be seen as a means by which the discipline has grown and developed. It remains aspirational and as such can be inspirational.

Principles of sustainability

The SPADES model attempts to identify the key elements, tools and techniques that can drive OL. In using a gardening metaphor there is an initial focus on the context and environment. The organisation is the context being considered and this presents the first principle of sustainability:

1   **Organisations are social constructs**
    Before planting any crop there is a need to consider the ground. Is it suitable for growing what is needed? Both the technical and cultural elements will constitute this environment and the relationship between the two is crucial. The ingredient that will ultimately determine the suitability of the ground is the ethics that underpin it. In drawing on Bauman's postmodern ethics there is emphasised the challenges associated with the contemporary context (complexity and plurality) and that this will mean that any ethical position will be based on what we might agree to be acceptable behaviour. For an OLP to be sustainable this agreement needs to facilitate and support the generation of tacit knowledge and its transformation into explicit knowledge. The basis of this is the experience of all individuals and this presents the second principle of sustainability:

2   **Individuals are the basis for the production of tacit knowledge**
    For knowledge to be made explicit, through whichever model of knowledge transfer that might be applied, this will require a choice to be made by the individual. Will they or will they not share their experience and what they have learnt from this experience? The relationship that exists between the individual and the organisation will determine the extent to which tacit knowledge will be transformed into an organisational

asset – it will shift from an individual to a collective/social asset. At the heart of the relationship between the individual and the organisation is trust and this presents the third principle of sustainability:

3   **For organisations to learn from the experience of individuals there must be trust between the individuals and groups that make up the social context of the organisation**

For individuals to trust the motives and actions of those around them there needs to be an explicit ethical basis for the actions of the organisation. Here the key relationship is a responsibility that an individual has for another. The individual accepts the responsibility for their own value. This challenges the *agentic state* of detachment and draws the individual to the centre. For the individual to accept this responsibility there needs to be a motivating factor largely based on the reciprocal nature of this responsibility and this presents the fourth principle of sustainability:

4   **Shared responsibility will drive the development of trust**

OL is a collaborative pedagogy, where individuals have both responsibility for their own learning and a recognised and accepted responsibility for making the value of their experience available to all. Where there is an embedded acceptance of this responsibility and where individuals recognise that there is a direct value for them as individuals in this collaborative learning, then OL will begin to become genuinely sustainable and this presents the fifth principle of sustainability:

5   **Individual experience is enhanced through collaboration, adding value to individual tacit knowledge which then feeds the cycle of experiential learning**

The LO is, in the first instance, an ethical statement or position. That position will allow individuals to build the trust that will initiate their positive engagement with the processes of knowledge sharing that will make their own tacit knowledge explicit. Where the experience of this process is positive then the individual will begin to accept a wider responsibility for their own learning and for this to be an explicit organisational resource.

The ethical basis will build the trust that will drive collaborative learning.

Pedagogy of experiential learning

The *principles of sustainability* identify the three key elements that will define the pedagogy of experiential learning. Essentially, these are based upon the principles of adult learning and modify Knowles' presentation of andragogy. Independence, self-direction and autonomy will drive the individual's engagement with their learning. They will have control of what and how they learn and will willingly share what they learn with others. The three key principles of the pedagogy of experiential learning are:

* Autonomy
* Responsibility
* Collaboration

Individual learners will have control, but this requires a reciprocal acceptance of enhanced responsibility. Individuals, however, are inclined to take control, they are motivated by the responsibility that comes from having this control over their own development, as it adds to their sense of worth and, ultimately, value. There is a natural impetus behind the autonomy and responsibility that will help to grow and sustain individual learning within the organisation. The transformation of this into an organisational asset is the successful embedding of collaboration. Again individuals will collaborate when they clearly identify this as a component element in their own creation or production of tacit knowledge.

It is the role of the OL practitioner to facilitate and embed the pedagogy of experiential learning, which itself has been based upon the principles of sustainability.

Planting, nurturing and growing

Each of the elements within the SPADES model are presented in accordance with the *principles of sustainability* and are aligned with the *pedagogy of experiential learning* already outlined. The technical and cultural environment will look to facilitate the development of rich dialogues.

> Dialogue is the free and creative exploration of complex issues involving active listening and suspending one's own views. The purpose of dialogue is to go beyond one's own understanding and become an observer of one's own thinking. This means suspending one's own assumptions and playing with different ideas. Dialogue means letting go of power differentials between team players and treating each member equally.
>
> (Jashapara 2004: 62)

Dialogue is, therefore egalitarian and aims to explore ideas and thinking. It is divergent, rather than convergent. It requires individuals to be able to articulate their own thoughts and ideas, to share these, have them contested and ultimately be willing to alter or amend their ideas. This is a challenge, as Jashapara (2004) indicates, because organisations often place individuals in defensive positions due to the inherent competitiveness of organisations. This competitiveness will erode trust or prevent it from becoming embedded and create a tendency to hide in order to avoid the possibility of being regarded as ignorant or poorly informed. This is not an environment where individuals take risks, play with ideas or actively seek to learn from others. It is not an innovative or creative context.

To counter the inherent competitiveness of organisations, in the first instance, individuals need to recognise the value of their own individual experiences. There needs to be mutual trust and respect. It is only once this is in place that individuals will be motivated enough to record and reflect upon their experience and to form it into a coherent and explicit form. This might be the use of a blog or an e-portfolio. The technical environment will provide these tools and the cultural environment will allow the individual the time and space to take control of this process and to produce a narrative that will be used to feed the wider organisational dialogue.

The OL practitioner will engage indirectly with these dialogues to assess and analyse the way in which the organisation is developing as a collaborative learning unit. They will look to identify the emergence of any barriers to learning, perhaps the eroding of trust by increased comments about the lack of contribution by *others*. The ethical basis of the entire programme is founded on the relationships that make up the collaborative learning experience and so it is vital that these are understood and nurtured. Critical discourse analysis is the principal tool and it should assist in the analysis of the OLP and any changes, alterations or tweaks that might need to be carried out in the design of the OLP.

Planting is the creation, development and assessment of the readiness of any organisation to successfully embed an OLP. This will not only quantify the technological assets but will also assess key cultural characteristics. The organisation may possess many technological tools, it may have invested in a learning management system, but it also needs to be able to support the autonomy required to develop successful learners in the first instance and then to allow the growth of a trusting environment that will facilitate both the uptake of responsibility and ultimately the collaborative sharing of the tacit knowledge generated by the experience of individuals. Many barriers to this collaborative environment may be present:

- Are structures too rigid?
- Is a command and control mentality creating a barrier?
- Are groups or individuals imposing themselves in such a way that intimidates others, perhaps the inappropriate use of seniority as a concept, which heightens levels of expectation?
- Does this manifest itself in the way that individuals and groups communicate with one another, is there a formality here that creates a barrier to open and fluid dialogues?

Providing the right environment is essential to the success of the OLP; if weak seeds are planted in a sterile soil then it can be no surprise that the return, or the harvest, will be disappointing, will not meet expectations and will likely fail. OL needs preparation and a clear understanding of the relationship between the technical and cultural environment. Any technical tool can either impede or facilitate organisational learning. A blog can be empowering, it can help make explicit key tacit knowledge or it can be a procedural burden that is perceived to add yet another 'thing' to an already busy workload. All of the tools and techniques associated with the nurturing, growing and propagating of the OLP have this inherent contradiction and it is primarily the planting stage, but also the nurturing stage that will determine whether or not individual learning will be able to transform itself into an organisational asset.

Nurturing will look to build the necessary relationship between the individual and the organisation. Onboarding is the start of this relationship, and it should be looking to encourage individuals to recognise that they have a specific responsibility, that they have control over what they do but that this draws them into a collaborative context where their individual position contributes to the collective. This is based on mutual trust and respect; any contribution will be reciprocal and individual learning will be enhanced by this in a positive and iterative collaborative engagement.

The organisation becomes a series of dialogues which in turn are formed by rich stories, told by individuals who have the capabilities to construct and present these stories. The nurturing process will identify the extent to which these capabilities are present within the organisation. Where they are not they will form part of the development plan for individuals and the OL practitioner should arrange and facilitate this as part of the ongoing process that supports individual professional development.

As relationships develop as part of the OLP then the *growing* of key practices will help to build the capabilities of the organisation as a platform for collective learning. Mentoring and the creation of stories around the potential development of the organisation with scenario planning are all conducted within the appropriate environment. Mentoring relationships will be identified based on already existing relationships, they may well be reciprocal with mentors acting as mentees and perhaps with the same individuals playing each role for each other. Trust is at the heart of this process and this has been formed and developed by the ethical basis of the organisation.

Propagating

An organisation that is capable of growing its learning, has an embedded learning culture adequately supported by technologies that are attuned to the needs of collaborative learning and has individuals who appreciate that they themselves will learn from and through this collaborative learning environment, will be capable of propagating their organisational learning.

Reflective individuals within CoP will be able to drive this collaborative learning. In doing so they should realise the claims made of this learning and of disciplines such as OL and KM. It is through the dialogues within the CoP that the organisation's knowledge structure will manifest itself. This will be formed or based on individual cognitive structures that are made explicit through dialogues that these individuals trust to be in their best interest. This is not solely the strategic goals of the organisation but also the individual's learning needs. Where the organisational dilemma is actively addressed the goals of the individual and the organisation become more fully aligned. This is the alignment of the strategy of the organisation as a whole with the OL strategy.

At this point the utopian aspect of the LO becomes apparent. It is talking about balances between learning processes, information systems, individual and group behaviour, the fluid and dynamic organisational environment and the strategic goal of the organisation. How can this be implemented and how can we measure or assess its success? As Harrison (2009) points out about the concept of the LO:

> The concept's underpinning philosophy tends to ignore or underplay issues of who controls that organisation and the uses to which new learning will be put and the concept itself reflects an essentially managerialist perspective. There are parallels here with the fundamental weakness already noted in much of the theorising about 'communities of practice'.
>
> (Harrison 2009: 132–3)

The concept of the LO needs to be seen as a macro-level consideration of the functioning of the organisation rather than a tinkering with micro-level processes. OL will largely be ineffective where there is an assumption about the willingness of individuals to learn for the organisation, in many cases they are not. It will also be ineffective where there is not a willingness to consider a radical shift in the design of individual tasks and roles. This will include:

> ... a radical change in management style.
>
> (Harrison 2009: 133)

Radical change appears to be necessary in order to be able to function in an environment that itself is characterised by radical change. Organisations that recognise that their environment is changing radically will need to expect that they themselves will need to change radically. The consideration of the LO and disciplines such as KM and OL are presenting models that can be perceived to form the questions that organisations need to address if they are to survive and thrive in this environment.

The key issue appears to be the unwillingness to recognise the nature of the questions that are being presented. Organisations want to implement OL without any real consideration of the implications of this. To an extent there is a smokescreen presented by technological developments coupled with this more managerialist perspective. The mechanisms for collaboration, the tools, are increasingly present through the development of Web 2.0 technologies and the functionality associated with social networking. Learning management systems promise to 'manage' learning to enhance the opportunity for this crucial collaboration. However, 'you can take a horse to water, but you cannot make it drink'. The failure of many KM projects has largely been centred on this high level of expectation based on the enhanced functionality of technology and the reality of poor engagement and uptake.

The key question for OL is not found in the operational processes but in the ethical position of the organisation:

> ... neither knowledge (as an umbrella term for all sorts of intellectual resources) nor management can be seen as unambiguous, well-defined concepts or practices. Knowledge management is not a box of tools; it is a mind-set, a way of thinking of organisations and firms in terms of being knowledge-laden.
>
> (Styre 2003: 80)

How an organisation operates within a context of uncertainty is through its own embedded knowledge. In order to be able to do this each individual will need to apply their experience to the goals of the organisation. The individual is drawn to centre stage and it is this that drives the ethical position of the organisation as it must, as a social system, recognise the position of the 'other'. An individual's own experience is constantly being formed and re-formed through this social system. This interdependence is the basis for collaborative learning and the key cultural characteristic of an organisation that is capable of learning.

> ... openness, support, a climate of trust and challenge and a commitment to continuous learning and knowledge creation from a base of individual and team reflection and experience all hold out the promise of achieving high-commitment organisations and solving hitherto intractable organisational problems.
>
> (Harrison 2009: 133)

Collaboration appears to be embedded in the wider social context, through social networking tools such as Facebook and Twitter. Similarly, Castells (2001) in his description of the development of the Internet highlights the altruistic creation of a tool (the Internet) that has gone on to form the basis of the information revolution. In doing so, this has illustrated the power of collaborative working where there is embedded trust and a willingness to share, to adapt and to respect the knowledge and ability of those engaged with the dialogue. This is despite its early association with the US military and what might be regarded as a traditional, hierarchical structure.

The development of the Internet would be an example of a community of practice at work, it illustrates the type of momentum that can be achieved where there is a genuine focus on a specific area of interest and where individuals, largely, are looking to share and re-share, to collaborate and adapt, to respect and to value the knowledge embedded in all of those making a contribution to the shared project. Rather ironically the 'hackers' described by Castells have become the embodiment of the individuals all organisations now need if they are to become organisations that are capable of learning.

Concluding remarks

OL is a collaborative dialogue. As such it is based on trust which in turn requires a firm ethical footing. A meaningful dialogue is between individuals who can trust one another and it is the role of the OL practitioner to assess the readiness of the organisation to engage with this. The SPADES model here, presents discrete tools and techniques that are focused upon the building of a relationship. There is nothing more certain than that the perception of these tools and techniques will continue to change and adapt. However, the goal of understanding the need to create this relationship will remain central to the OLP. We will need to adapt and change these tools, look for others, discard some and so on. This is the reality that underpins OL, that there is always a fluidity and dynamism to the context within which we operate and that our experience of it is the principle way we navigate through it. To create a sustainable way of learning from our experience, to be able to apply it and continually design and redesign it, is the goal of the SPADES model.

OL is an ethical position, it is the organisation's position within the postmodern. It is based upon trust that drives the application of experiential learning as an asset for the organisation. Along the way it challenges the structure of the organisation and motivation of the individual.

Bibliography

Adorno, T. W. and Horkheimer, M., (1979). *Dialectic of Enlightenment*. London: Verso.

Agger, B., (2006). *Critical Social Theories: an introduction* (2nd edn). London: Paradigm.

Aitchison, J., Bawden, D. and Gilchrist, A., (2000). *Thesaurus Construction and Use: a practical manual* (4th edn). London: ASLIB.

Al-Hawamabeh, S., (2003). *Knowledge Management: cultivating knowledge professionals*. Oxford: Chandos.

Allan, J., Fairtlough, G. and Heinzen, B., (2001). *The Power of the Tale: using narratives for organisational success*. New York: Wiley.

Alter, S., (1999). *Information Systems: a management perspective* (3rd edn). Reading, MA: Addison-Wesley Longman.

Altman, I. and Taylor, D., (1973). *Social Penetration: the development of interpersonal relationships*. New York: Holt.

Alvesson, M., (2002). *Understanding Organizational Culture*. London: Sage.

American Airlines (AA), (2015). *How American Airlines Uses Social CRM for Customer Engagement* available at www.slideshare.net/oursocialtimes/how-american-airlines-uses-social-crm-for-customer-engagement [accessed April, 2015].

Amstutz, D. D., (1999). Adult Learning: moving towards more inclusive theories and practices. *New Directions for Adult and Continuing Education*, 82, 19–32.

Anscombe, G.E.M. and Rhees, R., (1953). *Philosophical Investigations*. Oxford: Blackwell.

Appelhans, W., Globe, A. and Laugero, G., (2000). *Managing Knowledge: a practical web-based approach*. Reading, MA: Addison-Wesley.

Appelbaum, S. H., Hebert, D. and Leroux, S., (1999). Empowerment: power, culture and leadership – a strategy or fad for the millennium? *Journal of Workplace Learning: Employee Counselling Today*, 11 (7), 233–54.

Argyris, C., (1993). *Knowledge for Action: a guide to overcoming barriers to organizational change*. San Francisco: Jossey-Bass.

Argyris, C. and Schön, D., (1978). *Organisational Learning: a theory of action perspective*. Reading, MA: Addison-Wesley.

Armitage, A., (2010). From sentimentalism towards a critical HRD pedagogy. *Journal of European Industrial Training*, 34 (89), 735–52.

Ashforth, B.E. and Mael, F.A., (1989). Social identity theory and the organisation. *Academy of Management Review*. 14, 20–39.

Avison, D. E. and Fitzgerald, G., (1995). *Information Systems Development: methodologies, techniques and tools* (2nd edn). London: McGraw-Hill.

Axelrod, R., (1990). *The Evolution of Co-operation*. London: Penguin.

Bacon, J., (2009). *The Art of Community: building the new age of participation*. Sebastopol, CA: O'Reilly [Kindle edition].

Bandura, A., (1977). *Social Learning Theory*. Englewood Cliffs, NJ: Prentice Hall.

Bandura, A., (1986). *Social Foundations of Thought and Action: a social cognitive theory*. Englewood Cliffs, NJ: Prentice Hall.

Barnes, B. and Bloor, D., (1982). Relativism, Rationalism and the Sociology of Knowledge. In: Hollis, M. and Lukes, S. (eds), *Rationality and Relativism*. Oxford: Blackwell.

Barthes, R., (2009). *Mythologies*. London: Vintage Classics.

Barton, D. and Tusting, K., (eds), (2005). *Beyond Communities of Practice: language power and social context*. Cambridge: Cambridge University Press.

Baudrillard, J., (1994). *Simulacra and Simulation*. Michigan: The University of Michigan Press.

Baudrillard, J., (1998). *The Consumer Society: myths and structures*. London: Sage.

Bauman, Z., (1988). *Postmodern Ethics*. Oxford: Blackwell.

Bauman, Z., (2000). *Liquid Modernity*. Cambridge: Polity.

Bauman, Z., (2001). *Community: seeking safety in an insecure world*. Cambridge: Polity [Kindle edition].

Baumard, P., (1999). *Tacit Knowledge in Organisations*. London: Sage.

Becker, A. and Brauner, E., (2003). Management as Reflective Practice and the Role of Transactive Knowledge. In: *Proceedings 5th International Conference on Organisational Learning and Knowledge, Lancaster, England, 30 May – 2 June 2003*. Lancaster University.

Bell, D., (1974). *The Coming of Post-Industrial Society*. London: Heinemann.

Bell, D., (1996). *The Cultural Contradictions of Capitalism*. London: Basic Books.

Bennis, W., (2009). *The Essential Bennis*. San Francisco: Jossey-Bass.

Berger, C. R. and Calabrese, R. J., (1975). Some exploration and initial interaction beyond: towards a developmental theory of intercommunication. *Human Communication Research*, 1, 99–112.

Berger, P. and Luckmann, T., (1971). *The Social Construction of Reality: a treatise in the sociology of knowledge*. London: Penguin.

Berry, M. J. A. and Linoff, G. S., (2000). *Mastering Data Mining: the art and science of customer relationship management*. New York: Wiley.

Bertalanffy, L., (1950). An outline of general system theory. *British Journal for the Philosophy of Science*, 1, 114–29.

Bertrand, M. and Guillaume, S., (2003). The Learning Mix: a strategic tool to manage organisational knowledge. In: *Proceedings 5th International Conference on Organisational Learning and Knowledge, Lancaster, England, 30 May – 2 June 2003*. Lancaster University.

Birgerstam, P., (2002). Intuition: the way to meaningful knowledge. *Studies in Higher Education*, 27 (4), 431–44.

Blair, T., (1998). Foreword, In: Secretary of State for Trade and Industry. *Our Competitive Future: building the knowledge driven economy*. London: Cm 4176.

Boisot, M. H., (1998). *Knowledge Assets: securing competitive advantage in the information economy*. Oxford: Oxford University Press.

Boje, D. M., (2008). *Storytelling Organisations*. Los Angeles: Sage

Bolton, G., (2001). *Reflective Practice: writing and professional development*. London: Paul Chapman.

Boud, D., (2003). Combining work and learning: the disturbing challenge of practice. In: *Proceedings Second International Conference on Experiential: Community: Workbased: Researching Learning outside the Academy, Glasgow, Scotland, 27–29 June 2003*. Centre for Research in Lifelong Learning.

Boud, D. and Garrick, J., (eds), (1999). *Understanding Learning at Work*. London: Routledge.

Boud, D. and Miller, N., (eds), (1996). *Working with Experience: animated learning*. London: Routledge.

Boyatzis, R. E., (1982). *The Competent Manager: a model for effective practice*. New York: Wiley.

Bratton, J. and Gold, J., (2011). *Human Resource Management: theory and practice*. London: Palgrave.

British Standards Institution (1987). *BS5732 Guide to establishment and development of monolingual thesauri*. London: British Standards Institution.

Brookfield, S. D., (1996). Helping people learn what they do: breaking dependence on experts. In: Boud, D. and Miller, N., (eds), (1996). *Working with Experience: animating learning*. London: Routledge.

Brookfield, S. D., (2005). *The Power of Critical Theory for Adult Learning and Teaching*. Maidenhead: Open University Press.

Brown, A., (1998). *Organisational Culture* (2nd edn). Harlow, Essex: Pearson.

Brown, D. and Duguid, P., (1991). Organisational learning and communities of practice: towards a unified view of working, learning and innovation. *Organisation Science*, 2 (1), 40–57.

Brown, J. S. and Duguid, P., (2000). *The Social Life of Information*. Boston, Massachusetts: Harvard Business School Press.

Bryans, P. and Smith, R., (2000). Beyond training: reconceptualising learning at work. *Journal of Workplace Learning*, 12 (6), 228–35.

Burke, P., (2000). *The Social History of Knowledge: from Gutenberg to Diderot*. Cambridge: Polity.

Burke, W. W. and Litwin, G. H., (1993). A causal model of organisational performance and change. *Journal of Management*, 18 (3), 523–45.

Burr, V., (2003). *Social Constructionism* (2nd edn). London: Routledge.

C4LPT, (2015). Directory of Learning and Performance Tools and Services, available at http://c4lpt.co.uk/directory-of-learning-performance-tools/ [accessed April 2015].

CIPD, (2015). The CIPD homepage available at www.cipd.co.uk/ [accessed June 2015].

Callinicos, A., (1999). *Social Theory: a historical introduction*. Cambridge: Polity.

Cameron, D., (2001). *Working with Spoken Discourse*. London: Sage.

Castells, M., (2001). *The Internet Galaxy: reflections on the internet, business and society*. Oxford: Oxford University Press.

Center for Army Lessons Learned (CALL), CALL website available at http://usacac.army.mil/organizations/mccoe/call [accessed May 2015]

Checkland, P., (1981). *Systems Thinking, Systems Practice*. Chichester: Wiley.

Cheetham, G. and Chivers, G., (1998). The reflective (and competent) practitioner: a model of professional competence which seeks to harmonise the reflective practitioner and competence-based approaches. *Journal of European Industrial Training*, 22 (7), 267–76.

Cheung-Judge, M. and Holbeche, L., (2011). *Organisation Development: a practitioner's guide to OD and HR*. London: Kogan Page [Kindle edition].

Child, J. and Rodrigues, S., (2011). Social Identity and Organisational Learning. In: Easterby-Smith, M. and Lyles, M. A., (eds), *Handbook of Organisational Learning and Knowledge Management* (2nd edn). Oxford: Oxford University Press.

Chua, A. (2002). The Influence of Social Interaction on Knowledge Creation. *Journal of Intellectual Capital*, 3 (4), 375–92.

Commission of the European Communities, (2000). *Innovation in a Knowledge-Driven Economy*. Brussels, 567 Final.

Coopey, J., (1995). The learning organisation: power, politics and ideology. *Management Learning*, 26 (2), 193–213.

Coopey, J., (1998). Learning to trust and trusting to Learn: a role for radical theatre. *Management Learning*, 29 (3), 365–82.

Cope, J. and Watts, G., (2000). Learning by doing: an exploration of experience, critical incidents and reflection in entrepreneurial learning. *International Journal of Entrepreneurial Behaviour and Research*, 6 (3), 104–24.

Cox, B., (1994). *Practical Pointers for University Teachers*. London: Kogan Page.

Crossan, M. and Bapuji, H. B., (2003). Examining the Link Between Knowledge Management, Organisational Learning and Performance. In: *Proceedings 5th International Conference on Organisational Learning and Knowledge, Lancaster, England, 30 May – 2 June 2003*. Lancaster University.

Crowther, D. and Green, M., (2004). *Organisational Theory*. London: Chartered Institute of Personnel and Development.

Currie, G. and Kerrin, M., (2004). The limits of the technological fix to knowledge management: epistemological, political and cultural issues in the case of intranet implementation. *Management Learning*, 35 (1), 9–29.

Curzon, L. B., (1997). *Teaching in Further Education*. London: Cassell.

Davenport, T. and Prusak, L., (1998). *Working Knowledge: how organizations manage what they know*. Boston: Harvard Business School.

Davis, S. and Meyer, C., (1998). *Blur: the speed of change in the connected society*. Oxford: Capstone.

De Geus, A., (1999). *The Living Company: growth, learning and longevity in business*. London: Nicholas Brealey.

Delahaye, B. L. and Smith, H. E., (1995). The validity of the learning preference assessment. *Adult Education Quarterly*, 45 (3), 159–73.

Delbridge, R. and Keenoy, T., (2010). Beyond managerialism? *The International Journal of Human Resource Management*, 21 (6), 799–817.

Denning, S., (2001). *The Springboard: how storytelling ignites action in knowledge-era organisations*. Boston: Butterworth Heinemann.

Denton, J., (1998). *Organizational Learning and Effectiveness*. London: Routledge.

Dewey, J., (1991). *How We Think*. New York: Prometheus Books.

Dewey, J., (1997). *Experience and Education*. New York: Touchstone.

Dierkes, M., Berthoin Antal, A., Child, J. and Nonaka, I., (eds), (2001). *Handbook of Organizational Learning and Knowledge*. Oxford: Oxford University Press.

Dixon, N., (2000). *Common Knowledge: how companies thrive by sharing what they know*. Boston: Harvard Business School Press.

Donaldson, L., (2003). Organisation theory as a positive science. In: Tsoukas, H. and Knudsen, C., (eds), *The Oxford Handbook of Organisation Theory*. Oxford: Oxford University Press.

Dovey, K., (1997). The learning organisation and the organisation of learning: power, trasformation and the search for form in learning organisations. *Management Learning*, 28 (3), 331–49.

Driver, M., (2002). The Learning Organisation: Foucauldian gloom or utopian sunshine? *Human Relations*, 55 (1), 33–53.

Drucker, P., (1969). *The Age of Discontinuity; Guidelines to Our Changing Society*. New York: Harper and Row.

Dutta, D. K. and Crossan, M. M., (2003). Understanding Change: what can we 'learn' from organisational learning. In: *Proceedings 5th International Conference on Organisational Learning and Knowledge, Lancaster, England, 30 May – 2 June 2003*. Lancaster University.

Earl, M., (2001). Knowledge management strategies: towards a taxonomy. *Journal of Management Information Systems*, 18 (1), 215–33.

Easterby-Smith, M., Burgoyne, J. and Araujo, L. (eds), (1999). *Organisational Learning and the Learning Organisation: developments in theory and practice*. London: Sage.

Edwards, R., (1997). *Changing Places? Flexibility, Lifelong Learning and a Learning Society*. London: Routledge.

Entwistle, N. and Hounsell, D., (1975). *How Students Learn*. Lancaster: University of Lancaster.

Entwistle, N. and Ramsden, P., (1983). *Understanding Student Learning*. London: Croom Helm.

Evans, N. J. and Easterby-Smith, M., (2003). Can Organisational Knowledge Creation be Managed? In: *Proceedings 5th International Conference on Organisational Learning and Knowledge, Lancaster, England, 30 May – 2 June 2003*. Lancaster University.

Fairlclough, N., (2001). *Language and Power* (2nd edn). Harlow: Pearson.

Fairclough, N., (2003). *Analysing Discourse: textual analysis for social research*. London: Routledge.

Fairhurst, G. T. and Putnam, L., (2006). Organisations as discursive constructions. *Communication Theory*, 14 (1), 5–26.

Farr, K., (2000). Organisational learning and knowledge managers. *Work Study*, 49 (1), 14–17.

Fenwick, T., (2003). Inside out of experiential learning: troubling assumptions and expanding question. In: *Proceedings Second International Conference on Experiential: Community: Workbased: Researching Learning outside the Academy, Glasgow, Scotland, 27–29 June 2003*. Centre for Research in Lifelong Learning.

Fiske, H., (1990). *Introduction to Communication Studies* (2nd edn). Abingdon, Oxon: Routledge.

Fiske, H., (2011). *Introduction to Communication Studies* (3rd edn). Abingdon, Oxon: Routledge.

Flood, R. L., (1995). *Rethinking the Fifth Discipline: learning within the unknowable*. London: Routledge.

Foucault, M., (1980). *Power/Knowledge: selected interviews and other writings 1972–1977*. Brighton: Harvester Press.

Foucault, M., (1991). *Discipline and Punish: the birth of the prison*. London: Penguin.

Friedman, V. J., (2001). The Individual as Agent of Organisational Learning. In: Dierkes, M., Berthoin Antal, A., Child, J. and Nonaka, I., (eds), *Handbook of Organisational Learning and Knowledge*. Oxford: Oxford University Press.

Freire, P., (1996). *Pedagogy of the Oppressed*. London: Penguin.

Fuchs, C., (2013). *Social Media: a critical introduction*. London: Sage.

Fuller, S., (2002). *Knowledge Management Foundations*. Oxford: Butterworth-Heinemann.

Gabriel, Y., (2000). *Storytelling in Organisations: facts, fictions and fantasies*. Oxford: Oxford University Press.

Gadamer, H-G., (2004). *Truth and Method* (2nd edn). London: Continuum.

Gagné, R., (1985). *The Conditions of Learning*. New York: Holy, Rinehart and Winston.

Garfinkel, H., (1967). Studies in Ethnomethodology. Malden MA: Polity Press/Blackwell Publishing.

Garvey, B. and Williamson, B., (2002). *Beyond Knowledge Management: dialogue creativity and the corporate curriculum*. Harlow: Pearson.

Garvin, D.A., (1993). Building a learning organisation. *Harvard Business Review*, July–August, pp. 81–91.

Gear, T., Vince, R., Read, M. and Minkes, A.L., (2003). Group enquiry for collective learning in organisations. *Journal of Management Development*, 22 (2), 88–102.

Gee, J. P., (2005). *An Introduction to Discourse Analysis* (2nd edn). London: Routledge.

Gheradi, S., (2011). Organisational Learning: the sociology of practice. In: Easterby-Smith, M. and Lyles, M. A., (eds), *Handbook of Organisational Learning and Knowledge Management*, Chichester: Wiley.

Gheradi, S. and Nicolini, D., (2001). The Sociological Foundations of Organisational Learning. In: Dierkes, M., Berthoin Antal, A., Child, J. and Nonaka, I. (eds), *Handbook of Organisational Learning and Knowledge*. Oxford: Oxford University Press.

Gibb, G., (1981). *Teaching Students to Learn: a student centred approach*. Milton Keynes: Open University Press.

Gibb, G., (1992). *53 Interesting Things To Do in Your Lectures*. London: TES.

Gibbons, M., Limoges, C., Nowotny, H., Schwartzman, S., Scott, P. and Trow, M., (1994). *The New Production of Knowledge: the dynamics of science and research in contemporary society*. London: Sage.

Gill, J. H., (2000). *The Tacit Mode: Michael Polanyi's postmodern philosophy*. New York: State University of New York Press.

Glock, H-J., (ed.), (2001). *Wittgenstein: a critical reader*. Oxford: Blackwell.

Goldman, A. I., (1999). *Knowledge in a Social World*. Oxford: Oxford University Press.

Goleman, D., (1996). *Emotional Intelligence: why it can matter more than IQ*. London: Bloomsbury.

Graen, G. B. and Uhl-Bien, M., (1995). The relationship-based approach to leadership: development of LMX theory of leadership over 25 years, applying multi-level, multi-domain perspective. *Leadership Quarterly*, 6 (2), 219–47.

Gupta, U., (1996). *Management Information Systems: a managerial perspective*. Eagan, Minnesota: West Publishing.

Gupta, U., (2000). *Information Systems: success in the 21st century*. New Jersey: Prentice-Hall.

Habermas, J., (1986a). *The Theory of Communicative Action: reason and the rationalisation of society*, Vol. 1. Cambridge: Polity.

Habermas, J., (1986b). *Knowledge and Human Interest*. Cambridge: Polity.

Habermas, J., (1992). *The Structural Transformation of the Public Sphere: inquiry into a category of bourgeois society*. Cambridge: Polity.

Handy, C., (1985). *Understanding Organisations*. Harmondsworth: Penguin.

Harrison, R., (2009). *Learning and Development* (5th edn). London: CIPD.

Harvard Business Review, (1994). *Harvard Business Review on Leadership*. Boston: Harvard Business School Press.

Harvard Business Review, (1998). *Harvard Business Review on Managing Uncertainty*. Boston: Harvard Business School Press.

Harvard Business Review, (2001). *Harvard Business Review on Organisational Learning*. Boston: Harvard Business School Press.

Harvey, D., (1990). *The Condition of Postmodernity: an enquiry into the origins of cultural change*. Oxford: Blackwell.

Hassard, J. and Parker, M., (1993). *Postmodernism and Organisations*. London: Sage.

Hay, J., (2007). *Reflective Practice and Supervision for Coaches*. Maidenhead: Open University Press.

Hekman, S. J., (1986). *Hermeneutics and the Sociology of Knowledge*. Cambridge: Polity Press.

Hislop, I., (2005). *Knowledge Management in Organisations: a critical introduction*. Oxford: Oxford University Press.

Hislop, D., (2009). *Knowledge Management in Organisations: a critical introduction* (2nd edn). Oxford: Oxford University Press.

Hobsbawm, E., (1973). *The Age of Revolution: Europe 1789–1848*. London: Abacus.

Huotari, M.-J. and Iivonen, M., (2003). *Trust in Knowledge Management and Systems in Organisations*. New York: Idea Group.

Illeris, K., (2002). *The Three Dimensions of Learning: contemporary learning theory in the tension field between the cognitive, the emotional and the social*. Frederiksberg, DK: Roskilde University Press.

Institute of Business Ethics, (2015). Website available at www.ibe.org.uk/home/1 [accessed January 2015].

Institute of Training and Occupational Learning (ITOL), (2015). Website available at www.itol.org/ [accessed June 2015].

Jarvis, P., Holford, J. and Griffin, C., (1998). *The Theory and Practice of Learning*. London: Kogan Page.

Jashapara, A., (2004). *Knowledge Management: an integrated approach*. London: Financial Times/Prentice-Hall.

Johanessen, J.-A., Olaisen, J. and Olsen, B., (1999). Systemic thinking as the philosophical fouindaton for knowledge management and organisational learning. *Kybernetes*, 28 (1), 24–46.

Johns, C., (2013). *Becoming a Reflective Practitioner*. Oxford: Wiley Blackwell.

Johnson, P. A., (2000). *On Gadamer*. Belmont, CA: Wadsworth.

Kayama, M. and Okamoto, T., (2002). Collaborative learning in the internet learning space: a framework for a learning environment and knowledge management in the educational context. *Industry and Higher Education*, 16 (4), 249–59.

Keating, C., Robinson, T. and Clemson, B., (1996). Reflective inquiry: a method for organisational learning. *The Learning Organisation*, 3 (4), 35–43.

Knoco, (2015). Website available at www.knoco.co.uk [accessed June 2015].

Knorr-Cetina, K., (1999). *Epistemic Cultures: how the sciences make knowledge*. Boston: Harvard University Press.

Kogan, M., (2005). Modes of knowledge and pattern of power. *Higher Education*, 49, 9–29.

Kokkinidis, G., (2012). In search of workplace democracy. *International Journal of Sociology and Social Policy*, 32 (3/4), 233–56.

Kolb, D. A., (1984). *Experiential Learning: experience as the source of learning and development*. Englewood Cliffs, NJ: Prentice Hall.

Kolb, D. A. and Fry, R., (1975). Toward an Applied Theory of Experiential Learning. In: Cooper, C. L. (ed.), *Theories of Group Processes*. New York: Wiley.

Kramer, M. W., (2010). *Organisational Socialisation: joining and leaving organisations*. Cambridge: Polity.

Kusch, M., (2002). *Knowledge by Agreement: the programme of communitarian epistemology*. Oxford: Clarendon Press.

Kynaston, D., (2009). *Family Britain (Tales of a new Jerusalem), 1951–1957*. London: Bloomsbury.

Laszlo, K. C. and Laszlo, A., (2002). Evolving knowledge for development: the role of knowledge management in a changing world. *Journal of Workplace Learning*, 6 (4), 400–12.

Laudon, K. C. and Laudon, J. P., (2000). *Management Information Systems: organisation and technology in the networked enterprise* (6th edn). New Jersey: Prentice-Hall.

Lave, J. and Wenger, E., (1991). *Situated Learning Participation: legitimate peripheral participation*. Cambridge: Cambridge University Press.

Learning and Performance Institute, (2015). Website available at www.learningandperformanceinstitute.com/ [accessed June 2015].

Leonard, D., (1998). *Wellsprings of Knowledge: building and sustaining the sources of innovation*. Boston, MA: Harvard Business Press.

Levinson, P., (1997). *The Soft Edge: a natural history of the information revolution*. London: Routledge.

Lewin, K., (1997). *Resolving Social Conflict: selected papers on group dynamics*. USA: American Psychological Association.

Lewis, S., Passmore, J. and Cantore, S., (2011). *Appreciative Inquiry for Change Management: using AI to facilitate organisational development*. London: Kogan Page [Kindle edition].

Linstead, S. (ed.), (2004). *Organisation Theory and Postmodern Thought*. London: Sage.

Lipshitz, R., Friedman, V. J. and Popper, M., (2006). *Demystifying Organisational Learning*. London: Sage.

Little, S. E., Quintas, P. and Ray, T. (eds), (2002). *Managing Knowledge: an essential reader*. London: Sage.

Livingstone, D. W., (2001). Worker control as the missing link: relations between paid/unpaid work and work-related learning. *Journal of Workplace Learning*, 13 (7/8), 308–17.

Lynch, P. J. and Horton, S., (2001). *Web Style Guide: basic design principles for creating web sites*. New Haven: Yale University Press.

Lyon, D., (2001). *Surveillance Society: monitoring everyday life*. Milton Keynes: Open University Press.

Lyotard, J.-F., (1984). *The Postmodern Condition: a report on knowledge*. Manchester: Manchester University Press.

McCampbell, A. S., Clare, L. M. and Gitters, S. H., (1999). Knowledge management: the new challenge for the 21st century. *Journal of Knowledge Management*, 3 (3), 172–9.

McElroy, M. W., (2000). Integrating complexity theory, knowledge management and organisational Learning. *Journal of Knowledge Management*, 4 (3), 195–203.

McElroy, M. W., (2003). *The New Knowledge Management: complexity, learning and sustainable innovation*. Burlington, MA: Butterworth Heinemann.

McGill, I. and Beattie, L., (1995). *Action Learning: a guide for professional, management and educational development*. London: Kogan Page.

McGuire, D., (2014). *Human Resource Development* (2nd edn). London: Sage.

McLeish, H., (2001). Foreword, In: Scottish Executive, *Report on the Knowledge Economy Cross Cutting Initiative*. Edinburgh: Scottish Executive.

McLuhan, M., (2001). *Understanding Media* (2nd edn). Abingdon, Oxon: Routledge.

Mannheim, K., (1936). *Ideology and Utopia: an introduction to the sociology of knowledge*. London: Routledge.

Marsick, V., (1994). Trends in managerial re-invention: creating a learning map. *Management Learning*, 25 (1), 11–33.

Marsick, V. J. and Watkins, K. E., (1999). *Facilitating Learning Organisations: making learning count*. Farnham, Surrey: Gower.

Marsick, V. J. and Watkins, K., (1999). Envisioning New Organisations for Learning. In: Boud, D. and Garrick, J. (eds), *Understanding Learning at Work*. London: Routledge, pp. 199–215.

Masino, G., (1999). Information technology and dilemmas in organisational learning. *Journal of Organisational Change Management*, 12 (5), 360–76.

Megginson, D., Clutterbuck, D. and Garvey, B., (2005). *Mentoring in Action: a practical guide for managers*. London: Kogan Page.

Melé, D., (2012). *Management Ethics: placing ethics at the core of good management*. Basingstoke, Hampshire: Palgrave MacMillan [Kindle edition].

Moodle, (2015). About Moodle, available at https://docs.moodle.org/28/en/About_Moodle, [accessed April 2015].

Moon, J. A., (1999). *Reflection in Learning and Professional Development*. London: Kogan Page.

Morey, D. and Frangioso, T., (1998). Aligning an organisation for learning: the six principles of effective learning. *Journal of Knowledge Management*, 1 (4), 308–14.

Mortensen, C. D., (1972). *Communication: the study of human interaction*. New York: McGraw-Hill.

Newble, D. and Cannon, R., (1989). *A Handbook for Teachers in Universities and Colleges*. London: Kogan Page.

Newell, S., Robertson, M., Scarbrough, H. and Swan, J., (2002). *Managing Knowledge Work*. London: Palgrave.

Nonaka, I. and Takeuchi, H., (1995). *The Knowledge Creating Company: how Japanese companies create the dynamics of innovation*. New York: Oxford University Press.

Nonaka, I., Toyama, R. and Konno, N., (2002). SECI, Ba and Leadership: a unified model of dynamic knowledge creation. In: Little, S., (ed.), *Managing Knowledge: an essential reader*. London: Sage.

O'Brien, J. A., (2000). *Introduction to Information Systems: essentials for the internet worked enterprise* (9th edn). London: McGraw-Hill.

ODN Europe, (2015). Website available at www.odneurope.org/ [accessed June 2015].

O'Hara, K. and Shadbolt, N., (2008). *The Spy in the Coffee Machine: the end of privacy as we know it*. London: Oneworld Publications.

Organisation for Economic Co-operation and Development, (2000). *Knowledge Management in the Learning Society: education and skills*. Paris: OECD.

Orgnet, (2015). SNA software *in Flow* available at www.orgnet.com [accessed June 2015].

Partridge, D. and Hussein, K. M., (1994). *Knowledge-Based Information Systems*. London: McGraw-Hill.

Pavlov, I., (1927). *Conditioned Reflexes*. London: Oxford University Press.

Pedlar, M., Burgoyne, J. and Boydell, T., (1997). *The Learning Company: a strategy for sustainable development* (2nd edn). London: McGraw-Hill.

Peters, T. and Waterman, R. H., (2004). *In Search of Excellence: lessons from America's best-run companies*. London: Profile.

Phillips, J., (2000). *Contested Knowledge: a guide to Critical Theory*. London: Zed Books.

Plaskoff, J., (2011). Intersubjectivity and Community-Building: learning to learn organisationally. In: Easterby-Smith, M. and Lyles, M. A., (eds), *Handbook of Organisational Learning and Knowledge Management* (2nd edn). New York: Wiley.

Polanyi, M., (1963). *Personal Knowledge: towards a post-critical philosophy*. London: Routledge.

Polanyi, M., (1983). *The Tacit Dimension*. Gloucester, MA: Peter Smith.

Price, S., (1997). *The Complete A–Z Media and Communication Handbook*. London: Hodder and Stoughton.

Ramsden, P., (1992). *Learning to Teach in Higher Education*. London: Routledge.

Revans, R., (2011). *ABC of Action Learning*. Farnham, Surrey: Gower.

Ringer, F., (2001). *Towards a Social History of Knowledge: collected essays*. New York: Berghahn Books.

Robins, K. and Webster, F., (1999). *Times of the Technoculture: from the information society to the virtual life*. London: Routledge.

Roloff, K. S., Woolley, A. W. and Edmondson, A. C., (2011). The Contribution of Teams to Organisational Learning. In: Easterby-Smith, M. and Lyles, M. A. (eds), *Handbook of Organisational Learning and Knowledge Management* (2nd edn). New York: Wiley.

Rorty, R., (1991). *Objectivity, Relativism and Truth: philosophical papers*, Vol 1. Cambridge: Cambridge University Press.

Rosenfeld, L. and Morville, P., (2015). *Information Architecture: for the web and beyond*. London: O'Reilly.

Royal Dutch Shell, (2015). Shell Scenarios, available at www.shell.com/energy-and-innovation/the-energy-future/shell-scenarios.html [accessed May 2015].

Rumizen, M., (2001). *The Complete Idiots Guide to Knowledge Management*. London: Imprint.

Sacks, H., (1995). *Lectures on Conversations*, Vols 1 and 2. Oxford: Blackwells.

Saint-Onge, H. and Wallace, D., (2003). *Leveraging Communities of Practice for Strategic Advantage*. London: Butterworth-Heinemann [Kindle edition].

Sambrook, S., (2009). Critical HRD: a concept analysis. *Personnel Review*, 38 (1), 61–73.

Scarborough, H., (1998). Path(ological) Dependency? Core competencies from an organisational perspective. *British Journal of Management*, 9 (3), 219–32.

Schein, E. H., (1985). How Culture Forms, Develops and Changes. In: Kilmann, R. H., Saxton, M.J. and Serpa, R., (eds), *Gaining Control of the Corporate Culture*. San Francisco: Jossey Bass.

Schein, E. H., (1996). Culture: the missing concept in organisation studies. *Administrative Science Quarterly*, 41, 229–40.

Schön, D., (1967). *Technology and Change: the new handbook*. Oxford: Pergamon.

Schön, D.A., (1991). *The Reflective Practitioner: how professionals think in action.* Aldershot, Hants: Ashgate.

Scott, J., (2000). *Social Network Analysis: a handbook.* London: Sage.

Searle, J. R., (1995). *The Construction of Social Reality.* London: Penguin.

Seidman, S., (2003). *Contested Knowledge: social theory today* (3rd edn). Oxford: Blackwell.

Senge, P. (1993). *The Fifth Discipline: the art and practice of the learning organisation.* London: Random House.

Snell, R. and Chak, A. M.-K., (1998). The learning organisation: learning and empowerment for whom? *Management Learning,* 29 (3), 337–64.

Snowden, D., (1999). Story Telling: an old skill in a new context. *Business Information Review,* 16 (1), 30–50.

Society for Organizational Learning, (2015). Website available at www.solonline.org/ [accessed June 2015].

Solomon, N., Boud, D., Leontios, M. and Staron, M., (2001). Researchers are learners too: collaboration in research on workplace learning. *Journal of Workplace Learning,* 13 (7/8), 274–81.

Squires, G., (1999). *Teaching as a Professional Discipline: a multi-dimensional model.* Abingdon, Oxon: Routledge.

Stacey, R. D., (2001). *Complex Response Processes in Organisations: learning and knowledge creation.* London: Routledge.

Starr, J., (2014). *The Mentoring Manual: your step by step guide to being a better mentor.* London: Pearson.

Stehr. N., (1994). *Knowledge Societies.* London: Sage.

Stehr, N. and Meja, V. (eds), (2005). *Society and Knowledge: contemporary perspectives in the sociology of knowledge and science* (2nd edn). New Jersey: Transaction.

Stein, M. A. and Christiansen, L., (2010). *Successful On-boarding: a strategy to unlock hidden value within your organisation.* New York: McGraw-Hill [Kindle edition].

Stevenson, R. L., (1886). *Strange Case of Dr Jekyll and Mr Hyde.* London: Longmans.

Stewart, H., (2012). *The Happy Manifesto: make your organisation a great place to work – now!* London: Happy [Kindle edition].

Stewart, T. A., (1997). *Intellectual Capital: the new wealth of organisations.* London: Nicholas Brearley.

Stewart, J. and Rigg, C., (2011). *Learning and Talent Development.* London: CIPD.

Styre, A., (2003). *Understanding Knowledge Management: critical and postmodern perspectives.* Abingdon: Marston Book Services.

Sutherland, P., (1998). *Adult Learning: a reader.* London: Kogan Page.

Swart, J. and Pye, A., (2003). Collective Tacit Knowledge: integrating categories in the process of organisational learning. In: *Proceedings 5th International Conference on Organisational Learning and Knowledge, Lancaster, England, 30 May – 2 June 2003.* Lancaster University.

Tavistock Institute, (2015). Website available at www.tavinstitute.org/ [accessed June 2015].

Taylor, F. W., (1911). *Principles of Scientific Management.* New York: Harper.

Thibaut, J. W. and Kelley, H. H., (1959). *The Social Psychology of Groups.* New York: Wiley.

Tietze, S., Cohen, L. and Musson, G., (2003). *Understanding Organisations through Language.* London: Sage.

Tight, M., (2002). *Key Concepts in Adult Education and Training* (2nd edn). London: Routledge.

Trehan, K. and Rigg, C., (2011). Theorising critical HRD: a paradox of intricacy and discrepancy. *Journal of European Industrial Training,* 35 (3), 276–90.

US Army, (1993). A Leader's Guide to After Action Review: *Training Circular 25–20.* Washington DC Department of the Army.

Usher, R., Bryant, I. and Johnston, R., (1996). *Adult Education and the Postmodern Challenge: learning beyond the limits.* London: Routledge.

Van Dijk, J., (2006). *The Network Society* (2nd edn). London: Sage.

Van Dijk, T. A., (2011). *Discourse Studies: a multidisciplinary introduction* (2nd edn). London: Sage.

Vera, D. M. and Crossan, M. M., (2003). Reconciling the Tensions in Learning and Knowledge. In: *Proceedings 5th International Conference on Organisational Learning and Knowledge, Lancaster, England, 30 May – 2 June 2003.* Lancaster University.

von Krogh, G., (2011). Knowledge Sharing in Organisations: the role of communities. In: Easterby-Smith, M. and Lyles, M. A. (eds). *Handbook of Organisational Learning and Knowledge Management* (2nd edn). New York: Wiley.

Wade, W., (2012). *Scenario Planning: a field guide to the future.* New York: Wiley [Kindle edition].

Wallace, P., (2001). *The Psychology of the Internet.* Cambridge: Cambridge University Press.

Wasserman, S., (1994). *Social Network Analysis: methods and applications.* Cambridge: Cambridge University Press.

Watt, S. E., Lea, M. and Spears, R., (2002). How Social is Internet Communication? A reappraisal of bandwith and anonymity effects. In: Woolgar, S. (ed.), *Virtual Society? Technology, cyberbole, reality.* Oxford: Oxford University Press, pp. 61–77.

Weick, K. E., (1995). *Sensemaking in Organisations.* Thousand Oaks, CA: Sage.

Wenger, E., (1998). *Communities of Practice: learning, meaning and identity.* Cambridge: Cambridge University Press.

Wijnhoven, F., (2001). Acquiring organisational learning: a contingency approach for understanding deutero learning. *Management Learning,* 32 (2), 181–200.

Wilmott, H. C., (1994). Management education: provocations to a debate. *Management Learning,* 25 (1), 105–36.

Wilmott, H. C., (1997). Critical Management Learning. In: Burgoyne, J. and Reynolds, M. (eds), *Management Learning: integrating perspectives in theory and practice.* London: Sage.

Wilson, J., (2011). *Brian Clough: nobody ever says thank you.* London: Orion.

Wittgenstein, W., (1976). *Philosophical Investigations,* (translated by Anscombe, G. E. M.) (3rd edn). Oxford: Blackwell, p. 20.

Woolgar, S., (2003). *Virtual Society? Technology, cyberbole, reality.* Oxford: Oxford University Press.

Wright, J., (1982). *Learning to Learn in Higher Education.* London: Croom Helm.

Xenikou, A. and Furnham, A., (2013). *Group Dynamics and Organisational Culture: effective work groups and organisations.* New York: Palgrave Macmillan.

Yates-Mercer, P. and Bawden, D., (2002). Managing the Paradox: the valuation of knowledge and knowledge management. *Journal of Information Science,* 28 (1), 19–29.

Yolles, M., (2000). Organisations, Complexity and Viable Knowledge Management. *Kybernetes,* 29 (9/10), 1202–22.

Zack, M. H., (2003). What is a Knowledge-Based Organisation? In: *Proceedings 5th International Conference on Organisational Learning and Knowledge, Lancaster, England, 30 May – 2 June 2003.* Lancaster University.

Ziman, J., (1968). *Public Knowledge: an essay concerning the social dimension of science.* Cambridge: Cambridge University Press.

Ziman, J., (1978). *Reliable Knowledge: an exploration of the grounds for belief in science.* Cambridge: Cambridge University Press.

Index